Taxi!

Taxi!

A Social History of the
New York City Cabdriver

GRAHAM RUSSELL GAO HODGES

The Johns Hopkins University Press

Baltimore

© 2007 The Johns Hopkins University Press
All rights reserved. Published 2007
Printed in the United States of America on acid-free paper
9 8 7 6 5 4 3 2 1

The Johns Hopkins University Press
2715 North Charles Street
Baltimore, Maryland 21218-4363
www.press.jhu.edu

Library of Congress Cataloging-in-Publication Data

Hodges, Graham Russell, 1946–
    Taxi! : a social history of the New York City cabdriver / Graham Russell
Gao Hodges.
        p.   cm.
    Includes bibliographical references and index.
    ISBN-13: 978-0-8018-8554-9 (hardcover : alk. paper)
    ISBN-10: 0-8018-8554-X (hardcover : alk. paper)
    1. Taxicab drivers—New York (State)—New York—History. 2. Taxicab
drivers—New York (State)—New York—Social conditions. 3. Taxicabs—
New York (State)—New York—History. I. Title. II. Title: Social history
of the New York City cabdriver.
    HD8039.T162U636 2007
    388.4'13214097471—dc22   2006019856

A catalog record for this book is available from the British Library.

Contents

Acknowledgments

I have collected innumerable debts over the many years needed to complete this book. First in line are Kenneth Cobb and his team of archivists at the New York City Municipal Archives and the staffs of the New York Public Library General Circulation, the Billy Lee Rose Collection at Lincoln Center, and the Rare Books and Manuscripts Divisions of the Columbia University Library.

I was greatly helped by a series of terrific student assistants at Colgate University. Scott Miltenberger created an index to stories on taxis that appeared in the *New York Times* from 1851 to 1997. Kimberly Harrold analyzed cab memoirs and created an index to Hollywood films on taxicab drivers. Other students who helped me on this project are Nathaniel Urena, Megan Lyons, Rebecca Sadowsky, and Nancy Ng.

Numerous scholars helped with valuable tips about sources. They include Alan M. Wald of the University of Michigan and Steve Bachelor of Fairfield University. Gratitude is owed to Professor Dayong and my other colleagues at Peking University for their collegiality during the last stages of this book. Above all, Timothy Gilfoyle of Loyola University in Chicago and Joshua Freeman of the City University of New York took the time to read and offer valuable comments on full drafts of the manuscript. I learned much from their advice, and if I did not always follow their admonitions, the fault is mine and not theirs. Biju Mathew, author of the fine book *Taxi*, gave me pointers about the Taxi Workers Alliance and told me wonderful tales about his driver friends. Carl Prince of New York University listened patiently to many years of promises about completion of this book. I am grateful to Charles Silver of the Museum of Modern Art for his advice on hack men in motion pictures.

I owe a great debt to Robert J. Brugger, acquisitions editor at the Johns Hopkins University Press. He first signed on to this project almost a decade ago and then waited with patience and gave gentle prods about the manuscript. His constant belief in the value of this study has braced me immeasurably. Susan Lantz at the Johns Hopkins University Press performed an excellent and thorough copyediting.

My wife, Gao Yunxiang, always treated this project with great enthusiasm, and to her I owe much love and appreciation. This book is dedicated to the memory of my parents, the Reverend Graham Rushing Hodges and Elsie Russell Hodges, who always made me believe in myself and in this project. They will always be the best fares this hack man will ever have.

Taxi! ━━━━━━

Introduction ======================================

The New York City cabdriver personifies the energy and zeal of the world's greatest city. Tourists and residents view the Statue of Liberty, the Empire State Building, Times Square, and Central Park as the great spectacles of the city. Cabdrivers make up the human element of the New York City experience. While we admire the courage of the city's firefighters, especially since the events of September 11, 2001, and eye its police with wary respect, neither has the universal appeal of New York City's legion of taxicab drivers. Hard-driving and talking relentlessly, they have given generations of city dwellers and tourists moments that represent what New York is all about. It is hard to overestimate the psychic hold images of cabdrivers have on the American people. No film or television show about the streets of New York is complete without the presence of taxis and their drivers. In Las Vegas, a spray-painted image of a cab adorns a wall of many floors of the New York Casino. On eBay, the Internet auction service, vendors regularly sell such items of cabby kitsch as cookie jars, fountain pens, pins, shirts and blouses, movie photos, and even nail polish amid a myriad of toy cars from all eras and nationalities. Though taxi drivers provide a critically important mode of city transportation exceeded in patronage only by the subway, it is their place in the public culture of New York that makes them engaging.[1]

The history of the New York City cabdriver, from the first use of meter-equipped, gasoline-powered vehicles in 1907 to the present day, brings together all New Yorkers. A cabdriver culture exists within the garages, in holding pens at airports, in cut-and-thrust driving along the avenues and streets of the city, and in the minds of the taxi men themselves. As public carriers, taxi men interact with anyone who stoops into the back-seat of a cab, dodges their speeding vehicles, or stands rejected and angry as cabs roar past without stopping. Those relationships are also the story of this book.

Cabdrivers, until recently, have held a special place in the hearts of New Yorkers and visitors. Within the packed interior of the cab, driver and passengers create an evanescent intimacy by which life stories, political opinions, philosophies of life and love, and personal problems quickly surface during a ten-minute therapeutic ride. As a *New Yorker* magazine cover recently illustrated,[2] New Yorkers often offer their deepest feelings to cabdrivers masquerading as psychologists. In a city where most interactions are fleeting and meaningless, the cabdriver provides denizens with at least the illusion of camaraderie in a mutual performance. The cabby receives a bigger tip for words of wisdom or humor; the fare, often from the middle class, pretends for a moment that he or she is having meaningful human contact, and with someone of a "working-class family." A kind of class nostalgia affects public attitudes toward generations of cabbies. Poet Kate Daniels, meditating in the back seat of a cab, notices the wrinkles in the cabby's face and the voice, "loud and tired." She reflects, "He's just another person with a crummy job"— another lousy father, like her own. But she has learned to forgive:

> I know the way it feels
> To stay awake and work when all you want
> Is to lay your head in someone's lap and sleep.[3]

Few, if any, other tradespeople in New York evoke the personal and cultural fascination that Daniels conjures up. Of course, cabbies, as tradesmen working in a small shop on wheels, view their time with customers as money. Out in the streets, the cabby may consider himself (for they are nearly always male) his own boss, but thirty to forty times a day, passengers enter the cab believing they have the right to direct the driver as they please. The cabby may consider his taxi to be his shop and will bridle against any suggestion of inferiority, but unlike the shopkeeper, the taxi driver rarely encounters the same customer twice, and his momentary relationship with the fare relies on a metered cost for distance and time plus a tip that has become a mandatory part of the final price. Personality, rather than exceptional driving skills, is important in the making of a cabdriver. The expectation of a tip further complicates a class understanding of the taxi men. Few other shopkeepers expect a tip added to their charges, and the institution of this practice brought taxi men closer to the broadly defined class of service workers. As fiercely as taxi men might reject such a characterization, their interactions with fares and the chase for better tips make them resemble servants.[4]

That mixture of independence and servility is repeated dozens of times each day for a cabdriver. His shift consists of a long series of brief contacts with strangers whom he will rarely encounter again. His customers are found at random and do not know each other. Serving them exposes the cabby to numerous hazards and exigencies, including robbers, belligerent drunks, fare-jumpers, psychopaths and, in moments mandating heroism, the birth of babies. Despite cabbies' need for street smarts, few people regard them as skilled; in fact, many customers can drive and know the directions to their destination as well as their cabby does. They commonly treat him as if he were invisible. One-time cabby Clancy Sigal remarked that being a taxi man brought him closest to understanding what Ralph Ellison meant by the "invisible man," who is "looked at, spoken to, and seen through." As we shall see, relations between cabby and fares can move past class nostalgia to alienation.[5]

Such attitudes often stem from difference. Hacking tends to blur ethnic and racial boundaries among cabbies, but those divisions remain significant in the relations between cabbies and their customers. Recently, angry controversies have erupted when cabbies refused to pick up African Americans. The class status of cabbies mixes with ethnicity and race. In short, the story of the cabdriver tells much about the frustrations of the urban worker.

My research examines the relationships cabbies have with the city government, with employers and unions, with their fares, and with other cabbies. On one level, the saga of cabdrivers involves a frustrated quest for unity in response to the myriad regulations that govern the trade, to their boss at a large fleet garage or, today, to the brokers who hire drivers as independent contractors. Cabbies have struggled to organize into an effective union but have succeeded only for short periods. Their relationships with municipal government, their employers, and unions create a framework in which cabbies can be discussed as a class. In this book, I chart the tempestuous relationships that cabbies have had with the agencies that seek to control them. In so doing, I discuss how cabbies cooperate or compete with each other. As important are the often-stormy interactions cabbies have with their passengers. There is a routine quality to taxi rides for many passengers (the overwhelming percentage of patrons are businesspeople who live below Ninety-sixth Street in Manhattan and are going to and from work), but serendipity can occur anytime someone climbs in the back of a cab. Significant differences in class exist among cabdrivers. Owner-drivers, who own a medallion (a city permit to pick up customers on city streets or at the airports) are socially lower middle class, but are the elite of cabbies. These owner-drivers form associations to advance their mutual interests and protect the legal status of medallions that are currently worth hundreds of thousands of dollars and purchased through lengthy mortgages. Owner-drivers generally regard themselves as independent from the fleet drivers and have acted as strikebreakers. They epitomize the lower middle class, the petite bourgeoisie, while the fleet and lease drivers rank in the middle to lower depths of the working class, depending on their ability to organize, an accomplishment rarely achieved by cabbies.

Owner-drivers are distinct from fleet drivers, who historically have been employees paid under a commission system by taxi companies ranging in size from a few to hundreds of cabs or more. Regular fleet drivers, known as "steady men," relied on the company to give them a cab each day as long as their daily "bookings" (fare totals) remained sufficiently high. Many cabbies drove for fleets their entire work lives with no more job guarantee than the next day's earnings and, for decades, no promise of a pension. After the 1979 city law permitting "horse hiring," or daily leases, cabdrivers became independent contractors and lost any collective powers. Lease drivers rent their cabs daily or on long-term contracts, do not own medallions, and must pay a garage or broker a set amount before earning any money for themselves. The differing economic and social experiences of owner-drivers and fleet and lease employees stymie class consciousness. Only the sameness of their labor and public perceptions of cabbies enable us to understand them as a single class.

Lording over most cabbies are the fleet owners, who are tough, hardened, and ruthless businessmen. Accustomed to the rough-and-tumble world of making a living on the streets of New York, fleet owners are staunchly anti-union and determined to extract profits using as little company paternalism as possible. In recent years, fleet owners, known perennially as "bosses," have been joined by brokers, who represent individual medallion owners eager to rent out their monopolistic privilege.

A third set of masters are the elected and appointed city officials who make the rules by which cabdrivers work. Fleet or owner-driver cabbies work within a regulatory system defined by the city government. References to cabbies in this book are largely to medallion, "yellow cab" drivers (both owner-drivers and employees), though the term "taxi driver" for someone who drives customers in a car to a destination for pay can also apply to limousine or "black cars," to non-medallion livery drivers, and to "gypsy" cabbies. Limousine and livery drivers are licensed by the Taxi and Limousine Commission and are supposed to secure passengers only through radio calls. "Gypsy" cabbies roam poorer parts of the city without any supervision. In this book, I study these drivers as they interact with medallion drivers and as alternative taxi men, kept separate from yellow-cab drivers by city regulations and often by race.[6]

Whether owner-drivers or fleet or lease drivers, cabbies do share common burdens. An editorial in the *Taxi Times* decades ago described enduring laments of the fleet cabdriver:

> The lack of job security and the unspeakable working conditions, the constant striving to make ends meet on a miserly commission; the daily perils of driving in congested traffic at the beck and call of overbearing passengers, the degrading system of the shape-up and the petty shakedown artists in the garages, the biting sarcasm and harassment suffered on the streets of the city at the hands of law-enforcement agents of the industry over the past fifty years combine to produce "cabbyitis," an occupational illness of the taxi drivers, a chronic condition of anxiety; acute mental strain, and nervous tension, sapping the taxi driver's strength, debilitating the drivers' physical condition, breaking down the drivers' endurance and will to resist, eroding away their dignity and self-respect.[7]

The nameless writer hit upon timeless feelings of frustration and failure that plague the cabdriver. Whether consciously or not, writers, poets, filmmakers, and journalists evoke "cabbyitis," a unique occupational mentality that affects the interplay of hack men with the world and with each other. Many Americans know about cabdrivers through images created in Hollywood films. Hollywood has consciously crafted an imitation Manhattan for American viewers who might never venture to the big city. In urban dramas from the dawn of cinema to the present, cabdrivers have been omnipresent, sometimes as protagonists or more often as supporting figures. Inside the tiny interiors of the cab, cinematic drivers and passengers enact human dramas.[8]

There is something about the appearance of a taxi driver in a film or television show that animates the American public. Part of this has to do with the American fascination with the road. Like truck drivers, cabdrivers are iconic figures who inherit the restless, rootless, and marginalized traditions of cowboys, loggers, and miners. Americans and the rest of the world view cabbies as men on the loose, working on the fringes of society but bestowed with keen insights into human character. In the popular mind, taxi men's wisdom is mixed with laughter. The public sees cabdrivers as *luftmenchen,* a term that literally translates to "people of wind, smoke, and onion skin" and encapsulates men who are lone wolves, individualistic and without skills and social ties, or who are impractical people without a sure income.[9]

Novelists and poets populate their works with cabbies. As explorers and interpreters of the city, cabdrivers are frequently the heroes of detective novels. In children's books, cabbies become guides to language and to urban life.[10] Novelists and short-story writers use cabdrivers in character studies about city living. Cabdrivers are men of the crowds. Historically, cabbies and intellectuals have eyed each other warily. Writers enjoy lampooning cabbies but also have a grudging respect for their purported autodidactic knowledge. Cabdriver intellectuals and philosophers are legendary. Hack men are renowned by the public for their vigorous self-expression, jokes, wild political opinions, and knowledge (or lack thereof) of the city. Dave Betts, the self-described taxi philosopher, proclaimed: "Yeah, I hate driving a taxi, but I love my crowds, I love to hear em laughing, chatting, the way they dress. I love to see em happy an' I hate to see em look miserable." The quality of a good heart, he believed, came forth in a good tip, and he noted that the poorest passengers often "tip beyond their means."[11]

There are few histories of cabdrivers. More commonly, scholars have explored the regulatory phenomenon of the medallion and the finances of hacking.[12] I use these studies to draw out details and inform the story of cabbies. The story of the cabdriver fits into the history of New York City's laboring people, who have been well covered in Joshua Freeman's two important studies of the working classes of New York City since the 1930s. Although Freeman rarely discusses taxi drivers, his work provides significant contrast and context for this study.[13]

Many of the words in this book come from the taxi drivers themselves. In memoirs, interviews, joke books, restaurant guides, recordings, and documentary films, cabdrivers love to tell their stories and reflect upon their fares, experiences, political and social views, and the meaning of life. People love to listen to them. In this book, I draw from over thirty published autobiographies by hackies, which tell in detail how they got into hacking, how they have experienced New York, their work lives, and troubles with women, and what hacking has taught them. Above all, I have tried to let cabbies tell their stories, which often are stranger than fiction.

Hacking is, of course, a universal occupation, practiced in towns and cities all over the world. Hackies are folk heroes in Paris, Moscow, Beijing, Tokyo, and every city of any size around the globe. London's cabbies are commonly thought of as close relatives to New York hack men, but New York cabbies are proud of the differences between the two cultures. Diversity is one striking difference. In New York today, native-born Americans are just one of many nationalities of cabdrivers; there are Irish, Russian, French, Chinese, and Italian hack men, and over 50 percent of New York cabdrivers come from predominantly Muslim nations such as Bangladesh, Pakistan, Egypt, Morocco, and Nigeria, or from India, where the Muslim influence is strong. This massive social change has powerfully affected the relations between cabby and customer.

New York City is a place in process, and cabdrivers are the public face of the social changes of the city.[14] Taxi drivers everywhere write memoirs, endure government regulations, and have complex relations with their customers. Often, they bring their national perceptions of hacking to New York City streets to meld into a new global culture. Hacking has historically been regarded as one of the great acculturating forces in American society. Today, when ethnicity is a powerful force, contemporary cab drivers blend their home cultures with what they find in New York.[15]

Taken across the span of the past century, the history of New York City cabdrivers helps us move beyond sentimental clichés about their identity to uncover their uneven struggles to organize, survive, and create in a city that at once reveres taxi men and pushes them close to the bottom of its working population. This book is the story of that struggle, of what journalist Stanley Walker long ago termed that "dangerous and heartbreaking business," of driving a cab.[16]

1

The Creation of the Taxi Man, 1907–1920

Modern cab driving stems from a grudge. In early 1907, a thirty-year-old New York businessman named Harry N. Allen became incensed when a hansom cab driver charged Allen and his lady friend five dollars for a three-quarter-mile trip from a Manhattan restaurant to his home. Angered by this vehicular extortion, Allen vowed to create a new cab service. He recalled later: "I got to brooding over this nighthawk. I made up my mind to start a service in New York and charge so-much per mile." Word of Allen's plan circulated for months in advance. First reports appeared on March 27, 1907. Interviewed forty years later, Allen recalled how he went to France to scout out reliable, improved automobiles that were superior to the American versions derided as "smoke-wagons." In Europe, he secured over eight million dollars in underwriting funds from Lazarre Weiller, a French industrialist, and Davison Lulziell, an English railroad operator. Armed with foreign capital, he obtained a full financial package from his father, Charles C. Allen, a stockbroker, and his father's friends. Additional powerful backers included publisher William Randolph Hearst and political fixer Big Tim Sullivan. The police commissioner promised "moral" support. Hearst told Allen to ignore his critics because "they'll all be riding in your cabs sooner or later."[1]

On October 1, 1907, Allen achieved revenge by orchestrating a parade of sixty-five shiny new red gasoline-powered French Darracq cabs, equipped with fare meters, down Fifth Avenue. Their destination was a hack stand in front of the brand new Plaza Hotel on Fifty-ninth Street, across from the southeast corner of Central Park. Each driver wore a uniform designed to emulate a West Point cadet's. Allen instructed his employees to interact courteously with passengers to defuse an issue that had been a matter of public ire for decades. Irritation over rudeness and rate gouging by cabbies was perennial. Underwritten by his European creditors and by public enthusiasm for the new vehicles, Allen's New York Taxicab Company prospered. At the end of the first year, he gave faithful drivers a gold watch and announced he was starting a pension fund. In 1908, he had seven hundred cabs on the streets. Such sports as millionaire Diamond Jim Brady, an early skeptic of Allen's plan, bought five hundred dollars worth of discount coupons for rides. Modern taxicab service and its celebrated drivers soon became a reality for New Yorkers, pushing horse-drawn hacks into the dustbin of history.[2]

Harry Allen's success was momentary. Although production demands outstripped supply by mid-1908, Allen encountered serious labor problems. That autumn the first major strike by taxicab drivers destroyed his empire. On October 8, 1908, even as he announced a pension plan and handed out gold watches to the faithful drivers, five hundred of them walked out in a wage dispute. The drivers demanded a flat salary of $2.50 per day and free gasoline, claiming that gas costs alone were over eighty cents per day. There were other grievances. On top of maintenance and fuel costs, Allen charged the drivers a quarter per day for uniform use and another dime to polish the car brass. These fees cut their daily earnings down to less than a dollar a day. Allen rejected these appeals, arguing that good drivers made over $112 a month after these deductions, which he claimed was an excellent living wage.

Taxi drivers joined with the Teamsters Union to combat Allen. Negotiations collapsed. Violence flared with the introduction of strikebreakers. In one incident, angry taxi drivers invaded Bellevue to search for a scab who had eluded them by jumping into the river and then swimming to the back of the hospital. Allen hired "special policemen" armed with guns to protect his cabs, but the striking hack men continued their assaults. Although the regular police strived to create order in the streets, strikers found Allen near the Plaza Hotel and hailed him with a barrage of stones. Infuriated taxi men threw rocks through the large plate glass windows of the Plaza, the Knickerbocker Hotel, and another hotel on the Upper West Side. City police officers rode in Allen's cabs to intimidate the rioters, who in turn lured scabs down dark streets and beat them. One man died after a beating on East Seventy-second Street on October 15. Hired strikebreakers inadvertently shot and killed a small boy in the street. Strikers burned cabs and pushed them into the East River. Allen then hired Waddell and Mahon, a strikebreaking firm, with orders to smash the strike. Strikers responded with a note promising to bomb his company unless the private army was removed. When Allen refused, strikers hurled a bomb into a lot where Allen stored his cabs, barely missing a number of pedestrians. The strikers continued to attack taxicabs; in one instance in Harlem, sympathizers beat up two of Waddell and Mahon's goons and terrified several female passengers.[3]

On November 7, after a month of violence, the Teamsters Union suddenly halted the strike, abandoning its demands for recognition and accepting the New York Taxicab Company's requirement that the company be an "open shop," in which employment is not restricted to union members. The next day however, strikers voted unanimously to reject the agreement and continue the strike. Repudiating the negotiating committee, the strikers looked to other branches of the Teamsters Union for support. Within a few days, some drivers trickled back to work amid reports that the local's treasury was badly depleted. Angry negotiations between the company and the rank-and-file drivers went long into the nights. Out of money and disillusioned with the Teamsters, who had stopped supplying strike pay, workers returned on November 16, and it seemed as if Allen was triumphant. His victory ended soon after, when mounting legal costs stemming from the strike forced him out of the business.[4]

Labor peace was short-lived. Within a month, over three thousand coach and cabdrivers represented by a new union, the Liberty Dawn Association, went on strike in opposition to open-shop demands from employers such as the Morris Seaman Company, which was organized in 1907. They were soon joined by the taxicab drivers, meaning that technological innovations had not separated the interests of transport workers. Waddell and Mahon's private army of over a thousand strikebreakers reappeared. The strike shut down all transportation from the big hotels and on the streets. The *New York Times* warned that the "inconvenience of the strike" would inspire much ill-feeling. Although strikers threw rocks at the special police, within days the strike dissipated. The coach and taxicab companies had to employ goons to halt the labor action, as these strikes from October through December 1908 showed the depth of unrest among cabdrivers.[5]

Labor turbulence mirrored the extraordinary impact the new cabs had on the urban environment. Their appearance came after decades of searching for a reliable urban transport for the middle classes. Measuring the fare was not hard. Taximeters had appeared in Paris in 1869, and New York newspapers reported them at that time, but the innovation of gasoline-powered vehicles was new. One major reason for the rapid development of automobiles, as they became known, was public desire to replace horse-drawn vehicles. Many New Yorkers felt the replacement of horses was long overdue. Pedestrians had to be especially wary of horses. They considered horses to be unpredictable, smelly, and dangerous. Drivers knew the animals could not be reliably curbed and might run away, kick pedestrians, or be stolen. Horses required a professional stableman and usually an experienced driver. Inconvenience and cost meant that such transportation was out of reach for all but the wealthy. City life was hard on the animals. Scandals swirled around the condition of stables, which were prone to horrible fires that disrupted commerce and threatened homes. Horses were highly vulnerable to disease and had short work lives of about four years. A horse sometimes died in the street, and this required other horses to pull it away, packing the lanes. As business in Manhattan soared, horse-drawn vehicles created traffic jams. As express wagons pulled larger loads, owners used bigger animals, often teaming them in unreliable combinations. One scared horse could spook a whole team. Then there was the stench. Horse manure amounted to over a million pounds a day; huge piles of the stuff stored on the street corners for use as fertilizer caused a nasty odor that overwhelmed the efforts of sanitation men.[6]

Despite the demand for a replacement for horse-drawn vehicles, initial reforms failed. Bicycles showed some promise and, after the invention of the safety bicycle in 1889, attracted women who enjoyed new freedom in the streets, though the bikes hardly satisfied the need of mass transportation. Although steam-powered automobiles promised cleaner means of transport, they failed to persuade urban consumers to abandon horses.[7]

Horse-drawn hacks had taken passengers to destinations since the early nineteenth century. As the city spread rapidly up Manhattan Island and into Brooklyn in the antebellum years, New Yorkers no longer thought of their home as a "walking city." Horse-drawn and, later, steam-powered omnibuses plowed down major avenues but were slow, crowded, and unreliable. Seeking to avoid congestion and disease and fearful of violence, New York's new middle class moved further up the island and spilled into nearby towns. Mass transport took two forms. Horse-drawn omnibuses and horse-drawn railroads flourished in the lower part of Manhattan. In the upper sections of the city, steam-powered railroad lines carried over a million commuter passengers per year to upper Manhattan and Westchester County by the Civil War. Passengers then changed at Grand Central Station to the horse-drawn omnibuses that carried them the rest of the way downtown. Designed to prevent congestion, this method in fact increased it, because New Yorkers readily took to another form of private transport. Carriages, restricted to a tiny elite in the colonial and early national periods, became a choice method of transport for the middle classes by the Civil War. In the streets, throngs of carts and express wagons mixed with the steam- and horse-powered railways to pose an extraordinary danger for pedestrians, and inside, the omnibuses and railcars presented a kind of "modern martyrdom," for female passengers, already wary of the exploring fingers of urban male toughs.[8]

For those members of the middle class who could or would not afford a horse, carriage, and stable, hack drivers were plentiful. At first, most of these drivers were African Americans, who were licensed to drive by the city in the early nineteenth century. By the 1840s, as was the case with many semi-skilled and unskilled occupations, Irish immigrants pushed African Americans out of the trade. This early example of ethnic succession was more violent than later transitions, but it established a tradition of entering immigrant groups viewing hacking as a viable income and significant step up the ladder of economic mobility. Drivers toiled behind the wheel hoping that their sons could find better work. A second innovation was organizational. While African American drivers were primarily small entrepreneurs, the new Irish drivers did not own their rigs or horses and worked for wages for sizable fleets. The 1855 census counted 805 Irish coachmen and hack drivers, a figure that overshadowed 57 Germans and Anglo-Americans and scattered other nationalities. The Irish continued to dominate hacking and other street trades over the course of the nineteenth century.[9]

By the Civil War, fleets of several hundred hacks operated in the city streets. The reputation of hackmen was dubious. In the 1880s, hacks and cabs that traveled the city streets at night were called "nighthawks" and were notorious for preying on their customers. Their bad reputation came from cheating fares and from servicing nocturnal vice. There were also controversies over business methods; disputes over monopolistic behavior around key hotel doors were chronic. New Yorkers were accustomed to payment methods, at least. Fares based upon distance were not new, having been employed since mid-century.[10]

Gas power was not the first innovation in cabs. Previously, steam-powered automobiles had failed to attract consumer interest. Electric cabs had showed some promise; since July of 1897, twelve electric hansom cabs (an early innovation combining speed and safety), had plied the city streets. Organized by the Electric Carriage and Wagon Company, these novelty cabs competed with horse-drawn hacks. Despite their technological innovation, called by *Scientific American* in a March 1909 article "one of the most significant facts of city transportation," electric cabs varied only slightly in performance and appearance from horse-drawn vehicles. *Scientific Magazine* preferred the electric cab because it was silent and odorless. Even though the Electric Vehicle Company expanded its New York fleet to sixty-two in 1898 and then to one hundred the next year, its overall success was short-lived. Electric cabs were cumbersome, were unable to move faster than fifteen miles per hour, and required a battery recharge every twenty-five miles that took eight hours to complete. This problem limited use of electric taxis to single rides and made cruising impossible. Changing a battery also required use of an overhead crane and a spacious garage. Replacing the pneumatic tires required taking off the entire wheel disk, which caused further delays. Despite the clean and silent operation, passenger comfort was minimal. Fares sat in an open seat in the front of the cab, while the driver perched overhead. The brakes were applied forward, which in emergency situations meant that the entire car might topple over. Not surprisingly, electric cabs did not catch on. One contemporary writer observed that many people took one ride but rarely returned for a second, preferring horse-drawn hacks. A fire settled the issue. In January 1907, the Electric Carriage and Wagon Company went under when three hundred of its cabs burned in a garage fire.[11]

In their infancy, gas-powered cabs were but slight improvements over their predecessors. Besides their uncertain safety, the two-cylinder cabs had other limitations. A common model known as the Maxwell was noisy and would not go more than five miles before grease fouled the spark plugs. Its cab lamps blew out any time a wind rose. There were similar problems with the Pierson cab. One veteran cabby recalled, "I had to wrap a blanket around my legs to keep warm. I used to wear goggles to keep the dust out of my eyes and, boy, when the sun was hot, it cut a hole through the top of the car and roasted a fellow alive." Still, the cabby, Emil

Hendrickson, thought it was easier in the old days, when "a fellow got big tips and didn't have to push a hack for sixteen hours; when he didn't have to fracture his skull climbing over a cab in front of him; when the streets weren't crowded with trucks and cars." Hendrickson acknowledged that the Pierson was unreliable. On one occasion, the boss told him to get out the banana oil and shine the cab for a party of five. Over the Manhattan Bridge they went. At Forty-second Street and Fifth Avenue, the car stalled. Hendrickson and two of the gentlemen got out and pushed. A water belt slapped one of them and turned his fancy white shirt red. The trip from Brooklyn to Riverside Drive took nine hours. When the "quality people" came out of their dinner, the bearings on the car burned out. A tow truck took until 3 a.m. to arrive. Even then, the boss charged the passengers twenty-five dollars. Hendrickson wrote that he would not have blamed them if they had refused to pay anything.

Hendrickson recalled outwitting one of the three traffic cops in town. He received a ticket when his Steamer cab began to smoke on a back road in Brooklyn. The policeman ticketed him because the smoke hid the license plate numbers. In court, Hendrickson pointed out that the smoke was steam, and that "it is white and it evaporates." Case dismissed.

By the arrival of Allen's taxi drivers, the New York cabby had evolved into, as one observer put it, "an efficient race." Journalist Vince Thompson noted how the cabby displayed his considerable self-respect by bowling down the street and pushing aside other vehicles. Thompson regarded the world of hacking as "loose and lawless," and recommended that aspiring young men learn to drive cabs as a lesson in how to gain life goals ruthlessly and without rules. His complaints had the ring of truth. While the city aimed to license public hacks, thousands of other unlicensed drivers roamed the streets making up their own fares. Getting a license was no problem either. A man could "come out of Sing Sing [prison]," get "two greasy letters of recommendation," and obtain a license without the least background check. Thompson concluded that the "New York cabbie was the most slovenly in the world."[12]

Thompson's acerbic descriptions were not unique. Writers frequently compared New York's taxi men unfavorably with their presumed relatives in London and with a similar system in Paris. Though the New York and London cabbies are cousins, their development was in fact quite different. London cabbies were organized into a company, much like a guild, that allowed them to protect their trade interests and fostered independent, even middle-class sensibilities. Before getting a license, the

London cabby had to study the city terrain for several years and pass a rigorous examination that displayed his "knowledge" of the city's geography. Only then was the applicant allowed to get a license and purchase an expensive hack. His New York counterpart learned by on-the-job experiences and often drove shabby, poorly designed automobiles.[13] Though the quality of New York cabs has improved over the years, the differences in organization and preparation remain.

There were other historical differences between the London and New York cabmen. First, the introduction of fleets in antebellum New York meant that the bulk of New York hack men were employees, not owners. The lowly, underpaid status of the New York driver insured casual, transient employment. Never masters of their destinies, New York's hack men developed a different culture than London's. Though New York City government regulation of hack men derived from English and Dutch law, patterns of immigrant succession in the trade meant that New York taxi men were more international in origins.

The collision of Anglo-American law and immigrant culture made hacking one of the most visible means of becoming American. As Harry Allen's dress code for his drivers indicates, middle-class and elite New Yorkers viewed hack men as service workers. As cabs became commonplace in the 1910s, they served as readily accessible urban transport for the city's middle class. The urban bourgeoisie used cabs primarily to get from home to work or to entertainment. That mundane quality allowed class attitudes prevalent in the home to be extended easily into the interior of a cab.

Taxi men, as we will see, resented such characterizations. Yet the job allowed any newcomer to get a start in New York City. When becoming American meant acculturation, hacking took on a mythic quality as an entry-level trade by which an immigrant could work toward the success of the next generation in the American economy and society. Much later, with the shift toward racialized identity politics and the return of nativism in the late twentieth century, cabdrivers were perceived as incapable of assimilation into American life.

Considered later to be the quintessential immigrant job, hacking in the early years of the twentieth century was mostly restricted to the second generation and beyond. Irish New Yorkers had long dominated the hackney trade, dating back to the creation of fleets in the 1850s. Census data from 1900 indicates that second-generation Irish immigrants were even more likely than their fathers to become hack men. While few immigrants came to New York with the stated purpose of becoming a cab-driver, hacking jobs were a big step up from the unskilled day labor and street work in which many found themselves, and thus were considered good jobs for sons. The sons of Eastern European Jews and Italians were also more likely to be cabdrivers than their fathers. Italians prone to enter the world of hacking were the ones who arrived with few skills and fell into the poorest paying jobs. Although Jewish immigrants usually arrived with some skills, they faced discrimination in finding work. They could either seek jobs in expanding businesses such as textiles or labor in jobs that had low hurdles for employment. Hacking seemed to offer some stability to Jewish sons. Nearly 17 percent of second-generation Eastern European Jewish immigrants in New York City were hack men in the 1910s. By 1920, the number of Jewish cabbies was overwhelming. The *Taxi Weekly* quoted the *Jewish Daily Forward* in the 1920s as saying that about twenty thousand of the thirty-five thousand cabdrivers in New York were Jewish.[14]

If Jewish, Irish, and Italian drivers were not yet regarded as American (though the Irish were on their way), New Yorkers unquestionably wanted rides in their vehicles. Despite the turbulence in the industry, the taxi gradually took hold as an economic and social characteristic of the city. By 1910, the term "taxi" was in widespread use, though drivers continued to be known as hack men, hackeys, or hacks. The final blow for the horse cab may have occurred when the Darracq cabs replaced them in the ranks in front of the Waldorf Astoria Hotel. New urban edifices stimulated public use of cabs. After the construction of Pennsylvania and Grand Central stations, accompanied by the covering of railroad tracks and the creation of innumerable city blocks, the central areas of New York became dense grids with massive amounts of cross-town traffic. New York City's expansion as the center for banking, insurance, news media, department stores, and ancillary restaurants, theaters, and hotels created a demand for comfortable taxis. Subways and streetcars enabled city dwellers to move about, but the distances between subway lines and the lack of space for baggage limited their value. Prosperous New Yorkers wanted taxicabs to move mountains of baggage from home to hotel or train station. The need for taxis was not restricted to the upper class. More and more, hailing a taxi became a habit for the middle classes, who found the subway inconvenient. Hurried businessmen and middle-class New Yorkers now used cabs to travel to work or leisure in the burgeoning business districts. Tourism produced more taxi fares. Cabs attracted bohemian or voyeuristic New Yorkers who went slumming in Chinatown or around Times Square.[15]

The disappearance of hackney coaches by 1910 focused the struggle between taxicab drivers and their employers. The 1908 strike was a rehearsal for angry walkouts that occurred in the fall of 1909 and 1910. This meant more work for a "goon squad" of private policemen and spurred taxi companies to meet in the spring of 1909 to discuss plans to merge and form a taxi trust. The city government, viewing cabs as a public utility, responded with plans to regulate the new industry. Independent drivers, a force for the first time, decried the move toward monopoly. Price wars commenced as new companies emerged with plans to drop the initial fare from seventy cents to thirty-five; followed by quick promises to lower rates to twenty cents. The drivers' strikes during these two years had additional developments. There was less violence than in 1908, but the strikes were as protracted, and the 1910 strike witnessed a number of riots. Because the walkouts cost the city's economy about $4,500 a day, Mayor William Gaynor took a stronger hand in negotiations than did his predecessor and made the city police force more a part of the suppression of the strikes, a decision the cab companies applauded.

The 1910 strike was the first time that independent taxi drivers made an impact upon a work stoppage. As the fleet drivers went to the picket lines again and again in hopes of a closed shop for their union, independent drivers caught a windfall. There were reports that independent cabbies were making several months pay during the annual horse show and the opening of the opera season, which coincided in early November 1910. Many of the independent drivers sported deceptive signs on their cabs, proclaiming the vehicle to be a "union cab." That misnomer reassured gullible or desperate fares but also created greater confusion and cynicism about the potential for successful unionization for cabbies. It also marked the first instance of competition between fleet and independent drivers.[16]

A renewed attempt to unionize cabdrivers came in 1911 when the Chauffeurs and Helpers Union enabled drivers to work on a fixed daily salary for a stated number of hours per day. The original contract, for example, called for a $2.53 wage for an eleven-hour day. When the city government eliminated private hack stands and made them a public concession in 1913, it also encouraged fleet drivers to become owner-drivers.

As the advantages of being an independent driver outweighed working for a fleet and being a union member, the union lost a key bargaining position and membership.[17]

After the failure of these strikes, union-organizing efforts lapsed because of the pressure of competition from owner-drivers. More attention was paid to regulation. Initially, regulation of cabs fell under legislation passed in the previous century to govern hackney coaches. In May 1909, New York's municipal government passed ordinances to place taximeter inspection under the Bureau of Licenses, lowered the initial fare slightly, and required uniform fares. Fleet owners protested and took the city to court. This first effort failed to pass muster in the New York Supreme Court, which ruled that placing all passenger vehicles under a single law was unconstitutional. Soon after, fares bounced back up to $1.50 for the initial charge, or "drop." Reformers, led by Alderman Courtland Nicoll, a descendant of Richard Nicoll, the first English governor of New York, pushed for legislation that would negate the fleets' ability to avoid accident liabilities through a mesh of holding companies and limited partnerships. Nicoll also targeted the false distinction between public cabs and "special" vehicles that, if left unregulated, sold access to private hack stands on city streets to the highest bidder, caused traffic congestion, and insured corruption. After reforms guided through by Nicoll, the city government established open taxi stands along the major avenues and streets and in front of hotels, restaurants, and other major business sites.[18]

An additional concern was the power of private monopoly taxi companies. First organized in 1907, the Morris Seaman Corporation owned, by March 11, 1912, some 60 percent of the two thousand cabs operating in the city. Morris Seaman achieved dominant control through aggressive acquisitions of small garages. Through such expansive control, Morris Seaman Corporation was able to pay over $110,000 annually for street privileges in front of hotels, clubs, and restaurants. Drivers did not cruise the streets, but returned to hack stands owned by their corporation. Drivers were paid straight wages, not commissions, plus tips. In 1913, the daily wage was $2.50 with no special requirements for a license. Ownership of the best stands was the key to success, and the higher costs of these stands meant higher rates for passengers.[19]

Low wages, high competition for lucrative hack stands, and contact with hotel employees led taxi men to turn to tips for supplemental income. The practice of tipping was relatively new in American life.

Brought back from Europe by wealthy Americans notorious for over-tipping during "grand tours," tipping became an expected part of the wage by New York's service workers by 1910. Americans generally regarded New York as the capital of tipping. As the practice spread from hotel workers to other service laborers, cabdrivers were quick to demand tips, thereby creating tension with passengers. Many Americans believed that tipping undermined social equality and even campaigned against its use as a supplement to wages.

William Rufus Scott warned in his 1916 book *The Itching Palm: A Study of the Habit of Tipping in America* that tipping promoted "flunkeyism" and undermined democracy. Scott, who came from rural America, regarded taxi men as a good example of the itching palm. He believed that the taximeter charged the patron roundly for the service provided and that cabdrivers' demands for tips were avaricious. To Scott, tipping instilled servility and a slave mentality. Among passengers, tipping induced fear, pride, and graft. The only benefactors were the employers who could get away with poorer wages, according to Scott. Cabdrivers, however, learned quickly that tips could mean the difference between good and mediocre pay. They always remembered poor tippers. In one famous murder case in the 1920s, the defendant argued that he was nowhere near the scene of the crime. A cabdriver recalled taking the accused to the spot: "It was him all right. The reason I remember him so well is that he gave me a lousy nickel tip." Such clashes affected the reputation of famous Americans. Baseball player Ty Cobb of the Detroit Tigers became notorious for his surly response to a taxi man's request for a tip. After paying the fare but refusing to give a tip, Cobb snarled: "Want a tip? Don't bet on the Tigers today."[20]

Hack men's dependence on tips amplified reform efforts to reduce the hidden costs of closed lines, which restricted access to fares to a single company, at hotels and entertainment spots. Fleets customarily paid 10 to 15 percent of their gross receipts to these sites to monopolize hack stands, continuing into the motorcar era a practice dating back to horse-drawn hansom cabs. The Waldorf Astoria garnered thirty thousand dollars annually from taxicab fleets, while the Hotel Knickerbocker gained twenty thousand dollars each year; other clubs and hotels secured almost as much. Hotels and fleets obtained cooperation from the police through a system of bribes and free rides. Aldermen were corrupted through bribes and favors. Other fleets and independent drivers could not solicit fares at such stands and had to drive around, cruising relentlessly while monopoly owners got the best business. Such problems derived from the laissez-faire era of the nineteenth century, when the courts allowed companies to grab as much control over business as possible. But in the Progressive Era, with its emphasis on reform, and with the rapid increase in traffic congestion, such permissiveness seemed unfair and unhealthy in the 1920s. The Board of Aldermen passed an ordinance, the first specifically applying to the new industry, that abolished monopoly of hack stands, but further reform seemed elusive. At the same time, the aldermen lowered rates by about 15 percent, to fifty cents for the first mile and forty cents for each additional mile, with higher rates for groups of three or more passengers. The major fleets tried to respond to the new regulations by operating their cabs out of private garages linked to the restaurants and hotels and charged higher rates than the new commission allowed, arguing that their cars were private livery services. This dodge was stymied in April 1915, when the state appeals court ruled that every cab equipped with a meter fell under the ordinances. Although some fleets removed their meters, most fell into line.[21]

City efforts to loosen the fleets' control over hack stands did not immediately succeed. Terminal Transportation System and the Yellow Taxicab Corporation, which were taxi arms of major automobile companies, continued to control the lucrative hack lines at Grand Central and Penn Station until 1950. Interlopers met physical resistance and found their tires slashed and automobiles wrecked. The fleets hired thugs to intimidate drivers not employed by their corporation. For decades after the 1913 legislation that opened the hack stands at major hotels, hardened cabdrivers continued to warn newcomers not to try to get into the lines at the stations. Still, the legislation came to be known as the cabby's Magna Carta, because it ostensibly allowed equal and fair access to these lucrative sites.[22]

Lower rates meant better tips and more passengers. Drivers even opposed rate increases on occasion, arguing that a seventy-cent initial fare meant a thirty-cent tip, while an eighty-cent charge yielded a twenty-cent tip. Cheaper rates boosted the number of cabs on the streets, which rose from 2,800 in 1912 to 6,346 by 1918 and then to 13,449 in 1922. One casualty of the new regulations was Morris Seaman, who went into bankruptcy in 1916 and out of business the following year. Soon, the Yellow Cab Company became the largest fleet in the city, with 1,704 cabs by 1924. It reputedly chose the color yellow because it was easiest to recognize at a distance and at night. To combat the power of the Yellow Cab

Company, many smaller fleets created mutual benefit organizations, painting member cabs similar colors, placing telephones for use by fares at key points around town, and hiring drivers for the night shift.[23] Mutual benefit organizations also would enable small fleets to have a political voice.

During the early decades of the twentieth century, New Yorkers thought of cabdrivers less as hardworking immigrants than as petty criminals. There was some truth to that image. Despite the attempts by the city government and the fleets to create order in hacking, the rise of the new urban street culture attracted criminals to the trade. Loose regulations, lack of security checks, and the low prestige of the job meant easy access for lawless men. The city government hired hack inspectors to check meters and tires and warned the public about such driver schemes as flipping the meter twice to double the initial cost or initiating the fare as soon as the cab is hailed. As early as 1912, the *New York Times* reported that as many as two hundred ex-convicts owned hack licenses and used taxis for felonies. The same year, a cabby led a gang of thieves who executed a well-planned payroll robbery. Geno Montani, the cabdriver, had a regular job taking a payroll clerk from a main office to the bank. He conspired with a gang to fake an assault and robbery. The case fascinated city news readers for several months. More commonly, cabbies served as "go-betweens" for customers and prostitutes. The Committee of Fourteen, a self-appointed New York vice squad, regularly sent informants to hack stands, where they learned that cabbies were reliable sources for contacts with prostitutes.[24]

The Committee of Fourteen became interested in cabdriver crime at the close of World War I. The committee, composed of elite Republican merchants, professors, and settlement and religious workers, was aimed primarily at the abolition of prostitution. In a report revealing the demimonde of New York City, an inspector for the committee accosted a cabdriver at a hack stand. On October 24, 1918, seeking information about prostitutes on Broadway between Fifty-ninth and Sixty-ninth streets, the agent found none of the street loungers willing to help him "except one of the taxi drivers that hangs out in front of Healey's, Burke was the name." After some chitchat about a skating rink, the agent shifted conversation to "some of the girls that I had seen at the Palace and got him to believe that I was a regular guy and in with the crowd." The cabby accompanied the inspector into "Gihulys" for a drink. They spoke more about the girls, but the hack man informed the spy that few would come out into the streets because "we have a bastard of an inspector in this district and they have to be careful." Still, Burke added, there were plenty of homes around where women would receive him, "provided you don't look like a bull and if they know the man that brings you there." Burke and the inspector discussed hotels that would accept customers without baggage. Burke gave the inspector several fictitious names of pimps. Later, Burke, the inspector, and another cabby talked about the horse races and pool halls.

Although nothing came of this incident, it demonstrates the parrying done by cabdrivers and inspectors about the possibilities of vice. Although Burke seemed to be toying with the inspector, there was a veneer of truth to his meanderings. The inspector had better luck on another occasion. On Times Square, on a Friday night the same month, he spoke again to cabbies about women. He was again warned about inspectors but gradually learned much about the habits of prostitutes from the hack men. They told him of the prostitutes' apprehension of the inspectors. One practice was for streetwalkers to find "some one that looks O.K. they take a chance to hustle him and take a taxi for a ride through the park." If the prostitute failed to find a customer, the agent was told, they would go home quickly. Most of the prostitutes were "all broke now, if they get a john, they try to get as much as they can out of him." The next summer, the inspector learned more about the close ties between cabdrivers, pimps, and prostitutes. Looking for streetwalkers as always, the inspector found a cabby that directed him to a soft drink place that sold liquor after hours: "Said its on 48th Street, known as the Green Room, run by a woman named Rose Palmer, an old whore house madam, and her man is a lieutenant of the police, [but] he is not her husband, he is her pimp."

After receiving this lesson in police corruption, the inspector encountered a "fairly well-dressed man hanging around the Martinique [Hotel]," a pimp named Fred Wing, who owned a cab but drove it only for fun and for his women and rented it out to other cabbies while he pursued work as a doorman at a nearby rathskeller. Later, Wing, one of his prostitutes, and a customer took the cab for a ride to a hotel. On another night, Wing was lounging in front of the Martinique, then went inside to use their telephone. Within a few minutes, a prostitute appeared, soon to be whisked away in a taxi. Wing and the inspector talked extensively about "cat houses." Wing told the man that most were now closed but that there were a few around. The pair discussed prices of alcohol in such places; Wing parried questions about whether he was a go-between for customers and illicit groggeries. He did, however, recommend a "nice little Jane" who lived uptown in an apartment. From Wing and another driver named McCarthy, the inspector learned of houses of prostitution that cost from forty to sixty dollars for an evening of alcohol and sex. Both drivers told him that he could find them around the Martinique any time. Later, Wing and McCarthy became suspicious and stopped offering information to the inspector. Others, however, provided the inspector with the names of hotels where couples would be admitted without baggage or told him how to buy cheap, secondhand cases to carry in. As he expanded his acquaintances with the cabbies, the inspector was offered rides and introductions to women on the Upper West Side and in Harlem. One cabby offered that he knew "quite a few of the fairies," if the inspector preferred a male lover.[25]

Having become too familiar to the hack men around Times Square, who recognized him as overly curious, never willing to close a deal, but ever vigilant for differing forms of vice, the inspector went to the trouble of getting a job as a polisher at a cab garage on Eighty-sixth Street on the West Side. There he inveigled himself among the drivers and secured information about gambling. A driver took him to a saloon on Eighty-sixth and Broadway, where "in the back room were nine women, some with escorts and some without." There were soldiers drinking whiskey. Eventually, he went with a number of the servicemen and the women to an apartment called the Manhattan Court, which some cabdrivers had told him about before leaving the party. One night, the inspector said that he wanted something "fancy," and he was told that if no apartments were available, then "you take a taxicab, as there is always a taxicab around the door—they are always there for that purpose." The inspector's reports revealed the key role cabdrivers had in the nighttime underworld of illicit sex, alcohol use, and associated crimes. Most of the cabdrivers' work was humdrum—driving businessmen to work and housewives on shopping expeditions—but after dark, cabdrivers guided and transported willing New Yorkers into forbidden worlds.[26]

Notwithstanding the committee inspector's conviction that cabdrivers were innately criminal, the police and hack men learned to work together. The famous police detective Cornelius W. Willemse recalled borrowing a cab from its driver to avoid a police inspector intent on citing him for getting a shave while on duty. Desperately, the cop begged a cab from an "old sea-going hack," and told him to wait thirty minutes and then report a stolen vehicle. Meanwhile, Willemse drove the cab to the station, feeling foolish from the catcalls of other cops, who cried "Cab, Cab" to embarrass him, and reported that he had found an empty cab. The ruse worked and Willemse avoided trouble for a while.[27]

Willemse's solution to his predicament demonstrates how New Yorkers had come to accept cabs as part of the urban landscape. Taxicab driving quickly became synonymous with a new urban culture. Although contemporary journalists guessed that New Yorkers were not "cabby people," or regular taxi riders, songwriters celebrated the public mood for them. Edgar Selden and Melville Gideon's 1908 hit, "Take Me 'round in a Taxicab," included the lyrics:

There's a new-fangled cab that's designed to keep tab
To show you how are you may go
But if you're discreet
Its easy to beat
As any wise person may know
A register's there to keep track of your fare
While you watch the girl at your side
Now what is fairer than that as a squarer
So come, take me out for a drive.

Taxi men made new contributions to the street cant of New York. Too much partying gave rise to the term "taxi drunk," which described intoxicated passengers who loved to sit in the front seat and watch the meter jump. Annoying in themselves, such tipplers often became bigger problems when they could not pay their fares.[28]

The roaring presence of taxicabs made New York's streets far less safe. More dangerous than trolleys or wagons, the influx of automobiles lifted the numbers of fatal traffic accidents in the city far above the rates for London or Paris. Many of the victims were poorer children, who lacked safer playgrounds and were prone to play potentially suicidal games with the hack men.[29]

The new technology of film enhanced public acceptance of cabdrivers. During the infancy of the silent film industry, filmmakers commonly depicted working-class characters in their productions. They did so, not from any political or class consciousness, but from the growing influence of drama and because filmmakers often targeted their product to ethnic minorities and working-class patrons. These films concentrated on the pleasures and perils of urban life. Often the setting, not the actors, was the primary attraction. Real-life scenes in New York City were particular favorites. Most films involved hackneyed romances, melodramas, comedies, and adventures that rarely tried to solve social problems or uplift their audiences. There were however, a smaller group of films that focused on conflicts of labor and capital and provided political solutions.[30]

As silent films documented all of the working classes, taxi men frequently appeared in the productions. One theme that recurred in fantasies about working-class aspirations was impersonation of wealthier people, as one cabby does in *The Pretenders* (1916). There were a surprising number of films in which cabbies were involved in mayhem. In *The Closing Net* (1915), a hack man shoots and kills a "society crook," who is part of a band of dissolute gentry men. In *The Dictator* (1915), cabby John Barrymore fights another taxi man over a fare on the docks; both men fall into the river and the cabby drowns. Another socialite, this time a woman hot for thrills, takes cabs all over New York to gambling dens and other underworld locales in *The Adventure Shop* (1919). A taxi driver kills a dishonest socialite in the *Spurs of Sybil* (1918), after she has committed a series of crimes. Another taxi man runs over and kills a rejected suitor in *Half an Hour* (1920). A hack man drives over and mangles a character in *The Illustrious Prince* (1918); in the same film, after a wild night of drinking and carousing, a woman pushes her companion out of a moving taxi and kills him. A more heroic figure, a cub reporter, watches a woman being kidnapped in a taxi in *The Empty Cab* (1918); later he learns that she is safe and that the entire affair was a hoax designed to test his writing ability. A wealthy western tourist fondles a woman in a taxi; she struggles against him, falls out of the cab, and is badly injured. Because this is all fantasy, of course, they later fall in love and marry. A drunken cabby kills himself in *My Little Sister* (1919). Even darker intrigue occurs in *The Frame Up* (1917), in which a criminal syndicate takes over a taxi company in New York and turns it into a procurement operation to kidnap young girls for the white slave market.

Much of this can be blamed on the overuse of melodrama, but it is also plain that American audiences and film producers saw taxi men as sordid, untrustworthy, and violent denizens of the new urban landscape. Bad things happen to heroes and heroines in many movies, but when cabdrivers were involved in these early cinema productions, there was no redemption for their sins. As fringe members of the criminal underworld or conductors of vehicles in which crimes were committed, taxi men were characterized as highly unsavory in the early silent films.[31]

Only romance and the presence of women allowed for happy endings.

Sudden and unexpected love between two strangers, as in *A Damsel in Distress* (1920), permitted a release from the barriers of class. In *Babs' Burglar* (1917), a young woman, endowed with a thousand-dollar allowance from her father, promptly spends the cash on a new car and then drives it through a fence and backs into a milk wagon. After paying her fines, Babs, the heroine, has but sixteen cents left. She takes a job as a taxi driver to recoup her fortunes. After finding architectural drawings of her family house in the back of the cab, Babs concludes that her passenger was a burglar. She rushes to her family's home and sees him entering the house through a second story window. She fires a revolver to awaken her family. It turns out that the "burglar" was in fact her sister's suitor, who had come to elope with her. As the family enjoys the mistake, Babs is allowed to quit her job as a cabby and return home. In *Charge It to Me* (1919), a young woman, finding that she cannot buy her husband a birthday gift because their credit is overdrawn, takes a job as a taxi driver, dons a chauffeur's uniform, and quickly attracts scads of male customers. Soon, fares come bearing gifts to the husband after learning about the family plight from the lady cabby. The husband is not pleased; especially when he learns that one of the gift-bearers is a burglar. The police arrive; everyone is arrested until the wife/cabby explains everything. The cops release everyone but the burglar, and the wife quits her job and takes out her own charge account. While both films are nonsensical, they do contain elements of contemporary beliefs. Women could drive cabs, but only to help their mates or to get out of a temporary cash problem. Then they were expected to retreat to the female realm and leave the driving to the men. At the time, there were practically no female cabbies in New York.[32]

Cinematic fantasies could not hide the strife that characterized the introduction of automobiles and the creation of the cabdriver. In the brief period between 1907 and the end of World War I, the taxi driver was invented. As automobiles pushed horse-drawn hacks into oblivion, there was remarkable continuity in culture and personality from hack man to cabdriver. But though taxi men were a product of over a century of tradition, the newness of speed, competition, and the advance of a leisure society would create and plague the cabdriver, and his city, for decades to come. The new middle-class riding public seemed determined to view the cabdriver as a combination of servant and petty criminal. Fleet owners proved powerful adversaries to any hopes for cabdriver unity, and the city government seemed more interested in finding the right kind of regulation than in sympathizing with the needs of the cabdrivers. Yet through their strikes, attempts at union organization, and individual actions, the cabdrivers demonstrated a powerful will to affect their world. The next decade would test that determination.

2

Hack Men in the Jazz Age, 1920–1930

The era of Prohibition began on October 28, 1919, with passage of the Volstead Act that prohibited the use and sale of alcohol in the United States. It was intended to eliminate the use of alcohol from American society. New York City, with its entrenched drinking culture spread throughout the ranks of society and across ethnicities and work cultures, was an unlikely place for the prohibition movement to succeed. Civil authorities attempted to stop liquor sales and use, but the city's society and economy insured that such efforts would fail disastrously. The Jazz Age was celebrated in New York as nowhere else, and taxi men were eager participants in the whirlwind frenzy of nightclubbing, easy sex, and social liberation that made the 1920s in New York so notorious. Just as the nightclub world of music, dancing, and drinking blossomed in this decade, Americans' unbridled embrace of automobiles and the disorganized character of the business made hacking a major factor of the chaos in New York's streets.

The city government and its police at least tried to enforce Prohibition and to regulate taxi driving. As the taxicab matured into a full-scale urban utility in the decade after World War I, the city government and the fleets searched for order. An editorial that appeared in the *Cab News*, the magazine for fleet owners, described improvements to taxi service in New York City and goals for the future. The situation in New York was better than before, argued the writer, because of increased power of the fleets and because the "unorganized hacker with his make-shift auto, his discourteous manner and his low moral sense is disappearing and in his place, New York welcomes a responsible company that has sanitary cabs manned by responsible and capable men, stable rates and cars and service as prompt as it is trustworthy." The bias of this unflattering portrait of the owner-driver emanates, of course, from the fleet owners' desire for monopoly. Advertisements in the same issue of *Cab News* displayed, among the latest Checker and Yellow taxis, full-page illustrations of driver uniforms, gloves, and caps designed to convey the image of a reliable, courteous chauffeur for the middle classes. The fleets saw themselves as the most efficient factory to produce the perfect vehicular servant.[1]

Hack men viewed life quite differently and expressed their opinions vigorously. The 1920s saw the appearance of a new literary genre: the taxi driver memoir. The first of this type were Robert Hazard's *Hacking New York* and Dave Betts's *I'm Lucky at That*. Although cabdriver recollections were a staple of newspaper articles, Hazard's book was the first collection. Betts contributed regular columns to the *New York Telegram*. Hazard identified "all kinds of people driving hacks in New York." Rather than view his fellow drivers as decent middle-class people, he claimed that a lot of them were "gunmen, gorillas, etc, who serve a district leader at election time and get a certain amount of protection in return, and who drive taxi cabs as a convenient side line." Such toughs used closed lines, which were illicit descendants of the private hack stands a decade earlier. At the other extreme was the cabby "who had been hacking in New York ever since automobiles came in and he can tell some very good stories if you happen to meet him in one of the Coffee Pots about three o'clock in the morning."[2]

The memoirs by Hazard and Betts are filled with "good stories" that reflect the working-class attitudes of cabdrivers. Though the two autobiographies can hardly explain the mentalities of tens of thousands of cabdrivers, their comments are worth considering. Both held strong convictions about their jobs. Hazard complained about the long hours and the toll the job took on his body. After several years on the job, he offered to carry a sick woman up four flights of stairs, only to find himself badly winded after two floors. Hazard was aware of how the job damaged his marriage, telling one passenger he took Sundays off because otherwise he and his wife would never see each other. Loneliness was hardly the only occupational worry. Hazard experienced customers who would not pay; others wanted to fight him or were drunks, or sometimes both. At least drunks did not worry about accidents; one tipsy fare "went through the windshield," and did not even notice. Hazard was ambivalent about the police who could be problems or solutions. The License Bureau never did "anything but make jobs for politicians and make an opportunity for a shake down."[3]

The cabby memoirists' words reveal ethnic hostilities rampant among New York's working classes. Hazard mocked the accent of his Jewish dispatcher and regarded him as corrupt. Betts was more sympathetic toward Jews and felt they taught him about life. Betts was much more liberal than Hazard about race, arguing, "There's bad and good in all races. If people emphasize the bad eggs, then they are letting the meanest, dirtiest cussedest things in human nature . . . control us, cussed prejudice." Hazard regarded Chinese people as excellent customers and enjoyed working in Chinatown, although he reported that the neighborhood had a bad reputation. He wrote that Scots were cheap and complained about the meter immediately, though he was more amused than annoyed by their voices.[4]

Hazard and Betts agreed about the general duplicity of women. Betts in particular disliked women who "roped some gink" and became rich, and who thought they "can act just like the Parkavenoo's act." Betts admitted that he lacked experience with women and hoped for marriage. Hazard, who was married, had run-ins with women he considered bossy. He traded insults with a woman who accused him of running up the fare. When she told him there would be no tip, he retorted: "That's old stuff. I knew that long ago. It's enough to get rid of you."[5]

One reason for the hostility both hack men showed toward women may have been lack of exposure to them due to the paucity of females in the business. Few women drove cabs during the 1920s. Initially, about a dozen women drove, a number that soon dropped to only two by 1928. One of the women, a widow named Mrs. Edith Baker from the Bronx, drove to keep her son in school. She stayed in the business because she found "the profits worthwhile, saw that the work was not beyond my capacity, and concluded that I could get along as well as any man." She usually hacked outside of the Ansonia Hotel during the evening shifts and found that other hack men treated her with respect.[6]

Hazard preferred hacking on his own to working for rich people. Through the anecdotes of a fictional hackie named Mack, Hazard told of the need to "break in" rich people and then "watch your step and you're all right." Mack's employers, a rich corporation lawyer and his wife, were continually mistreating doormen and waiters and then were surprised at the bad service they received.[7] Betts was also quite willing to confront the wealthy. In a memorable encounter with banker J. P. Morgan, Betts showed a feisty egalitarianism. Betts considered Morgan a friend, having "hauled him four or five times." At the end of one trip, Morgan, getting out of the cab, "pays me off then cocks his head skyward, looks like more rain don't you think, he says." Betts briefly considered the banker's importance and power, and then concluded, "this big man was asking a little man's opinion," and, while the safest thing to do was agree, Betts "didn't figure that way at all, it wasn't the way to open the book." Betts replied, "Yer all wrong, it ain't going to rain." Morgan regarded Betts curiously and asked what made him think so. Betts quickly mentioned the flowers in Madison Square. "Yes," said Morgan, warming up, "when we were both kids, both of us would stick a brick where the parson would stumble on it, but neither of us would trample the flowers, because we both loved them." "Right," said Betts, and those flowers "is sorta perked up, sorta holding their heads up, like they was saying, we don't need no more water, we're feeling fine." Morgan agreed with a smile and as he left, shook hands with Betts. On subsequent trips, the cabby traded similar "kid stories" with the financial giant "an he never forgot me after a long missing spell." Betts was aware of the huge disparity in their status and incomes, but plainly did not feel intimidated by Morgan. During this era, class differences did not intrude upon their mutual memories. Morgan, one of the most powerful men in the world, could engage in class nostalgia, while Betts could temporarily view himself as the banker's equal.[8]

Betts and Hazard gained readers because journalists discovered that cabdrivers were expert guides to the city in the 1920s. Morris Markey, who wrote for a number of newspapers before becoming a full-time contributor to the *New Yorker* when the magazine debuted in 1925, chronicled one night touring the markets and working-class bars. With his companion, a hack man named Mr. Leary, Markey began his nocturnal investigations at three o'clock in the morning on West Street, below Fourteenth, where hundreds of men were "moving swiftly in every direction and shouting to each other, horses stamping on the cobblestones, wheels rumbling and truck motors grinding away." Hundreds of wood fires burned to keep away the cold. The men were buying and selling the day's produce, brought by truck farmers from out of town. From there, Markey and Leary drove to the Susquehanna Bar, where the bartender shrugged and told them, as he served them drinks: "We never paid much attention to prohibition." From there, they moved on to dives where angry men yelled about "the top hats," or businessmen, while few listened. On the way back uptown, the pair encountered a traffic jam. There was no resentment or excitement about the delay, just a general acceptance that there was not enough room and that truck drivers had a right to block the street while unloading. Truck men, hack men, and Markey stood by the inert mass of vehicles and talked about horse races and the New York Giants until the jam eased. Markey and Leary then headed north for breakfast at a chili joint.[9]

Describing hack men as streetwise philosophers, as Hazard, Betts, and Markey did, could not disguise the harder realities in workplace relations. The fantasies of obedient and docile cabbies envisioned by the city government and the fleets collided with the hopes of owner-drivers for income and of the fleet drivers for unions, better pay, and improved working conditions. For fleet drivers, the answer lay in collective organization. In the wake of World War I, cabdrivers strived to create a union that would confirm gains made in the previous era. Cabdriver walkouts in the late 1910s were restricted to actions against particular fleets. On February 27, 1919, drivers for the Black and White Taxicab Company went on strike in protest of the firing of two drivers. After the company owner reserved the right to fire employees, the strikers sought arbitration through the New York State Department of Labor. Eventually, the company satisfied the drivers not by rehiring the two men but by providing wage increases, health benefits, and better death benefits. There was an additional walkout in late April by drivers who held out for rehiring of the fired cabbies, but the company stood firm.

The following year, the Greater New York Taxi League, an organization of independent drivers formed in 1919, went on strike against the Pennsylvania Railroad Company over their preferential use of a fleet known as the Black and White Taxicab Company. The Taxi League, intended to pressure the interests of the small owner-drivers, had larger ambitions and soon after announced plans to organize all the cabbies—both fleet and independent—eliminate felons from their ranks, and insure safe cabs. The league also proposed the creation of a licensing board that would grant permits only to "morally and physically fit" men and would insure a standard fare for all cabs. This rare attempt by owner-drivers to unite with fleet drivers drew the attention of the city government. It responded to the league's plans by creating its own scheme to put licensing under control of the police department. Mayor John Hylan opposed the last idea, believing that it would overburden the police.[10]

As the Teamsters faded from power, company unions took their place.

The Black and White Chauffeurs Union organized in 1921 to work with the fleet of the same name. In 1921, the Black and White Chauffeurs successfully negotiated an increase to $4.50 per day plus a commission of 20 percent on all earnings above eight dollars a week. These demands indicate that cabbies were seeking a manageable wage and wanted to avoid dependence on tipping. American attitudes toward tips, as noted, were often hostile and at best were unreliable. Unfortunately, the union's method effectually created a minimum earnings expectation for the company's drivers. Those who earned less would lose their jobs. The result was a sudden surge of reckless driving. The fleet had less responsibility and could expect a guaranteed amount weekly from drivers. The Mogul Checker Cab Company created a company union in 1923, which spurred workers to hustle for a 50 percent commission worth about nine dollars per week. Because companies pushed their own unions, officers lacked independence. Drivers resented the terms of company unions and were reluctant to join them. Even so, the effect of company unions was to increase turnover among drivers and make the streets less safe.[11]

A much larger issue was demands from independent drivers and insurance companies to limit the number of taxicabs in the city. With the abolition of monopoly control over hack stands, cruising became the normal way to find fares. Empty cabs relentlessly racing each other for potential passengers clogged the streets. One article claimed that the lack of regulation of the number of cabs had created a "Yellow Peril" in the streets.[12]

Chaos reigned in the streets in the early 1920s. Over seventeen thousand drivers using different colored flags to signify the rates they charged competed fiercely for fares. Due to this cutthroat competition, prices were about 20 percent below the maximum allowed. Hack men battled with their fists for spots in the hack lines in front of hotels, restaurants, and other popular venues. The jump in competition spurred more reckless driving and accidents, problems that necessitated laws requiring a minimum of $2,500 in liability insurance per cab. Fleet owners and independent operators alike demanded mandatory fare increases in hopes of stabilizing prices and avoiding ruinous competition. All sides agreed that the root problem was the overabundance of cabs and drivers.[13]

First calls to limit the number of taxis came in 1923 from the city government and from the editorial pages of the *New York Times*. The response in the streets was a jump in the number of licensed drivers to nineteen thousand the next year, sending rates down further and exacerbating battles for fares. According to the *Times* and *New York American,* many drivers were criminals. The Hotel Association chimed in with more complaints, claiming that cabs were dirty and that drivers could not speak English and had little knowledge of their destinations.[14]

Public association of cabbies with racketeering became more pronounced. William McAdoo, a New York magistrate, contended in 1925 that thugs were using cabs in conjunction with burglaries, safe-blowing jobs, and holdups. One scam reported by Morris Markey involved cabdrivers who took gullible suckers out for fun to rip-off bars. After a drink or two, the customers would be forced with threats of violence to pay their bills with blank checks, on which would be written much larger amounts than the cost of their beverages. Another good example of the gangster cabby was Larry Fay, who operated a series of clubs with his partner, Texas Guinan, known as Queen of the Nightclubs. Fay came out of Hell's Kitchen, west of Times Square. Owner of a police record of forty-six summonses for brawling, but no convictions, Fay started adult life as a cabdriver. One night, shortly after the advent of Prohibition, he drove a rich bootlegger clear to Canada and learned about rum running from his fare. After a winning bet on a horse race at odds of 100–1, Fay bought a fleet of cabs and adorned them with swastikas (used for thousands of years as symbols of good luck before they were adopted by the Nazis), modeled after the blanket on the horse that won him his stake. Fay hired very tough cabbies, including ex-convicts, former prizefighters, and bruisers from Hell's Kitchen. Allied with gangster Owney Madden, Fay used strong-arm methods to control the hack stands at both Penn Station and Grand Central. After losing his cash gambling, he went back to hacking with aspirations to make himself the czar of independent drivers.

When that scheme flopped, Fay turned again to nightclubs and opened the famous El Fey Club with Guinan. An immediate success because of Guinan, who refined her famous "Hello, Sucker," greeting at the club, the El Fey became the "granddaddy of the all night speakeasies." The hottest place in town, the club attracted celebrities. Arriving by taxi at El Fey were visiting royalty, baseball players, rich Park Avenue hostesses, bankers' wives, editors, and even Mayor Jimmy Walker. Their comings and goings were chronicled by famous journalists such as Walter Winchell and Heywood Broun, Mark Hellinger, and Ed Sullivan. The club jump-started the careers of entertainers Ruby Keeler and George

Raft. Padlocked by the police one night, the club briefly closed. Fay tried to reopen it, but the magic had moved on.

After Fay tried to cut corners by reducing staff wages, one of his cabbies shot him dead outside the club. Fay's demise seemed a realistic warning to hack men who tried to move into the fast life. Many retreated back to crime on the local, neighborhood level. In Greenwich Village, cabdrivers joined neighborhood social clubs that combined politics with gambling, pimping, and speakeasies.[15]

If New Yorkers regarded hacking as badly in need of regulation, they could find little solace from its political handlers. Regulation of the growing industry became a political football. The Board of Aldermen tried to hand over responsibility to the police department, which demurred, arguing that governing the cabbies would tax police resources. Mayor Hylan supported the police and vetoed the measure. That did not end the issue, as aldermen and the public again and again demanded the police take charge. In 1925, Mayor Hylan signed into law the Home Rule Bill, which transferred the control of cabs from the Bureau of Licenses to the New York City Police Department. On April 9, 1925, the police assumed total control of taxicabs and created a special police department that became known as the Hack Bureau. The reaction was mixed. The city chamber of commerce praised the new method of control; a leading fleet owner criticized the police. The issue became more heated when the police decided not to issue any more hack licenses until their new system was in place. This de facto means of limiting the number of cabbies raised suspicions among fleets and hack men that the cops were preparing to curb the numbers. Conflicts over police control of hacking went into various courts, but inevitably the city and its police prevailed.[16]

After the police department took control of the cab industry, it moved, in cooperation with the fleets, to regulate cabbies. In mid-June, the police department ordered that cabbies wear a uniform including a cap, a white linen shirt with a collar, a necktie, and a coat. Soon after, it declared that cabbies must be "temperamentally fit for the job." The newly formed Hack Bureau gained gratitude from the fleet owners when it arrested cabbies who had tampered with their meters. The *Taxi Weekly*, a newspaper dedicated to the welfare of cabbies, headlined a claim that constant campaigns were necessary to keep the good name of the industry before the public. Cabdrivers disagreed and campaigned in 1926 for the ouster of John Daly, the deputy police commissioner in charge of licenses, whom they believed was waging war on them. One tactic of the Hack Bureau that enraged cabbies was the seizure of licenses from hackmen who were delinquent on debt payments. Although this bread-and-butter issue energized the cabbies and helped them show unusual solidarity, they did not succeed in getting rid of Daly.[17]

Cabdrivers had many complaints about police harassment in the aftermath of the establishment of the Hack Bureau. Hack men complained that policemen believed nearly all cabbies were "wise guys." One cabby was angry because he was arrested after another motorist hit his car. Several felt their licenses were seized without reason. In the summer of 1928, the Hack Bureau began randomly taking identification cards from taxis while their owners were not in them. Cabdrivers did have a sounding board for their complaints. Editor Hugh A. Brown, a University of Virginia graduate, World War I veteran, and member of the Social Register, a listing of elite New Yorkers, started *Taxi Weekly* in 1925. By 1927, it had a guaranteed circulation of 12,500, which allowed a small profit. Despite his patrician origins, Brown sympathized with the cabbies. He tried to reform the industry by pushing for limits on the numbers of cabs and for fare increases. He once defended a Jewish driver fired for refusing to pick up a passenger on Yom Kippur, and, most importantly, forced the opening of the police department's "star chamber," or secret, trials of cabdrivers and helped taxi men avoid paying over one million dollars annually in petty graft. According to cabbies, the police used regulation to extract money from them. The *Weekly* helped cabbies collect fares from cheats and provided free counsel in their grievances. Only once did it misstep. One year Brown went on a business trip and returned to a summons from a process server. The cause was a column by hack man Otto Lewis, describing one Herbert T. Darling of Jackson Heights as "The Meanest Rider." Lewis complained that Darling grumbled the entire ride from Queens to his office at Fifty-second Street and Sixth Avenue. Darling sued. It turned out that the grump was not Darling, but someone who worked in his office. The *Taxi Weekly* apologized.[18]

There were indications that the police department oppressed cabbies by making showy arrests each year. For example, on August 18, 1922, the cops arrested cabby Samuel D. Jacobson for calling orchestra leader Nathan Franko, a "cheap skate." Magistrates found Jacobson guilty but suspended the sentence and ordered Franko to pay the disputed fare. This gesture was ineffectual and avoided the bigger problems. The police seemed determined to paint all cabbies as criminals. To inspire more positive images, fleet owners, the city government, and the taxi media created awards in the 1920s to stimulate courteous behavior and honesty. Santa Damico was nominated for Most Courteous Driver in 1927 after returning five thousand dollars in jewelry to a Mrs. William P. Morgan. That meritorious act did not win Damico the award however; it went to Russian-born Alexander Diaman. Newspapers reported extraordinary cases of cabdriver honesty. Cabby John Cody turned in seventy-five thousand dollars worth of jewelry left in his cab by a woman in a rush to catch a train. A few years later, driver William L. Kuebler turned in to the police a box with nearly two thousand dollars in it belonging to two African American passengers. There were independent examples that belied stereotypes of cabdrivers as common criminals. J. B. Carrington, a Yale graduate and stockbroker, enjoyed hacking at night. Kenneth La Roy was an aspiring singer. A CCNY professor drove a cab during the summer, then returned to teaching in the fall of 1927.[19]

Despite these commendations, cabdrivers retained a poor reputation. One constant difficulty was their penchant for squabbles with middle-class women. During the Christmas season of 1926, four cabbies were arrested for attacking female passengers; one hack man received a thirty-day jail sentence. Another cabby went to Sing Sing Prison for driving his cab while intoxicated and killing a female passenger in an accident.[20] Cabdrivers were still synonymous with crime. As Dave Betts, the taxi philosopher, put it: "A taxi-cab driver we all know is a guy who hovers an snoops among the foothills of the Mighty Rockies of the underworld." Betts believed in a "sorter code which makes us keep our mouths shut, we don't aim to be snoopers, and we aint policemen." Still, there were cabbies on the wrong side of the law. Some committed minor violations such as fixing their meters to run faster. Other cabbies were cited for attacking passengers, including one who got into a violent argument with a woman who failed to hire his cab, though it was first at the stand.[21] Even honest cabbies had to deal with crime. Veteran drivers later recalled the early 1920s, when racketeers regularly robbed cabbies. The routine was to steer the driver down a dark street where other "mugs" waited to rob "the sucker for all they could get off him."[22]

The Volstead Act gave legal sanction to efforts to stamp out drinking and ancillary pleasures. It spurred the Committee of Fourteen to redouble its efforts to uncover violations of the new law. More than ever, cabdrivers became a focus of committee entrapment methods. In addition to reckless driving and clogged streets, excessive competition and rate wars pushed many cabbies into illicit by-employment. The Committee of Fourteen's inspectors were quick to find work scrutinizing the behavior of the beleaguered cabdrivers. As before, the standard procedure was to pose as a tourist from out of town looking for women or alcohol. The inspectors never consummated any deals arranged with their prey, but invariably extracted sufficient information about their work habits, houses of assignation, liquor sales, and associates to report to the police who then made arrests.

These reports show how cabbies sought extra cash through prostitution and bootlegging. Taxi men gained access to outside earnings because of the enormous jump in the numbers of nightclubs, professional sports teams, hotels, and motion picture houses, and because of the rapid development of an illicit network of speakeasies and brothels to quench the thirsts of eager patrons. Cabbies took inspectors through tours of the settings of vice: nightclubs, saloons, and speakeasies, to drug stores, cigar shops, newsstands, hotels and apartment buildings, and even their own cabs. Cabdrivers bargained with potential customers and regularly steered them to prostitutes.[23] Characteristically, drivers took inspectors on rides to where "girl friends" might be found.

Race was no barrier in such transactions. On one occasion, a cabby took his fare around to several places before going up to Harlem to West 143rd Street. Upon arrival, the inspector demanded to see "white women" but was informed that the girls who were "on the way" were "nearly white." The inspector noted sufficient information to have arrest warrants sworn for the Jewish cabdriver and the African American madam, indicating a business relationship between the two. One cabdriver asked the inspector if he minded "a mulatto." When the inspector demurred, the cabby insisted the women were "nearly white, just a little yellow." Actor Jimmy Durante recalled how cabdrivers waited outside the clubs after midnight, offering to take customers to peep shows and to "Japanese dancing girls and all other kinds of acts on their lists."[24]

Hack men were active links in the chain of illicit entertainment. Called "the best business getter for the clandestine clubs," many cabbies worked closely with hostesses at night spots. Drivers carried cards that advertised "blondes, brunettes and red heads" and gave the address of a club. Drivers were ready guides to speakeasies and restaurants that served alcohol and were frequented by unescorted women. Cabdriver Robert Elliott, police department taxi license number 28,006, who "hacks around 49th and 8th Avenue," advised his passenger to go to a speakeasy where "they charge 25 cents for a glass of beer." Asked where the place was, Elliott produced a card and told the inspector to ask for Fred and tell him that Bob sent you. A second cabby told the inspector to go to an apartment on West Eighty-eighth Street and ask for "Miss Fox and tell her that Jerry sent me."

Inspectors, prostitutes, and cabbies were particularly active during the 1924 Democratic National Convention. Cabdrivers took inspectors posing as delegates to Harlem apartments, hotels, and cabarets. Men interested in sex, but without an apartment or hotel, were advised by cabdrivers to "get in the taxi with her and I'll drive you through some dark streets." Although true lovers also used cabs for cuddling, as journalist Stephen Graham put it, "The meter counts the kisses in dollars and cents." One driver offered to "stop on a side street and I'll put the top up." The cabby left the window open, however, and listened to the conversation in the backseat, asking the couple not to dirty the seat. Another prostitute suggested to the inspector, "Maybe we could take a taxicab to make it quicker." A taxi driver secured a woman for the inspector and offered the use of his cab and the lady for ten dollars. When the inspector refused, the cabby suggested that they rent the apartment he shared with three other cabdrivers. One driver drove a prostitute around with him in his cab.[25] Cabdrivers preyed on seamen, picking them up on payday, "to drive them around town until he gets his cut."[26]

The connections between hack men and prostitutes became part of urban lore. Conrad Aiken wrote a poignant short story about the tough, intertwined lives of prostitutes and cabdrivers. In it, a cabby named O'Brien comes back from the lunchroom on a rainy night to find a young prostitute in the back seat of the muddy hack he had tucked away in an alley. She has "several gold teeth. Her hat was sodden in the rain, the fur piece round her neck was bedraggled, her wet pale face glistened." When the cabby opens the back door to drag her out, they fight hard, then share a cigarette and talk. He learns she is seventeen years old and has just been kicked out by her pimp because she is pregnant. Gradually, the cabby and the prostitute find warmth in each other and fall asleep leaning against each other. As the girl closes her eyes, her head on the cabby's shoulder, she imagines the rain makes the impression of "snow on the taxi roof like a wedding cake," giving the pair a momentary intimacy in a harsh world.[27]

Taxi-dance halls, or dime-a-dance halls, originated in New York around the time the number of cabs expanded. The taxi dancer was so-called because "like the taxi-driver with his cab, she is for public hire, and is paid in proportion to the time spent and the services rendered." Cabdrivers regularly serviced taxi-dance halls, delivering passengers and young women to favored spots, where some engaged in prostitution. At times, taxi dancers were observed arriving at the club in the front seat of the cab, which suggested a relationship with the hack man. Hack men could also be found among the dancers' customers.[28]

Generally, taxi dancing was deemed perilous for virtuous women. The Hollywood production of Robert Terry Shannon's novel *The Taxi Dancer* featured Joan Crawford as a Southern belle searching for stardom as an actress in New York. A cabdriver takes her to a hotel occupied by young taxi dancers. She then becomes involved with gamblers, caddish dancers, and a slumming millionaire. Only after a murder was Crawford reunited with her lover, a reformed gambler.[29]

Taxi-dance halls were particularly known for the racial mixture of their women and patrons.[30] While midtown was the primary locale for taxi dancers and their cabby associates, astute drivers transported thrill seekers all over town. Jazz-age Harlem was a prime spot for partygoers of any sexual predilection. In Blair Niles's novel of homosexual jaunts around Harlem in the late 1920s, *Strange Brother,* fun seekers regularly took taxis from one hot spot to another. Taxis seemed always parked outside the latest "in" club, waiting for post-midnight patrons.

Cabdrivers, like doormen, porters, and club operators, earned cash by connecting customers with prostitutes or at least with the establishments they frequented. Hack men made interracial connections between customers, prostitutes, and taxi-dance hall girls. White cabdrivers had extensive awareness of black-operated brothels where commercial mixed-race sex was acceptable. Such knowledge and practices came from the taxi men's openness and involvement in relations across racial lines. Even as Americans, and urban workers in particular, committed horrible hate crimes, the 1920s must be seen as a time when, among cabbies, racial barriers mattered little when cash beckoned.[31]

As cruising became the norm, a variety of car companies introduced cabs into New York City, allowing consumers multiple options to choose between and giving rise to trends in cab models. Robert Hazard, the cab memoirist, recalled how, in succession, Brown and White cabs were popular, followed by Yellow cabs, and then the Checker cabs came in and had "all their own way the best part of two years, and finally they had sold cabs to half the independents in town." When the Checkers took over, Hazard reported, the Yellow Cab Company took back about two thousand cabs over one summer from owners who could not make payments. Hazard found that passengers ignored him until he drove a Checker. Passengers were quick to make their own choices. In F. Scott Fitzgerald's novel *The Great Gatsby*, Myrtle Wilson, Tom Buchanan's girlfriend, let four cabs go by before she "selected a new one, lavender-colored with gray upholstery." There were so many cabs to choose from, noted travel writer Stephen Graham, that "no one wants to walk far in New York; taxis are numerous and cheap."[32]

Staring out of cabs, passengers gained a new perspective on the streets. One character in Blair Niles's *Strange Brother* "noticed how all along the Avenue, the green traffic lights, which showed at every corner, cast green lanes of reflected light on the glistening black pavements, and how the lights of the advancing cars were reflected in motion." Stephen Graham complained that the "taxi cuts off the view. You feel some bumps and you surmise you are on 8th Avenue, or a blaze of light tells you that you are on Broadway."[33]

Taxicab riding inspired its own kind of songs, making it part of the romance and loneliness of Broadway. Songwriters quickly realized the romantic possibilities of a taxi ride for two. The 1919 hit "Taxi" included the lyrics:

Taxi (whistle)
None Anywhere
Taxi (whistle) Now I've Got a Fare
And he tells me he wants a double-seater. He's all dolled up like
he's going to meet'er
Taxi (whistle) Drive Anywhere
Taxi (whistle)
They'll never care
He's thinking of little turtle dove
They only take a taxi When they love, love, love.[34]

Not everyone found happiness in a taxi. F. Scott Fitzgerald gauged the quality of loneliness of the city streets in *The Great Gatsby:* "Again at eight o'clock, when the dark lanes of the Forties were five deep with throbbing taxi cabs, bound for the theater districts, I felt a sinking in my heart. Forms leaned together in the taxis as they waited, and voices sang,

and there was laughter from unheard jokes, and lighted cigarettes out-
lined unintelligible gestures inside." His narrator understood how apart
from that world he stood.[35]

In a story unpublished in his lifetime, Fitzgerald indicated how distant success was for even ambitious cabbies. In "The Pearl and the Fur,"
which was intended for the *Saturday Evening Post,* Fitzgerald described
the relationship between a teenage girl and an honest cabby she encounters. Gwen goes for a ride in a cab past large apartment buildings that
"sparkle upward like pale dry ginger ale through the blue sky." In the
backseat of the cab, she finds a chinchilla cape. She and the cabby, a poor
but struggling young man who is trying to earn college tuition, realize
that the fur belongs to a socialite who is about to depart on a cruise ship
for the West Indies. As the pair approach the ship, Gwen senses a world
of "tropical moons and flashing swimming pools and soft music on
enchanted beaches." She declines a reward of a free trip to the islands,
instead asking for and receiving money that will enable the cabby to go
to college for a year. Gwen's true nobility is rewarded when the socialite's
son takes her dancing at the Rainbow Room, the mecca of debutante
society. The cabdriver is kept out of such glamour and is restricted to the
honorable, if pedestrian, climb up the ladder via his own merits and a
large tip.[36]

The pay was poor, but the chance to drive fast gave hacking a romantic air. Young sports found allure in the reckless speed of hacking. Switching identities with cabdrivers was the conceit of George Agnew Chamberlain's 1920 comedy, *Taxi*. In this popular book, the wealthy young hero
Robert Hervey Randolph swaps his clothing and buys a cab from Patrick
O'Reilly, driver no. 1898 of the Village Cab Company, becoming Slim
Hervey, ace cab driver. Hervey's plan is to hide himself until he can earn
enough money to match the fortune of his high-society girlfriend, who
demands that he have at least one hundred thousand dollars before she
will consider marrying him. Hervey quickly becomes one of the best
drivers in town and specializes in the area around Wall Street. There he
picks up stock tips and, after hustling his old Yale schoolmates in a poker
game, invests everything in insider trading. Armed with his new fortune,
he quits his cab job, buys fancy clothing, and successfully asks for the
girl's hand. O'Reilly, now back in his hack clothes, drives them to the city
clerk for the marriage license. Chamberlain's slight comedy reveals the
close association of young swells with the coarser cabdrivers and suggests
that a dip into the tough, dangerous world of hacking might be good for

any young gentleman on the way up. A secondary character in the novel is a young taxi dancer upon whom Randolph takes pity.[37]

Hollywood exploited the comic potential of reckless driving in Harold Lloyd's 1928 comedy, *Speedy*. Its main character, Harold "Speedy" Swift, bounces through a series of jobs until he finds work driving for the Only One Garage, run by an aged omnibus driver with a beautiful daughter. Lloyd's character takes the girl around to New York City sights as he determines that his love must save the father's job from a criminal syndicate bent on monopolizing the business. Speedy races his cab around New York, terrifying his passengers (including Babe Ruth in a terrific cameo) and prompting the police to threaten to seize Speedy's hack license. After a number of extraordinary dashes around New York City, Speedy saves the old man's franchise, wins a huge settlement for him, and gets the girl. In a similar if more serious vein was the 1928 Marshall Neiland film *Taxi 13*, in which cabby Angus MacTavish (Chester Conklin), who supports his careworn wife and ten children, hires out his hack unwittingly to a gang of safecrackers. When MacTavish and his daughter help the police capture the thieves, he is given a five-thousand-dollar reward, with which he buys a new taxi. In movies such as this, Hollywood presented hack men as somewhat peculiar but good-hearted workmen who deserve the beautiful heroine or at least better working conditions.[38]

Hollywood theatrics and the tawdry dramas of the taxi-dance halls notwithstanding, there was dailiness about hacking. Drivers worked hard, went to social events such as prize fights, flirted with pretty women, and discussed the latest cabs from Checker and Ford. The *Taxi Weekly* interspersed stories about heroic cabmen with solicitations to raise funds for injured hackies and perennial complaints about jaywalkers. It reported on annual picnics for drivers of major garages. In 1928, it warned New York governor Al Smith that Hack Bureau abuse of cabbies would turn about seventy-five voters a week against him. The newspaper reported anger among cabbies when the Hack Bureau required drivers to wear caps.[39]

There was a movement to form a Hackman's Political Party in the late 1920s to pursue the interests of the trade. The *Taxi Weekly* quoted drivers as saying that cabmen were either under the control of their district leaders or were too independent to pay any attention to politics. Still, by autumn of 1928, the party claimed over twelve thousand members and scheduled primaries to vet candidates. It promised to work with either major party according to how its candidates treated hack men.

The *Taxi Weekly* boasted that hackies' votes could be pivotal in assembly and congressional races and later voted to eschew involvement in national politics in favor of local races. The party soon created a legal aid society to help cabbies in need of defense from Hack Bureau charges.[40]

In the late 1920s, individual owner-drivers banded together to form the White Horse Company and announced plans to operate five thousand cabs, charging lower metered rates than those allowed by the police department. Members of the company planned to purchase from their cooperative smaller, less expensive cars on the installment plan so they could make a living at the lower rates. The police department immediately went to court to invalidate the new rates. Over the next year, various courts rejected and then upheld the drivers' plans. Ultimately, the drivers' scheme failed because the industry could not sustain the prices; nonetheless, in 1930, New York City had the lowest taxi fare rate of any major city in the nation. Also in the 1920s, the number of cabs in New York City increased from 13,632 to 16,917, with a supply of about three-and-a-half drivers per cab.

By the end of the decade, insurance had become a knotty problem. One of the few achievements of the 1920s was a ruling in municipal court that owners of taxicabs were liable for damages committed by employees. As the number of accidents soared, insurance costs and, later, gasoline costs became significant issues for the fleets, who strived to turn these expenses over to the drivers.[41]

The hack man was an essential player in New York City's Jazz Age. Despite the hopes of the city government for order and of the fleets for monopoly, cabdrivers epitomized the anarchy of the town in this raucous decade. All of that came to a sudden collapse with the crash of the bull market on Wall Street in late 1929. Wall Street's debacle brought an end to the Roaring Twenties and made hacking a refuge for the economic casualties. Middle-class professionals and rowdy young sports who had benefited from the sizzling economy of the 1920s looked to cab driving when their careers imploded. They joined the thousands already driving to compete for fewer and fewer fares, making the tumult on the streets even worse. As the boisterous good times of the 1920s tumbled, the systemic problems of the taxi industry and of its drivers were plain to see. Auto companies had supplied an overabundance of inexpensive cars, and the city government lacked a workable licensing system. Despite the efforts of large fleets to control the industry and evict small drivers, the business remained open to any male—and a few females—who could navigate a taxi through the city streets. Driving was an adventure; now the excessive numbers of younger drivers joined grizzled veterans in the chase for the diminishing number of fares. The cabdrivers' trade needed a shakeout, and in the next decade, hack men and the city government strove to sort out this taxi anarchy.[42]

3

The Search for Order during the Depression, 1930–1940

The Great Depression hit the working people of New York City hard. By 1934, about one-third of former skilled manufacturing employees were on relief. The construction industry, despite such new projects as the Empire State Building, the George Washington Bridge, and the Lincoln Tunnel, lost much of its former bread-and-butter business of apartment buildings and offices. Unskilled workers suffered the most. Over 40 percent of African American male workers were unemployed. With no alternative but the overwhelmed relief services, which many disdained, thousands of New Yorkers used their knowledge of the city and their one remaining marketable skill—driving a car—and got hack licenses. By 1931, over seventy-three thousand men held hack licenses, allowing them to compete for positions behind the wheels of the twenty-one thousand cabs in the city.[1]

New York City became quieter as the raucous good times of the 1920s faded. The slowdown was evident in Times Square. Previously, clubs and restaurants stayed open until the wee hours. Cabmen adeptly took fares to late night sexual assignations or to speakeasies. Now the theater crowds finished their ice cream sodas or beer and sandwiches and vanished down into the rumbling melancholy of the subways. By midnight, the policeman in the information kiosk closed his doors and went home. The yellow news ticker on the Times Building "ceased its guarded narrative of the world's confusion." Off in the distance, down the side streets, a few leftover hot spots held on, and a handful of steerers still loomed in the shadows looking for suckers. But Times Square was dark. The only sounds came from the radios of vacant taxi cabs whose drivers lounged on the sidewalk trading bad jokes with gaudy prostitutes. When even the banter died after one o'clock, the hack men eased back into their cabs, made U-turns "with violent protest of their tires," and tore away without any fares. The post-midnight crowd had already gone to bed.[2]

The easy money gone, hack men, owner-drivers, fleets, and the city government used differing strategies to survive the Great Depression. Independent cabbies and fleet drivers shared common objectives of survival in an era of falling income and merciless competition. Fleet owners strove to sustain profits by cutting commissions and lowering costs. The city government increasingly realized that the number of cabs had to be decreased and that further regulation was necessary. These forces collided in the strike of 1934, which set the stage for the reorganization of the trade under the Haas Act of 1937.

Reform began under Mayor James Walker, who announced in January 1930 a plan to franchise the operation of all cabs in the city to a single vendor, making it illegal to be an owner-driver. Monopoly would relieve congestion, elevate driver earnings by reducing competition, and earn cash for the city. Ten years earlier, Grover Whalen, the city's commissioner of plants and structures, had proposed a similar plan, which went nowhere. In 1930, initial reaction to Mayor Walker's scheme was unenthusiastic throughout the industry. At the same time, the Board of Aldermen planned to reduce fare wars by setting minimum rates for cabs. The mayor vetoed this plan and instead convened a committee to study the industry and make recommendations.[3]

Researchers assigned to study the industry for the commission warned that unlicensed "wildcat" taxicabs would choke New York and other American cities. Among the problems created by a lack of regulation was excessive cruising, which led to congestion, lack of liability for accidents, and unreliable service. Wildcatters, who cut rates down further, had practically eliminated the difference in price between cabs, buses, and subways.[4]

The committee's report, issued on September 22, 1930, found that the industry was in a "thoroughly unhealthy condition." The taxicab industry suffered from "many avoidable accidents" by drivers who lacked the financial responsibility and insurance to assume liability. The dangerous conditions on the streets stemmed from excessive cruising by drivers who were compelled to work long hours to make ends meet. Such conditions meant that the industry had failed to provide safe, economic, and avail-

able transportation to the public. The commission recommended dras-
tic cures. It noted that taxis carried 346 million passengers a year and had
an income of over $120 million in fares with another $24 million from
tips. It asserted that this volume warranted the cab industry's recognition as a full-fledged utility. While the commission preferred regulating
the industry under a single franchise, it purported to consider the "interests of all parties" presently working. This meant the creation of a
government entity that instilled cooperation between fleets and individual owner-drivers by regulating both kinds of drivers. That new agency
would be the Taxicab Control Bureau.[5]

The committee's report honed in on a number of key problems. Committee members sent surveyors into the streets to count cabs with and
without passengers. During the morning and evening rush hours, the
surveys found that nearly half of the cabs passing the corner of Seventy-
second Street and Park Avenue were empty of passengers. Around the big
hotels, the situation was even worse; 70 percent of the cabs circling the
Penn Station area were empty of passengers.[6]

Contradicting its earlier claims and popular beliefs, the commission
found that cabbies were not the reckless drivers the public perceived them
to be. The frenzied search for fares had not translated into dangerous
streets. Cabdrivers, the commission found, drove about one-third of the
vehicular miles in the city annually, but were responsible for about one-
quarter of the injuries and about 15 percent of the deaths. New York City
had an astounding total of over one thousand traffic deaths in 1929.[7]

The commissioners did decide, unsurprisingly, that cab driving,
whether for a fleet or as an independent operator, was a tough way of
making a living. Operating expenses including gasoline costs, maintenance, and insurance ate up the net revenues earned by large and small
fleets and by owner-drivers. Average returns on investment ranged from
about fifty cents per day for large fleets to over a dollar and a quarter for
small fleets to nothing for owner-drivers.[8]

The committee recommendations formed a significant part of the
regulations that were developed over the next five years. The Taxicab
Control Bureau became the first umbrella city regulatory agency for
taxis and their drivers. It planned to issue permits that lasted no more
than three years and set standard fare rates and performance qualifications for drivers. The bureau created a squad of hack inspectors to insure
adherence to the regulations by drivers and companies. In January 1932,

the bureau ruled that no taxicab could operate in the city streets without a license. The big cab companies viewed these actions with approval, but the independent drivers were sure the bureau was created to crush them and vowed to fight. Small fleets were equally concerned. One struggling garage purchased fifty cabs from a manufacturer. When the garage had problems making the payments, the cab factory convinced it to take fifty more. As this bright scheme collapsed, the garage simply returned all one hundred cabs to the factory and put the license plates on cheap, used vehicles purchased elsewhere. The manufacturer ran to the control bureau, which then cracked down on the small garage.

The downfall of Mayor Walker and the end of the Taxicab Control Bureau came later in 1932. In the midst of the Seabury Commission's investigation into racketeering in city government, Walker's ties with J. A. Sisto and Company, key backers of the Parmelee taxi fleet, came to light. With a large interest in the city's biggest taxi fleet, Sisto was positioned to seize monopoly control over the industry. He had much to benefit from taxicab service "under a single franchised corporation." As part of his lobbying campaign to get the mayor to approve a single contractor for taxi service, Sisto gave Walker a private discussion of oil stock. Sisto explained to Judge Seabury that his discussion with the mayor had to do with protecting his business. Sisto told Seabury, "My conversation with the Mayor was in connection with newspaper accounts about some racketeers getting into the taxicab situation and disrupting our investment; wanting to cut some rates down to five cents a mile or two cents a mile. I asked him if there wasn't some redress against those types of people going into an industry and protecting a large investment which the taxicab owners had in the business." Sisto was typical of newcomers to the idea of taxi regulation, whom contemporary journalists described as: "carefully dressed gentlemen from Wall Street with envelopes full of gilt-edged bonds in their pockets, and known by the sort of practical midwifery understood by other gentlemen in politics."

Building on the earlier conversation and showing his tangible gratitude to the mayor, Sisto gave Walker $26,000 worth of bonds, which the official put in his safe. Parmelee was not alone in pursuing interest with the mayor. Terminal Cab Company, another large fleet, paid a similar amount to state senator John Hastings, one of Walker's allies. After information on this insider trading and bribery became public, Walker was forced to resign from office. With his removal, the Taxicab Control

Bureau soon died. Interim Mayor Joseph McKee abolished the board in December 1932 during a drive to curb city costs in the midst of the Depression.[9]

As the Depression deepened, the number of drivers soared while daily tallies of fares declined sharply. In April 1932, a city commission counted over 75,000 drivers ready to work for 16,732 taxis. This meant that more drivers were competing for fewer cabs than even the year before. High rates of unemployment in every sector of the city's economy, but especially in construction, transport, and recreation, pushed more men into hacking.

Driving a cab was not as lucrative as it had been in the 1920s, and the sudden drop in wages created friction between employers and hack men. Hack men now rarely made over twelve dollars a week and often had to dip into their own pockets to protect their jobs. To insure income, smaller garages instituted illegal "horse hiring." In this method, the owner hired the driver but forced him to rent the car for five dollars a day and pay for gasoline and oil. About the only hope for escape from the daily grind were the now rare out-of-town trips that could earn a week's wages in a few hours. Many cabbies turned to petty crime to help make ends meet. Worried, the city government ordered a survey of cabdrivers. Conducted on various street corners in lower Manhattan by police officers, the survey of some 330 hack men portrays the struggles of long-term drivers to make ends meet. Over two-thirds of the cabbies had driven for twelve years for the same company or were owner-drivers. The police interviewers learned that at least one-third of the cabdrivers were family men, many with three or four children. Nearly all stated that they were not making enough to support their families. Over eighty took assistance from their family or relatives, while about one hundred were borrowing money. Very few had wives who worked outside of the home.[10] To earn an average of twelve to fifteen dollars per week, cabbies worked more than twelve hours per day, with more than a fourth of them working thirteen hours or more per diem, figures that remained stable over six months. A day trip to the end of Long Island could bring over fifty dollars to the lucky cabby. Unlike in the prosperous 1920s, there were few such magical moments during the Depression years.[11]

A *New York Times* article published in February 1934, summarized the condition of the industry and its drivers over the previous five years. As the effects of the Depression deepened in New York, the number of cabs for hire in the streets remained close to the twenty-two thousand available during the "high times" of 1929, but the plentitude of passengers dropped precipitously. Of these, the three large fleets, Parmelee, Terminal, and the Keystone Transportation Company, each operated about four thousand cabs. Parmelee typified the power of the fleets. It used Checker cabs exclusively, held a strong share of fleet cabs nationally, and used a vertical system of control over supplies, gasoline, and maintenance costs. Its method of "preventive maintenance" won praise in the industry. President Morris Markin of Parmelee was one of the most respected industry leaders.

About eight thousand cabs were operated by independent drivers, while the rest were owned by fleets with as few as five and as many as two hundred cabs. There were now only 53,700 licensed cabbies in the city, a number that had decreased since 1929; of those, about thirty thousand were actively working. Those drivers earned a total of about $115 million plus about $15 million in tips, sharp drops from the $168 million earned in fares in 1929. The average daily pay had fallen from $21 in 1929 to $8.50 in 1933. Weekly and annual pay had also declined precipitously. Costs, especially for independent drivers, chewed up much of their earnings, and owner-drivers commonly drove sixteen hours a day just to break even, making the benefits of ownership over fleet employment an open question. Fleet driver incomes had fallen so badly that many drivers abandoned the work and garages were desperately seeking new laborers. The *New York Times* argued that the sizable role taxicabs played in transporting New Yorkers was critical to the public interest; in 1930, the last year for which statistics were available, cabs carried one-third of all passengers in the city, and the industry's earnings amounted to just under the totals for subways, elevated trains, and buses combined. Cabs were a public utility, the paper concluded, but were operated privately and inefficiently.[12]

Their numbers and their plight made cabbies important targets in the pivotal mayoral election of 1933. The ballot pitted Fusion Party candidate Fiorello LaGuardia against John O'Brien, the Democratic Party's Tammany candidate, and Joseph McKee, the nominee of the anti-Tammany Recovery Party. As LaGuardia and McKee publicized themselves as reform candidates, each needed an advantage that they believed lay in the "ethnic" votes. Irish voters tried to decide between O'Brien and McKee; Italian voters favored LaGuardia, while the Jewish vote split between LaGuardia and McKee. Much of the campaign aimed at winning Jewish support. Scholars have long credited LaGuardia's eventual persuasion of

Jewish voters to the discovery of an anti-Semitic article penned by McKee in 1913. LaGuardia's campaign emphasized getting out the vote using neighborhood and street rallies aimed at Jewish voters.[13]

In a number of these street-corner rallies, LaGuardia appealed specifically to Jewish and Italian cabdrivers, attacking Tammany Hall for its support of a nickel tax on each fare. The controversy had its origins on September 14, 1933, when the Board of Aldermen, facing a financial crisis, worsened the woes of the cabdrivers by legislating a nickel per ride tax, effective October 1. Cab riders filed suit to mandate that the nickels go to benefit the poor. A month after this tax began, the state Supreme Court ruled it illegal and ordered it halted, pending an appeal by the city government. That appeal was denied in January 13, 1934.[14]

During the election, LaGuardia offered not to push the city's appeal any further if the proceeds from the tax were turned over to the drivers, a clear political appeal to the trade. The fleets rejected this offer and pushed for a settlement that would award only 40 percent to the drivers. Protest meetings sponsored by the Taxi Men's Committee for Fusion held rallies against the tax. The Taxi Men's Committee urged cabbies to march to a LaGuardia rally at Madison Square Garden on November 2, promising every participant a reserved seat. Hack men sang a song deriding O'Brien, claiming he "put the city in the pawn shop." The lyrics said of LaGuardia: "You're the man we need, to wipe out, to stamp out, all the Tammany greed." Cabdriver William Gandall was named head of the taxicab driver support committee for LaGuardia. Owner-drivers were unconvinced and favored O'Brien. *Taxi,* the weekly newspaper devoted to the interests of the owner-driver, hailed O'Brien as a "liberator," and urged cabbies to cast their ballots for him. In the election, LaGuardia scored heavily in ethnic and working-class neighborhoods, where laborers, including three thousand cabbies, supported the Fusion candidate.[15]

After his election, The Little Flower, as Mayor LaGuardia was called, worked mightily with cabdrivers to avert a strike. In the aftermath of LaGuardia's victory, a court decision overturned the nickel tax, and the money was given to drivers with no explanation for how the windfall should be divided. As dissensions deepened over this issue, union organization attempts, and management bullying, frustrated drivers walked out and set up picket lines. A number of them made personal appeals to the mayor about their dire straits and asked him to intervene. As the crisis deepened, Mayor LaGuardia demanded concessions from the fleets, but they seemed recalcitrant.[16]

During his election campaign, LaGuardia learned from interviews with representatives of over seven hundred cabdrivers that they overwhelmingly wanted the nickel tax removed and expected that its departure would increase their earnings. His aides provided detailed observations about daily exchanges and the new importance of tips to cabdrivers. One of his aides, Lester Stone, filed a memorandum of a meeting in which the strikers spelled out their grievances. Their principal complaint was that the nickel tax "depresses business and lessens their tips." The memorandum further explained that "passengers generally speaking used to give an average tip of ten cents to a driver but the driver today gets a tip averaging five cents," because of the tax. The drivers contended that tips amounted to 30 percent of their income. They did not want, however, a decrease in the initial fare from twenty to fifteen cents per ride, an action that would produce competition for fares. That request may indicate that cabbies did not want to entrust their income to tips, especially during such hard times.[17]

These were not the only worries that drivers had. Many complained of "skip-outs," or customers who ran up six- or seven-dollar fares and then ducked into buildings to avoid paying. Cabbies felt that the police were hostile and unhelpful in dealing with fare stealers, drunks, fares who bargained for lower rates, and outright robbers. When cabbies asked cops for assistance, the reply would be "Scram, bum!" Things had gotten so bad that cabbies, in order to give the boss some money and avoid being laid off, resorted to "riding the ghost," or "throwing the hat in the back seat," which meant putting the meter into operation without passengers and paying their own money to drive the cab.[18]

LaGuardia attempted to mediate the strike and to assure the cabbies of his support for their concerns. He stated that he would not tolerate hiring of replacement workers. He explained that he would not endanger the people of New York with inexperienced, youthful drivers, and he forbade the police commissioner from issuing new licenses. He cautioned the drivers, however, that there should be no "rough stuff," warning, "I can get plenty rough myself."[19]

Despite LaGuardia's intervention, twelve thousand cabdrivers went on strike on February 3, 1934 over the distribution of the five-cent proceeds from the now-banned excise tax. As New Yorkers awoke to empty streets, cabbies searched the city for scabs. One striker vividly recalled how cabbies would "come out of a meetin', and we went up Broadway, and the bastids that was scabbin', we pulled the doors off their cabs." Nor were the cabbies fearful of the police. The striker remembered walking through the streets, clogging traffic and wrecking any taxi still on the job. The hack men slashed the tires of the police cars and threw bags of marbles underneath the feet of horses.[20]

There were two sources of opposition to the strike. One came from the ranks of part-time drivers. A law student who drove a cab to pay his way through law school wrote Mayor LaGuardia that the strike was damaging his chances for a livelihood. Far greater resistance to the strike came from the independent cab owners. Though publicly the *Taxi Age,* the newspaper of the owner-drivers, supported the strikers in stories and editorials, about two thousand independent drivers continued to work the streets. The Columbus Circle Taxi Group, an association of private drivers, wrote the mayor in anguish on February 5, demanding police protection against rampaging strikers.[21] As one association, the United Auto League of Drivers and Owners, explained to Mayor LaGuardia in a letter dated February 4, 1934, "we are not working for the people the strikers are striking against." It argued, "Not one of us is a thug from Chicago," and asked LaGuardia to arrest Samuel Orner, president of the Taxi Workers Union. The league complained, "Our withdrawal from the streets will in no way help the strikers or hurt their employers." The general manager of the Columbus Circle Taxi Group reported to LaGuardia that "I personally saw an independent cabdriver being stopped this morning at 149th Street and Mott Avenue by a mob of strikers and they took his switch key away from him and when he appealed to the Police Officer," the officer, told him he could do nothing about it. Owner-drivers then were called to a special meeting in the Bronx to hear about new regulations, listen to sympathetic politicians, and "organize in one solid central organization."[22]

Within the first day, LaGuardia's hopes for a nonviolent strike were smashed. One thousand drivers marched through Times Square during the evening theater rush. The hack men stopped cabs with uncooperative drivers, ripping off doors and forcing the fares to get out and walk. A woman in an evening dress was hurt when she was hit by a large piece of ice flung through a cab's window. After disrupting the theater crowd, the marchers made their way to Madison Square Garden, where five thousand drivers held a meeting to discuss the negotiations between their representatives and the employers. The crowd booed a proposal reported by William Gandell, chairman of the meeting for the union, from the fleets by which the drivers would get 40 percent of the revenues from the discredited excise tax.[23] Soon the angry cabbies rampaged through the streets again. They attacked more than 150 cabs; set fire to some, slashed tires, and beat up a number of "scabs."

On February 5, the strike moved into its third day. As estimates calculated that the taxi industry had lost half a million dollars, Mayor LaGuardia announced a settlement. Under his plan, the drivers and the companies would split the estimated half a million dollars in tax nickels. The drivers would also get 40 percent of a new fare increase of five cents. The public would benefit from a one-third reduction of meter fares for three successive Mondays. LaGuardia dispatched taxi negotiators to meetings of drivers around the city to explain the new plan. Within hours, the drivers rejected the settlement and added to their demands. They now wanted a minimum pay of twenty dollars for a sixty-hour week. The strikers backed up their demands with their fists, getting into fracases with the police in front of the Waldorf Astoria at Fiftieth Street and Park Avenue and at the Casino de Paree on Forty-fourth Street and Eighth Avenue. Strikers burned independent cabs at Forty-second Street and Broadway and in Brooklyn and Queens. Strikers attacked passengers as well. Two women were dragged from their cab on Ninth Avenue and Fifty-seventh Street. The next day saw increased violence as five hundred taxi strikers rioted on Broadway and wrecked and burned cabs. Similar incidents were reported around the city. In Harlem, the *Taxi Age* reported, "Negro strikers" punctured the tires of strikebreakers. The actions in Harlem may well have been against a black-owned garage; Harlem entrepreneurs William H. Peters and Samuel Hamilton owned over 250 cabs and employed 750 drivers and other personnel.[24]

The Communist Party's role in the strike was of critical importance. The party had adopted a policy of trying to organize a single industry by concentrated efforts on one shop at a time; it was also energetically striving to organize bus and subway workers. Its aims coincided with those of the Clan na Gael, a radical Irish organization, with which it shared leadership and tactics. The Communist Party's methods in part stemmed from their weakness in overall numbers. Because the party rarely could claim membership of more than a few percent of the workers in the transit occupations, it had to use the "concentration" method. At the same time, the party had to contend with LaGuardia's avowed sympathy with the striking cabdrivers and his skillful balancing of the factions in the conflict.[25]

Initially, the Communist Party tried to tap into cabby anger by denouncing LaGuardia's plans for distributing the nickels and for the holiday from fares as a "sell-out." The new head of the Taxi Workers Union, Joseph Gilbert, accused the mayor and his top aide, Morris Ernst, of deception. Gilbert continued attacking LaGuardia over the next few days as a means to rally unity among cabdrivers in the union. The communists further accused Ernst of putting cops in cabs to deceive and arrest strikers and allowing the Parmelee garage to fire union men. More importantly, in a demonstration of their deep distrust of mainstream political figures, the communists blamed the mayor and Ernst of trying to use the National Recovery Act (NRA), which the Roosevelt administration had enacted in 1933 to enable unionization, to install company unions.[26]

Not all communists wanted to organize the taxi men. The Trotskyite Communist League of America watched the 1934 strike in amazement, saying of the cabbies: "the thinking of many of them stands closer to that of the underworld and the cop than it does to that of the working class-movement." The Trotskyites regarded the cabbies as "men horribly exploited, unorganized, a prey of politicians, racketeers and crooks, without tradition of trade union principles or even the most elementary understanding of the class struggle." One party organizer rallied cabbies by exhorting them that "for the first time in their lives hack men are not lice or scum of the earth, but workers rendering service just like the worker in a big factory or plant." The Trotskyites stayed out of the strike actions and later blamed owner-drivers as scabs.[27]

His communist critics may have forced the mayor to temper his response to the strikers. LaGuardia reminded the police of the rights of the strikers and, during the first days of the strikes, took away billy clubs from the police to prevent abuses. His lenience proved ineffective. On February 7, 1934, the striking drivers again roved through the midtown streets, smashing car windows, ripping off doors, and roughing up drivers. After some delay, the police moved in. Police commander John O'Ryan and the mayor disagreed about tactics as the violence continued. O'Ryan wanted to use quick suppression. LaGuardia regarded the actions as free speech and was reluctant to use strong force to put down the strikes.

Mayor LaGuardia reported a new peace the next day on much the same terms he had proposed before, promising the drivers half of the $500,000 collected from the nickel tax. Showing his impatience, he threatened to revoke the strikers' licenses. In a more friendly vein, he promised to allow the National Recovery Act deputy for the New York region negotiate a minimum weekly wage and promised that jobs would be saved. La-Guardia was anxious to please the federal government as he was also negotiating for new subsidies for bridge and housing construction. The following Monday, New Yorkers enjoyed the first "bargain day" of cut-rate fares. Newspapers reported that most passengers gave the rebate back to the cabbies as a tip, demonstrating solidarity with the drivers.[28]

In the next few weeks as negotiations continued, LaGuardia's NRA representative pushed for a new industry code and urged a reduction of five thousand taxis, while assuring the drivers that no layoffs were necessary. On March 4, the city negotiators proposed a minimum wage of twelve dollars a week, a sum that the drivers quickly rejected. Hack men denounced the amount as insulting to veteran drivers with families. The cabmen worried as well about LaGuardia's plan to limit the number of cabs. Soon, about ten thousand of the drivers organized against the mayor in a new group called the Taxicab Emergency Council.[29]

Even that driver-backed coalition could not curb new strikes. As the Labor Board sought peace, about 20 percent of the 2,300 drivers for Parmelee, the biggest fleet in the city, went on strike. At issue were competing unions, one sponsored by the company, the other proposed by the drivers. Within days, the rest of the fleet's drivers went out. By March 16, hundreds of cabbies marched down Broadway. Some attacked cabs and, allowing long-simmering tensions to come to the surface, dragged out their female passengers. Still, Mayor LaGuardia refused to intervene.[30]

Organized drivers, now known as the Taxi Workers Union of Greater New York, called for a general strike on March 18. The response was mixed. Some independent cabdrivers continued to work the streets, despite threats from strikers. The city's negotiating team reported that drivers would no longer meet with them. Angry citizens blamed the mayor's leniency and demanded arrests. Even as this call arose, three hundred striking drivers attacked a scab taxi, clubbed the driver, and dragged three women out of the vehicle. Violent protests increased over the next few days. On March 23, the police and striking hack men fought for much of the night in Times Square. For the first time, on orders from the mayor, the police used nightsticks on the angry cabbies. Undeterred, the cabdrivers set fire to a cab in Times Square, broke into new riots around Manhattan, and disregarded calls by LaGuardia and the NRA negotiator to end the strike.[31]

The Communist Party appealed to other unions to support the striking cabbies with their own walkouts, but gained support only from ideologically friendly organizations. Workers from seafarers', leather dressers', and needle and furniture workers' unions and various committees of the local AFL pledged support. Race was not a boundary for strikers. In Harlem, already roiling with reports of the sham trial for rape of nine African American youths known as the Scottsboro Boys in Alabama, cabbie grievance and anger over racism coalesced. In a direct appeal to racial solidarity, a black driver from Harlem stood before white drivers at a rally. He assured them, "Boys, when you say you're with us, mean it. Mean it from the bottom of your hearts! We's been gypped ever since 1861 and we're from Missouri. If you show the boys up in Harlem that you mean what you say, then you're getting the sweetest little bunch of fighters in the world; for them spades driving the Blue and Black taxis up there can do one thing—and that's fight. And when we fights together, us black and white, man, they ain't nobody can stop us."[32]

Upset over criticism that he was partial to the drivers, LaGuardia called a conference on March 24 of both sides of the strike. After this meeting, LaGuardia believed he had an agreement to hold a plebiscite on a union at Parmelee. After the leaders of the Taxi Workers Union reported the agreement to its membership, the peace collapsed. The strikers went back to the streets on March 25 and 26 and used guerilla actions instead of directly confronting the masses of police guarding Times Square, the major hotels, and Fifth Avenue. Elsewhere in Manhattan, striking cabdrivers hurled stones at noncompliant cabs, frequently hurting the passengers. A number surrounded LaGuardia's car and hissed at him. LaGuardia was incensed that the agreement had broken down. Private citizens angrily wrote LaGuardia that he was failing to do his duty to protect them. A grand jury convened to determine if the police were honoring their responsibility to protect innocent citizens. LaGuardia became so frustrated that he refused finally to meet with the strikers even as they roved through the streets close to City Hall. After he called the union a bunch of racketeers, the organizing committee sent him a telegram offering to open its books to him. LaGuardia responded with an apology, which may indicate that his concerns were more about violence than about corruption.[33]

Mayor LaGuardia was aware that much of the drivers' animosity came from the recalcitrant attitudes of the major fleets, including Parmelee and Terminal, which refused to negotiate with the strikers and insisted on the primacy of the company unions. LaGuardia angrily denounced the fleets as wanting their "own way on everything." Privately, he urged the fleets to be conciliatory. Meanwhile, in the streets, the police arrested more drivers and revoked their licenses.[34] LaGuardia decided to counterattack the communists, whom he now believed were instigating opposition to his compromise plans. Condemning communist influence, LaGuardia cited a meeting at Cooper Union led by Ben Gold of the Needleworkers Union, Louis Weinstock of the Rank and File Committee of the American Federation of Labor (an organization repudiated by the main body), and Willard Bliss of the Radio Telegraph Union, which was controlled by communists. The police identified Samuel Orner and Joseph Gilbert of the Manhattan branch of the Taxi Workers Union as members of the Communist Party. Within a day, the strikers announced the expulsion of Gilbert and other communists and declared a willingness to settle. In the next few weeks, taxi service returned to normal. Orner and other officers were expelled from the Taxi Workers Union, and the union voted, after urging by socialist leader Norman Thomas, to align with the American Federation of Labor. While newspapers praised the mayor, a grand jury criticized him and the police for inaction. LaGuardia responded that the blame for the strikes lay with the cab companies. He then appointed a commission, headed by chief negotiator Duetsch, that recommended massive revisions in the regulation of the cab industry.[35]

What the mayor had in mind was a reduction in the number of cabs, a raise in the fees for licenses from ten to forty dollars, and support for a stable cab fare. The independent taxi drivers opposing these measures feared that the fleets would soon control the streets, despite the mayor's assertions that the numbers would be divided equally between single owners and the fleets. The fleets, in turn, were concerned about a paucity of drivers, and twice within a year complained that the Works Progress Administration had lured drivers away. Such complaints were predictable, but what was impressive about the two years following the bitter strikes of early 1934 was that ordinary cabdrivers supported the mayor and were still willing to work with him.[36]

Despite that good will, cabbies had difficulty organizing effective unions. The Independent Taxicab Union first appeared in 1935. Gangsters in the Louis Lepke Gang created fronts disguised as unions, forced drivers to pay dues, and created "protective associations." Cabdrivers who resisted the gang were subjected to stench bombs, ripped upholstery, and burned cabs. According to historian Charles Vidich, gangsters ruined the chances for genuine union organizations for cabdrivers after 1934.[37]

Activist drivers found themselves jobless in the aftermath of the 1934 strike. Strikers who were arrested returned to their fleets to learn that they had been fired. One example was Joseph Smith of 73 West 134th Street. Smith was arrested for disorderly conflict on February 7, then again on March 23. Both cases were dismissed, but Smith was told to bring his credentials to the Hack Bureau, where on April 2 his badge was revoked. Another driver, Samuel Spiro, of 70 East Fifty-fifth Street in Brooklyn, wrote LaGuardia that, despite the mediation of Morris Ernst, the Parmelee garage had fired him for his participation in the strike.[38]

Artists and writers, absorbed by the human drama of the strike, supported the cabbies. Albert Halper, a prominent left-wing writer, penned a short story entitled "Scab" that appeared in the *American Mercury* in June 1934. Halper expertly dissected the troubled psyche of a penniless cabdriver who defied the strike. The driver fearfully navigated the streets, wary of mobs of his fellow cabbies. He learned that his fares were indifferent to his anxieties and tipped no better than usual. When a blonde female fare ordered him to go to Greenwich Village, he encountered a gang of striking drivers, many of whom knew him. They dragged the woman from the car and smashed its windows. When the scab returned to his garage that afternoon, the owner was far more concerned about the vehicular damage than about the driver's woes. Upon returning home, the driver realized his predicament and resolved not to scab again.[39]

Hollywood declined to portray the 1934 taxi strike in films, but the Theater Union and the Taxi Drivers Union produced an independent film in the months after the strike. Entitled *Taxi,* the film incorporated newsreel footage of the strike and used actual cabdrivers in many roles. This well-intentioned plan proved problematic, as drivers could rarely show up consistently. As a result, a number of people played the same role. Shooting was hampered by extreme cold, which limited takes to five minutes each, followed by warm-up periods. The plot concerned the plight of unemployed cabbies, especially those blacklisted for communist sympathies. The film criticized company unions and scabs and called for stronger unions. It is unclear if the production was ever completed or shown, but the effort indicates the desire of cabdrivers to portray themselves and their grievances.[40]

Of larger impact was the groundbreaking theatrical performance of Clifford Odets's *Waiting for Lefty.* The play opened as a Group Theater production on January 5, 1935, at the Civic Repertory Theater. It was intended to commemorate the strikes of the past year. The production, brimming with sympathetic portrayals of the fallen professionals among the ranks of the hack men, made theatrical history with its openly militant politics, its depiction of the lives and speech of ordinary New Yorkers, and its powerful emotional appeal to the tumultuous present. In the one-act performance set in a union hall, characters step forth to proclaim their descent into hacking and their realization of working-class consciousness. In one scene, Edna berates her husband Joe, a hack man, for his fear of striking. Edna repeatedly accuses Joe of unmanly behavior and then compares him unfavorably with her father, who joined a successful strike to battle for higher wages during World War I. Edna reminds him, "You're not a kid and you do have to think about the next minute. For God's sake, do something, Joe, get wise. Maybe get your buddies together, maybe go on strike for better money." Edna threatens to leave Joe for another man if he does not show some courage, telling him, "When a man knocks you down, you get up and kiss his fist. You gutless piece of baloney!" Edna has few good words for the union, which she regards as rotten. In another scene, Harry Fatt (the name says all), the union head, speaks approvingly of President Franklin Roosevelt and tells the cabbies that now is not the time to strike. The men elect Lefty to be the new chairman, while Fatt engages in some classic red-baiting. At the end, the announcement of Lefty's death provokes the drivers to stand, fists aloft, and shout, "Strike, Strike, Strike!" At performances of the play, actors from the Group Theater hidden among the audience repeated the call in loud voices. The audience quickly joined in, and within minutes the auditorium would rock with cheering and crying. Odets recalled, "You saw for the first time theater as a cultural force . . . The proscenium had disappeared, When that happens emotionally and humanly, you have great theater." The performances electrified left-wing theater for the rest of the decade and galvanized a wide variety of other artists, including photographers, composers, novelists, poets, folk singers, and fashion designers. Odets had captured artistic and political fascination and identification with the ordinary cabbies who sustained the dramatic strikes the year before.

Photographers from the emerging New York School of photography found inspiration in the rapid movement and nitty-gritty qualities of hacking. Photographers Weegee, Ted Cromer, Berenice Abbott, and Robert Frank took candid images of cabdrivers and their hacks. Hack men represented the vigor, reckless energy, and speed of the city's modernity. At the same time, hack men had a timeless traditionalism that such realist photographers found reassuring. For years, the arts in America remained enraptured with images of hack men.[41]

Most Americans knew of cabdrivers through the silver screen. Cabbies became ubiquitous in films. For many Americans, James Cagney's performance in the 1932 hit movie *Taxi* crystallized the everyman quality of the cabdriver. In the film, the dapper Cagney plays Matt Nolan, an independent owner-driver, caught in the struggle against Consolidated, a taxi cartel. He falls in love and marries Sue Reilly (Loretta Young) after her father is sentenced to prison for killing a truck driver who deliberately wrecked Nolan's cab to get control of his hack stand. Though somewhat domesticated, Nolan retains his hot temper and quickly reverts to violence to wreak revenge against his father-in-law's attackers. Advertisements for the film describe Nolan leading the forces of the "independent drivers against the strong arm tactics of the taxi chain." The film portrays cabbies sympathetically and hints at the possibilities of collective action.

The *New York Evening Standard* contended that Nolan was the personification of "every cab driver who ever gave you an argument or handed you a load of blarney through the window." The reviewer watched as patrons lined up in the rain to watch Cagney, and wrote that they recognized in his character "the self-assured wise guy with whom they play pool, and the women, the cocky redhead with whom they strut fancy steps in the dance hall." The press book for the film emphasized the masculine, roughhouse quality of Cagney's performance, hyping it: "Honk! Honk! Here comes Jim. Rough, ready, romantic. The fighting-ist, loving-ist red head that ever skipped a stoplight. He knows what's what . . . He's wise to every bright light on Broadway and speeds through life to love." *Taxi* is a dramatic cross-section of the sidewalks of New York. Cagney combined his Irish personality with Jewish culture by gleefully speaking Yiddish in *Taxi,* using a popular method of introducing ethnicity into films about the working classes.[42]

The film is significant in its positive portrayals of cabby masculinity and sexuality, but relies too heavily on Cagney's performance rather than any general comments about the occupation. Cagney's character deploys an individualistic approach to overcoming tyranny and corruption, rather than emulating the collective efforts found in the strikes of the era. Commentators in the left-wing monthly *New Theater* bemoaned the retrograde qualities of *Taxi.* Lincoln Kirstein, one of Cagney's early critical champions, compared *Taxi* with *Waiting for Lefty,* and saw in the Odets play the kind of drama Cagney should have made.[43]

Taxi was not the only Hollywood representation of New York cab-drivers, or even the most heroic. In the film *Big City* Spencer Tracy plays Joe Benton, an independent cabdriver who is married to Anna Benton (Luise Rainer), a Russian woman, and brother-in-law to Paul Roya (Victor Varconi), another cabby. Both cabbies are beset by the syndicate and try to infiltrate the fleet to uncover plans to ruin them. Paul is accused falsely of placing a bomb in the garage and is shot by the night watchman. Government officials distort the inquest to try to deport Anna. Her pregnancy delays legal actions, during which time the independent cabbies, aided by boxer Jack Dempsey in a cameo role, come to the aid of the Benton family and prove their innocence. The baby is given the names of dozens of cabdrivers to commemorate their courage and solidarity.[44]

Other productions in this decade enunciate the special talents hidden in cabdrivers. In *Broadway Gondolier,* Dick Powell plays an operatic taxi driver. He is discovered, but he misses his first audition. However, the producer's secretary, played by Joan Blondell, finds him attractive. The cabman is encouraged by his teacher to go to Europe and learn singing there. After a quick trip to Venice, Powell's character returns to hacking in New York. Despite the fierce opposition of Blondell's boyfriend, she and the cabdriver are united at the end. Presumably, he will then leave taxicab driving for the opera.[45]

Reflecting the class anxieties under the surface of *Taxi* were a number of films of the 1930s that involved switched identities. Usually, higher-status people fall into cab driving before being restored to their heroic statuses. Cab driving becomes desolate labor in *High Gear,* which features James Murray as a fallen race car champion who is ashamed of driving a cab and works hard to keep a beautiful woman from discovering his new job. After his son is badly hurt protecting Murray's cab from goons, Murray regains his courage and wins a lucrative racing match. In the 1936 production of *They Met in a Taxi,* cabdriver Jimmy Donlin (Chester Morris), becomes the willing dupe of Mary Trenton (Fay Wray), who pretends to be fleeing her own wedding but later turns out to have stolen a pearl necklace from a real wedding. The necklace proves to be a fake, but Donlin helps her find the real one. After that, they profess love.[46] Hacking was often a cover for nefarious deeds in films of the era. A gangster impersonates a cabdriver in order to rob a wealthy foreigner of his jewels in *Step Lively, Jeeves!* (1937).[47] Other cabdrivers pretend to be what they are not. Admitting that one is a cabdriver is often more than a Hollywood character can bear. In *Star for a Night* (1936), Fritz Lind, played by Dean Jagger, drives a cab but tells his mother in Austria that he owns an automobile factory.[48]

Cabdrivers were portrayed as criminals in other films. Brian Donlevy plays a murderer and counterfeiter who is killed by members of his own gang in *Midnight Taxi,* a 1937 release from Twentieth Century Fox. Hopton Russell played a cabdriver intent on murdering his passengers for the diamonds they carried in *Below the Deadline* (the title is a reference to the diamond district). After overhearing a woman describe her true identity in the backseat, a cabdriver attempts to extort cash from her in *Alias Mary Dow.*[49]

Love is the driving force of many Hollywood films. In the cabdriver epics, romance assumes class connotations. Cabdrivers and taxi dancers are natural lovers who overcome obstacles in *Midnight* (1939). Claudette Colbert plays a European showgirl who convinces a soft-hearted cabdriver to help her look for work, despite not having enough cash for the fare. The cabby, played by Don Ameche, falls in love with her, although she tries to dump him. The cabby then organizes all of his friends to search New York for her. Now a socialite, the former showgirl is horrified when her cabdriver admirer shows up at an elite gathering and proclaims to be her future husband. Eventually she accedes, and they march off to the marriage bureau.

In *Dance Hall Hostess,* a 1933 production about Irish-Americans, Nora Marsh (Helen Chandler) jilts her cabdriver finance, Jerry Raymond (Jason Robards) for a rich man who promises to buy her a new pair of silk stockings every day of the year. Furious, Jerry wrecks his cab, is fired, and begins beer-running to keep Nora in stockings. After Nora marries the rich man and has a child with him, his well-to-do family rejects her. Anguished, the rich son commits suicide, and Nora and Jerry wind up together with her child and a taxicab. Love with a cabby legitimizes a fallen woman in *Pickup* (1933). Here a cabby played by George Raft picks up a streetwalker (played by Sylvia Sidney) and, despite his initial suspicions, takes pity on her. Their love prospers and she takes a job at the taxi garage. Later, her career in the badger game comes out, and the cabdriver has a fling with a society girl. Eventually, after several murder attempts by old enemies, they are reunited. Each of these movies, as historian John Bodnar has argued, are cautionary tales about attempting to cross class, ethnic, and legal borders, which contribute to an ongoing cultural debate about the alternatives and fates of tough young people.[50]

Hollywood films borrowed from the street culture of hack men and in turn influenced their public persona. The public credited cabdrivers with oracle-like knowledge about politics. An article just before the 1936 election cited cabbies as the "chief source of public opinion" about the candidates. The article described how cabbies keep "a finger on the public pulse." It may have been a sign of growing cultural unity that cabbies developed contemporary slang. A "schoolboy" was a new driver. An "elk" was a progressive driver, from a union standpoint. A "tail light" was a driver who was sycophantic around the boss. A "stiff" was a low booker. Policemen in radio cars were known as the "Dolly sisters," while patrolmen were called "the arm" after the term "strong arm."[51] Some trade terms survived from the horse-and-rig days. Hacking, of course, was one such term. So was "bilking," which a fare did by running off without paying. In the 1930s, such thieves were called "skips." "Horse hiring" came from the 1880s, meaning renting cabs by the day. The steady rise in competition in the 1930s produced new terms. Cabbies trying to sneak in front of a hack line were called "chiselers" who "crash" the lines. The "boffing crews," who were prepared to bump a chiseler with their front fenders, resisted anyone who tried to crash. Persistent crashers suffered "the needle" when a sharp instrument punctured their cab's tires.[52]

The cabbies' tough talk and cinematic images induced government researchers to record the sayings and legends of the taxi men. Works Progress Administration (WPA) investigators collected cabdriver stories from the streets of New York. One cabby recalled how he had taken a man "with about six or seven large bundles," around town. Assured by the customer that the trip would be worth twenty or twenty-five dollars, the driver patiently waited as the fare stopped twenty times each in Brooklyn, Manhattan, and the Bronx. Ultimately, the fare stiffed the driver, who later learned that he had been driving around a numbers runner.[53]

Despite their public myths and working-class argot, cabdrivers still lacked any genuine unity, a factor that worried those in government and business who were associated with the trade. The strike of 1934 had sufficiently alarmed the city government, the media, and the newly organized mutual society the League of Mutual Taxi Owners (LOMTO) that further reforms seemed necessary. Despite the recommendations of commissions, the mayor's attempts at reform, and the appeals in the newspapers, the excessive number of drivers, high turnover, no job security, long hours, and low wages plagued the drivers. At the same time, critics charged that lowering the number of drivers would inevitably lead to monopoly. Alderman Lew Haas proposed a bill in February 1937 that limited the number of licenses, known as medallions, to 13,595 and fixed the number allocated to fleets and to owner-drivers in the status at the time. That way, fleet owners and individual drivers could not encroach on the others' allotments. The city government would control access into cab driving.

The Haas proposal came about during another threat of fare wars that would push drivers and garages into ruinous competition. The Sunshine-Radio System, which operated the much-loved DeSoto Skyliner taxi, planned to slash rates by one-third, despite job actions threatened by their drivers and competing fleets' cabbies. The weather intervened. A heavy rainstorm created an instant bonanza, loosening the discount stickers enough that drivers could eagerly peel them off their cabs. First attempts to push through the Haas Act failed, despite Mayor LaGuardia's support. After intense lobbying, the bill passed on March 1, 1937, by a vote of 50 to 4. On May 11, the New York State Supreme Court upheld the act, ruling that the police did have the right to limit the number of cabs in the city. So empowered, the city stabilized the number of medallions at 13,595.

Major fleets supported the new law and urged company unions to support it. The *Brotherhood Register,* the newspaper of the Parmelee Garage Company Union, hailed passage as the "climax to a long fight to stabilize the hack business." The Brotherhood, which claimed 3,500 members, stated that it had argued for three years that only the principal of limitation, enunciated in the Haas Act, could solve the woes of cabdrivers. Shortly after passage of the act, the trade's ills were so bad that the number of licenses dropped further to 11,787, as drivers, fatigued and discouraged, returned their medallions to the city government. Moreover, the new medallion system had little effect on faltering prices. Fleets and individual drivers had difficulty getting cabs on the streets. Although the new regulations had little short-term effect, they gradually formed the working agreement for the taxi industry into the 1970s.

After the passage of the Haas Act, no one expected the medallions to ever be worth more than the ten-dollar license fee. One of the drafters of the bill later commented: "It was a fluke; no one ever foresaw that these licenses would ever be valuable." By limiting licensed drivers to those who owned a medallion or worked for someone who did, LaGuardia's administration did not modernize hacking, but reached far into the municipal past for a method to bond hack men and society together. Just as cartmen, butchers, grocers, tavernkeepers, and other licensed occupations of the colonial and early national eras accepted regulation in order to limit their numbers and to create a franchise that brought them significant political and economic powers, so the Haas Act created a license that eventually would bind the city and cabdriver together and give these semi-skilled laborers sizable political power and some prosperity.[54]

The Haas Act also instituted strong protections for owner-drivers by mandating that individual cabbies own at least 42 percent of all cabs. This measure halted a powerful consolidation that had swept the trade after 1930. At the beginning of the decade, almost 95 percent of all cabs were individually owned. Most of the twenty-seven fleets that owned fifty or more cabs were small. Only five fleets operated over 250 hacks. Five years later, those percentages had changed dramatically. Fleets of one hundred or more cabs now accounted for 38 percent of the 12,578 cabs operated in the city. The trend was decisively toward the monopoly envisioned by Mayor James Walker in 1930. One major difference was that the fleets were no longer subsidiaries of big auto companies. The Checker Company had three fleets in 1930, but only one (Parmelee) in 1935. The Yellow Cab Company, which formerly had a fleet of three thousand cabs, filed for bankruptcy in 1935.[55]

The Haas Act stimulated further union organization. Despite violent opposition from the Teamsters, the New York Taxicab Chauffeurs and Service Men, a branch of the United Automobile Workers of America assisted by the Transport Workers Union under Mike Quill, first organized the Allied, Parmelee, and Terminal garages and then moved to create closed-shop agreements with other fleets. Throughout the summer and fall of 1937, the TWU held mass meetings targeted at each major garage at the Transport Workers Hall on West Sixty-fourth Street. It published bulletins in each garage advising the drivers about recent achievements and arguing against the company union. The Brotherhood, which claimed to represent the vast majority of Parmelee drivers, lashed out at the TWU in its editorials and claimed that the company union had achieved better pay and benefits for them. The TWU held meetings in Harlem and regularly included officials from black labor organizations. Norman Thomas also appeared at rallies.

In October 1937, the TWU encountered some protests at the Sunshine-

Radio System, where drivers opposed to the union threatened to strike. The TWU blamed management for inciting the action, which spread to over one thousand drivers. Ironically, the TWU found itself in the position of supplying Sunshine-Radio System cabs with drivers to break an unauthorized "wildcat" strike. In mid-October, the strikers returned and, despite some further grumbling, accepted a closed shop. Another threatened strike in December 1937 was covered in newspapers all over the nation. As the city government now understood the power of union organizing, the TWU secured a contract for fifteen thousand cabdrivers, with a commission system based upon time of work. Its victory in the Sunshine garages was overwhelming; it won by a vote of 1,365 to 99. Similar accomplishments occurred in other garages. The TWU flexed its muscles by threatening general strikes to push their demands. At the end of the year, the TWU successfully negotiated with fleets for increased commissions and for minimum weekly salaries of eighteen dollars or 40 percent of a weekly gross billing of $36 and 50 percent of anything over $38. The TWU then moved in its next contract to eliminate part-time drivers by limiting union membership to a maximum of fifteen thousand drivers. As this move threatened the stability of the fleets, the major companies abrogated the contract by the spring of 1938. In March 1938, two large fleets locked out over six thousand drivers. The TWU claimed to have placed these drivers elsewhere, while blasting the companies for using scabs and "coolie single shift" drivers. Within a few days, the companies reinstated the drivers. The TWU and the fleets agreed upon an open-shop clause a week later. There were reports that the fleets used hired muscle to drive out unionized cabbies and that the police were acting as strikebreakers. The union issued a broadside asking for public support against "czaristic fleet owners.[56]

Mike Quill, head of the TWU, won election to the city council in 1938. Joined by two other councilmen, Quill introduced a measure to guarantee a minimum wage of $18 per day for day drivers and $21 for night men. TWU flyers proclaimed its benefits. Undoubtedly, such arguments referred to fleet owners, who used lockouts to break the union. New opposition emerged from the independent drivers, who regarded the proposed bill as destructive of their position in the taxi business. Independent operators protested to LaGuardia that although they had nothing personally against Quill, they questioned the propriety of his dual powers as a councilman sponsoring the bill while simultaneously serving as president of the TWU. The independent drivers distributed flyers that warned that the new legislation would create a politicized taxicab board of control that would set fares, hours of operation, double fees for individual drivers, and even jail those who did not comply with its edicts. The TWU reached out to the owner-drivers, holding mass meetings for them featuring Quill and Eugene P. Connolly as speakers. At the meetings, Quill discussed plans for a credit union and cooperatives for automobile parts and service. Still, distrust marked the relationship between the owner-drivers and the TWU. Eventually, the proposed bill was referred to a commission, where it languished.[57]

The accusations revived old recriminations by owner-drivers that the unions were extortionists. It appeared, however, that the TWU was as concerned as any other party about criminals. In April 1938, the district attorney indicted five men on racketeering charges. The TWU had compiled files on the men, who had worked for the union, and turned them over to the district attorney to aid in his investigation. The TWU had been sufficiently anxious about rumors of misconduct that Eugene P. Connolly had advised Quill that the organization should publicize its own efforts to find and oust extortionists.[58]

Although the influence of the Communist Party among cabdrivers reputedly was gone in the aftermath of the bitter 1934 strikes, TWU organizing plainly demonstrates the influences and achievements of the party organization. Identified as members of the negotiating team were John Santo, international secretary-treasurer; Harry Sacher, general council; Eugene P. Connolly, director of the taxicab division, and Warren G. Horis, general taxicab organizer.

According to Joshua Freeman's exhaustive study of the TWU, Santo, Sacher, and Connolly were significant officers in the Communist Party. Although Santo customarily preferred to remain in the background, in part because of his strong Hungarian accent, he was by the mid-1930s openly leading the union negotiations and briefly was the official head of the union. His presence at the taxi negotiations indicates how important the TWU and the Communist Party considered the drive. Freeman notes that Santo, who had joined the party in Hungary in 1928, was very much an orthodox communist. Despite his preferred role as insider, in the cab negotiations he was right in front. Eugene P. Connolly was later a top official in the American Labor Party, while Sacher was a leftist member of the TWU inner circle. Frequently involved in the parlaying was Austin Hogan, who came from a family of Irish Republican Army activists and was an effective communist organizer in the early 1930s

and beyond. Finally, among the most important exhorters and organizers for the TWU and its efforts with the cabdrivers was the legendary
Mike Quill, who in his early years was a conduit between the union and
the Clan na Gael, the influential radical Irish labor organization.

Even with the presence of communists at the bargaining table, the
TWU was able to work with the city government and with the fleets because LaGuardia, in the face of acerbic criticism from the Roman Cath-
olic Church, the Hearst newspapers, and Tammany Hall, refused to attack
philosophies with weapons reserved for criminals. He strongly guaranteed First Amendment rights. Unlike many of his contemporaries, La-
Guardia generally treated the Communist Party pragmatically. In turn,
the TWU strived for many of the same objectives LaGuardia deemed
essential for reform of the taxi industry. It urged greater regulation and
curbing the excessive numbers of cabs and drivers that resulted in "cutthroat competition among cab owners [that] constantly cut into the already sub marginal earnings of these workers."[59]

In fact, the TWU could not duplicate among cabdrivers the solid
achievements that they secured for bus and subway drivers. In the years
after the TWU organized these workers, it gained more money and benefits for them. Salaries went up, with limits on hours worked and, for the
first time for many, real paid vacations. The TWU created medical, educational, and sports programs for transit workers other than cabbies. It
strived to overcome racial, ethnic, and occupational divisions. Helping
transit workers forget about the stings of past defeats, the TWU achievements sustained a sense of manliness among them.[60]

These accomplishments did not occur among hack men. The TWU
did try to implement a credit union, sponsored dances organized by the
Ladies Taxi Auxiliary, and put on performances of *Waiting for Lefty*. But
it could not muster among cabbies the sizable community it sustained
among bus and transit workers. The constant turnover, the hypercompetition among drivers, and the roughshod methods used by fleets to
oppose the union made organizing a constant battle. There was a sense
of anomie and despair. WPA recorders talked to participants in the 1938
taxi strike. One man called his fellow hack men "the worst people in the
world, exploited I mean." He stated that thirteen hours a day was average with earnings of about four dollars a week. The biggest concern was
job insecurity: "The hack goes down to the garage, an he don't even know
if he'll get work." Low bookers, or those below average, were especially
vulnerable. Moreover, the fleets intimidated drivers not to pay their

dues, thugs brutalized shop stewards, and many drivers were forced to sign petitions denouncing the union before they could get a cab at the daily shape-up.[61]

There were several other reasons for the union problems. Cabbies did not benefit from the influx of radically minded immigrants who worked among bus and subway workers. Few Depression-era immigrants to New York City moved into hacking. White-collar work, skilled labor, and domestic service attracted far more immigrants than the taxi trade.[62] Cabdrivers were primarily native-born American men trapped into work they took as a last resort. They were "Depression virtuosos," often well-educated artists and intellectuals, who began driving a cab to make ends meet and wound up driving permanently. Because of their hopes to claw back up the work ladder, they had little commitment to permanent organization or were too embittered and cynical to achieve any real unity.

The typical cabdriver was hardly a radical but probably a fleet driver like Harry Faber. *Fortune Magazine* profiled Faber's career in 1939. He held hack license number 37046, had driven a cab for about fifteen years, and for five years had hacked a Checker cab for Parmelee. Faber held a decidedly negative view about his job, concluding that hacking was about "the lousiest $%%## way to make a living there is." He acknowledged that he and his Checker were practically indistinguishable from the other 1,999 hacks at Parmelee, except that he shaved three times a week, unlike some of the "other stiffs who go around looking like gorillas. They're palookas." He prided himself on his high bookings and wanted to appear successful to his fares to encourage better tips. In the wintertime, Faber wore a cap, suit, and battered overcoat, but in the summer, he switched into an old alpaca jacket, a sport shirt, and a pair of odd pants. He changed his shirts three times a week. Although the job was physically draining, he was generally fit, with a wiry body. He did, however, complain of kidney troubles, stomach ulcers, sore back muscles, and hemorrhoids.

Faber had developed a daily routine. He spent most of his time along with about twenty other regulars playing "off the board," or not cruising the streets, by waiting in line on Forty-fourth Street between Fifth and Sixth avenues near the Harvard Club, the Hippodrome, the New York Yacht Club, and the Royalton, Algonquin, Seymour, and other hotels. After each fare, Faber generally headed back to Forty-fourth Street. The block produced about 250 calls per day in the winter and about 150 in the summer. During dead periods, Faber relaxed by talking about politics, women, fares, and traffic cops. He befriended many New Yorker writers. Although city laws required that any cab driver be allowed to wait in the line, outsiders that tried would be frozen in place by hacks who parked behind and ahead of the offending cab. After the intruder gave up, the group made up a pot of cash for the two vigilantes. Their actions indicated that control of the hack line was still practiced twenty years after it was declared unlawful.

By sticking close to Forty-fourth Street and not cruising, Faber averaged about fifteen fares per day, earning around $4.49 for the company and about $3.30 for himself, plus about $1.25 in tips. Hacking did not pay as well as it had during the twenties, when Harry could clear as much as one hundred dollars per week and nearly always forty a week. Now, the Depression, the general lack of money, and the extension of the subway and bus services meant fewer customers.

Lower bookings meant that tipping had become a vital part of cabbies' daily income, but Harry knew that each day would find at least two skunks, or non-tippers, in his cab. He considered men to be good tippers, women less reliable, and tourists the worst, as they did not understand New York mores. Usually, Faber avoided cruising except on rainy days, a custom that cut down on wasted miles and avoided confrontations with policemen who guarded avenues where cruising was forbidden. Faber and his friends regarded Jake Miller, the "arm" at Fifty-sixth Street and Fifth Avenue, as the meanest cop, and "an —— who wouldn't give you a break no how."

Harry's workday had a predictable pattern. He labored about eleven hours per day. He reported to the Parmelee Garage Number 6 on Twenty-third Street and the East River at 6:50 a.m. to pick up his freshly washed, swept, and refueled Checker. The garage, one of sixteen Parmelee operations in the city, consisted of a large parking lot, a cheap diner, and a low brick building containing offices, gas pumps, and wash equipment. Harry first headed to Forty-fourth Street and the stand at the Harvard Club in hopes of being first in line, or "head up," for the morning icebreaker, or first fare of the day. While waiting, he would wolf down some breakfast. It was on such an occasion that he got the best fare of his career, a $13.50 ride to Coney Island with two Englishmen seeking some thrills. Harry got the call from Chester, the doorman at the Algonquin Hotel. Chester and Tommy, the Harvard Club doorman, made sure that no cruising cabs got any business at their establishments. In return, Faber and his pals on the hack line pooled together a Christmas tip for the two doormen. One day, Tommy rewarded Faber with a significant thrill by calling him to pick up Mrs. Franklin D. Roosevelt downtown. Harry told the first lady that he was a pro–New Deal Democrat, and she liked that. Cabdrivers liked Mrs. Roosevelt, who had a reputation as a great tipper, and they often encouraged her to sit in the front seat so they could talk with her more easily.

To insure the best mileage, Faber split the rest of his day by lurking about the railroad stations in the morning rush hour, then during the next few hours he worked around the office buildings and department stores. Lunch hours were for diners, and the early afternoons were for female shoppers. The late afternoon was best spent in the financial district, then the hotels and restaurants were busy until nine o'clock. For the next two hours, the action slacked off, and so Harry and his fellow hacks customarily ate their dinners, read the newspapers, gossiped, and then lined up for the post-theater crowd. Harry had learned little tricks such as hanging around a darkened office building from which lucrative fares might suddenly emerge; he was convinced that late nights at the office were more for sin than hard work. Big hotels disgorged late-night partiers; after midnight, hackies stuck around nightclubs waiting for drunken patrons who missed the last train to the suburbs. These hackies may well have steered the customer to a clip joint in exchange for the standard commission of 40 percent of the sucker's bill. Though that was illegal, hacks taking customers to smaller hotels for a dollar referral fee was legitimate. Shadier were the cabby pimps. Faber estimated that only about 2 or 3 percent of hacks operated as procurers. Occasionally, a customer from the Harvard Club would ask him for an address of a beautiful young woman, but Harry would respond, "Sorry that don't happen to be my line of work," knowing that the tip would be smaller as a result.

Harry was born to Russian-Jewish parents on the Lower East Side in 1939, completed school through the eighth grade, got a job as a shipping clerk, did a two-year hitch in the navy, and was a trolley conductor on the Eighth Avenue Line. He started driving a cab in his early twenties with Yellow Cab (the precursor to Parmelee), then borrowed a thousand dollars from relatives and two thousand more from the manufacturer and got his own cab, a Mogul-Checker. He was able to pay off his debts in a year and drove the Mogul for three years. When the odometer hit 185,000 miles, he got a new cab, which he drove until 1932. The hard times forced him to give up his own business and work for a year with Benny Engle's

Five Borough Garage, a small firm that went bankrupt shortly thereafter. Harry then joined "the Yellows," as the Parmelee garages were called by cabbies. He was known as an exceptionally good booker and a safe driver, with only about a dozen citations and two small accidents in a fifteen-year career.

Harry was married in 1928 to Esther Weitzman, one of the crowd of young people who would go to Coney Island together and then dance at Knapp Mansion on Bedford Avenue, near where the couple now lives. Esther worked for a while in the garment district, then quit to take care of their only child, a daughter, and her mother, who had diabetes and was semi-invalid. Harry gave Esther at least eighty dollars per month, with which she managed the household. The rent was thirty-five dollars per month for a six-room walkup, which they shared with her brother, who drove a truck for the Joe Salwen Paper Company. Mrs. Weitzman was Orthodox, and while Harry and Esther were Americanized, he did not drive a cab on the holy days, a time when the absence of Jewish drivers caused a drought of available cabs in the city. Their amusements were simple: radio, magazines, occasional movies, and visits to the Knapp Mansion or, more frequently, to some of Esther's many relatives. On Saturdays, Harry knocked off work early, bathed, put on his good suit, and spent the evening playing pinochle and hearts with his pals while Esther went to her ladies' club. On Sundays in the summer, they headed for Coney Island or perhaps borrowed a car to drive upstate. Harry never took a vacation, but Esther would go upstate for two weeks in the summer to a Jewish resort where she paid twenty-five dollars, American plan, to dance and be entertained with other people from Brooklyn and the Bronx. She liked it upstate and wanted Harry to quit hacking and open a grocery store there. He thought more practically of going back to the trolley business but admitted that the grocery idea wasn't a bad one, as selling food could not be any riskier than hacking and, if times were slow, you could eat wholesale.

Faber's life epitomized the blurred boundaries between the lower middle class and the working classes. At times, he owned his own business, but much of his career was spent in the working classes, laboring for a giant corporation. Despite the popular reputation of the cabby as independent spirit, Faber's work life was mundane; it had rare moments of excitement but always within the routine of fares.[63]

Nowhere in the *Fortune* article on Harry Faber was the issue of union membership mentioned. He may not have been a member, as cabdriver unity with the Transport Workers Union again flagged in the late thirties. In 1939, negotiations between the TWU and the major fleets failed again. Dissension within the ranks and the TWU's precarious hold over its members set up a major reversal in the next round of elections held in January 1939. Though the TWU did well in the major fleets, it won only six of the twenty-eight fleets overall and held only a small margin over company unions. After several months of threats, the union called a brief general strike in January of that year. Strike bulletins were issued at major garages. One significant issue was the upcoming World's Fair. The TWU worried that the mayor would allow an increase in the number of cabs on the streets during the planned festival. It also denounced a plan to give the Parmelee organization an exclusive right to a huge waiting area next to the fair. The upcoming fair gave the TWU some leverage over the fleets; a strike then would cause chaos and large cash losses. The TWU was not above the use of violence. Twice, officials of the union were arrested during early 1939 for beating up uncooperative cabbies.[64]

Mike Quill, the head of the Transit Workers Union, considered the botched strike as one of his greatest failures. Quill blamed the cabbies, who he said had never come to the aid of the bus and subway drivers. Accordingly, those drivers mistrusted the cabbies and became openly hostile of them. One veteran TWU organizer spoke contemptuously of the hack men: "We had a feeling they were not like us. We were known for our generosity when members of other unions were in trouble. We gave money, collected food, and marched on their picket lines. Taxi men wanted no part of such activities. They didn't understand the meaning of solidarity." Quill also blamed the fleet owners, about whom he said, "notoriously unscrupulous, they reneged on agreements, written or oral." But he regarded the cabbies as "in continuous turmoil." The TWU organizers cautioned cabbies not to strike precipitously, but the hack men "in a rowdy, ill-tempered meeting, voted to strike." Quill recalled the meetings, one held after the night shift at three a.m., as "the best show in town after midnight and it was free." John Garfield and the Group Theater would come regularly to the Transport Hall to watch "the performance of the cabdrivers." Unfortunately the strike was a fiasco, "the young TWU's first and only disaster." The TWU pulled out all stops, hiring a chef recently laid off from the Waldorf Astoria to run the strike kitchen. The TWU Ladies' Auxiliary showed up to help, but none of the cabdrivers' wives made an appearance, creating more resentment. The TWU put in sizable amounts of dues from the bus and subway drivers' locals but, Quill claimed, the cabdrivers showed little appreciation. They would park their cabs far from the Transport Hall, come and eat a gourmet meal, and then leave to scab a strike the union had advised them not to hold. Quill regarded the cabbies as not only exploited by vicious bosses, but also as individual entrepreneurs. When the riding public's purse strings are tight, Quill noted, the taxi man is "in cutthroat competition with his fellow workers; solidarity with them is very nearly the last emotion a cabby feels."[65]

At the end of the 1930s, few could see that the TWU effort to organize the cabbies would eventually decline. At the end of the decade, cabdrivers had weathered the depression that shook American society. With a sympathetic mayor working to ameliorate the hypercompetition of the streets and aided by a militant union, cabdrivers curtailed their numbers and created value to their jobs. They demonstrated willingness for sharp class-based activism, as manifested in the violent 1934 strike. That action made even the sympathetic LaGuardia regard cabdrivers as badly in need of regulation. At the same time, their union efforts rested on a shaky alliance with the Transit Workers Union, headed by Mike Quill, a major labor figure who viewed cabbies with distrust. Owner-drivers survived the decade with an insured percentage of the cab labor force. Cabdriver culture, seen only discreetly before, took on a more recognizable visage in the 1930s. The strength of the large fleets produced career men such as Harry Faber. The hack men's determined effort to organize and gain economic leverage attracted left-wing writers who portrayed taxi drivers as proletarian heroes. More conservatively, Hollywood cinema mainly focused on taxi drivers as individualistic but attractive working-class males, though some cinematic cabbies were criminal. Trapped by economic disaster into a low-paying job, cabdrivers themselves created a tough, streetwise persona. In the late 1930s, the medallion system seemed like just another license fee, but eventually it would become the basis for the cabbies' franchise, economically and politically. Larger world events would elevate the medallion to a value far beyond the intentions of its inventors.

4

Prosperity during Wartime, 1940–1950

World War II revived the taxi industry in New York City. Rationing of gasoline and automobile parts by the Office of Defense Transportation (ODT) curtailed excess production of cars. Generally, the government lauded the taxi industry for its cooperation with the war effort. Showing their patriotism, in 1944 cabdrivers in New York City oversubscribed to the war bonds effort. They could afford to do so. Fewer cabs on the streets meant more business, less cruising by empty cabs, and less competition. The military draft removed the oversupply of drivers. Fed-up drivers continued to turn in their medallions, avoiding the ten-dollar-a-year renewal fee, and leave the job. During World War II, the number of drivers serving their country in the military and working for better wages in the munitions factories reduced the number of medallion holders to 7,500, the lowest number since the system was introduced. As veterans returned to reclaim medallions, the pool of medallion holders returned to its prewar level. Demand was so strong that shortly after the war ended, the city government issued new medallions to additional returning veterans, raising the number of permits to 11,787 in 1946, a total that lasted for decades. Not all veterans benefited from the city's expansion of the number of medallions. By 1947, fleets sold unused medallions for about $2,500, a figure that the police and newspapers considered extortionate, but which began open speculation on the tin permits.[1]

Even before the war began, the arrival of extra-fancy taxis heralded a new age of prosperity. Even in the late years of the Depression, automakers paid close attention to public desires. In 1936, roll tops were the rage, followed quickly by shatterproof glass tops. Roll tops had their disadvantages, such as excessive gas fumes, but were good for transporting linoleum rolls or for making speeches when drunk. Tourists also liked them. In 1940, the Checker cab offered the greatest innovation, a disappearing all-metal landaulet top. The driver turned a crank that caused the roof section over the passengers to disappear into the body of the cab, allowing fresh air and sunshine. Checker cab paid attention to the driver's comfort with better ventilation and heat and adjustable cushions for the front seat. New attachments helped prevent rolling on the hills and indicated when the gas tank was filled. The DeSoto Skyview continued to feature retractable roofs and added more trunk room for spare tires. Salesmen whimsically contended that a barrier in the trunk was required to prevent transport of dead bodies. The durable taxis could descend from original owners to newer New York drivers and then survive to be taken as discards to smaller cities in the South.[2]

The Transit Workers Union continued its efforts in the early years of the 1940s. The union again urged Mayor LaGuardia in March 1940 to limit the number of cabs even further. When negotiations between the TWU and the two largest fleets, the Terminal and National cab corporations, broke down in April 1940, the union ordered a walkout by over six thousand drivers. Accounts of the success of the strike varied. Unlike the strikes of the 1930s, in which the mayor showed sympathy for the strikers, this time the police monitored the picket lines and warned cabbies that any violence would not be tolerated. Special police details were assigned to the big hotels and taxi garages and at major intersections. Nonstrikers, especially owner-drivers, profited quickly from the absence of thousands of major fleet drivers.[3] Despite Mike Quill's misgivings about the failure of the 1939 strike threat, the TWU improved its performance after the failed attempt to strike during the problem-ridden World's Fair. Four thousand Parmelee drivers had gone on strike on April 25; the following month, fourteen strikers were arrested for picketing at the World's Fair. LaGuardia was displeased with both sides: at the cabbies for striking and at the garages for refusing an arbitration proposal. The owner-drivers made their position clear. They accepted the wisdom of police rule, in place since 1925, over the industry and argued that though the fleet drivers had the right to demand a higher commission, they did not feel the economic situation warranted an increase. As the police guarded the city's infrastructure and monitored the movement of owner-drivers carefully, LaGuardia convinced the TWU to end the strike on May 29 and promised to remedy conditions in hacking. Parmelee refused to go along with the mayor's demand, however, and taking advantage of the strike's collapse, fired over two hundred drivers.[4]

The TWU responded sensibly to the wartime crisis by vowing not to strike during the battle against fascism. It continued to organize, working steadily on the Parmelee garage throughout 1943 and 1944. By June 1944, it claimed to have organized many of the fleet's units, including one in which the "Negro drivers are enrolling." The TWU stated that it would keep part-timers out of the taxi business, revise Hack Bureau regulations, and seek a CIO union shop contract for all garages, an agreement that would require job security, vacations with pay, seniority rights, arbitration, payment for time spent on automobile breakdowns, and bonuses based upon bookings for cabbies. That it had not yet achieved these goals, already a part of agreements with bus and train drivers, demonstrates the troubles the TWU had with hack men.

The TWU could point to some successes, however. It scored another major victory at the massive Sunshine Garage, gaining drivers an increase in wages, paid vacations, union security, arbitration of discharges, and a pay bonus of 1 percent retroactive to the previous year. Despite these victories, the TWU faltered at other garages, and by late 1944, the owner-driver newspaper the *Taxi Age* crowed that the TWU was rapidly losing strength. Mike Quill, the TWU president, dismissed the cabbies as willing to capitulate to the fleet owners for a small bribe.[5]

What Mike Quill regarded as a "small bribe," the taxi men regarded as the road to prosperity. The war shortages produced a "taxi driver's golden age." Rationing of gas and of private car use and fares flush with wartime earnings made cab driving easier and more profitable than ever. One driver reported buying his wife a new fur coat and having savings of seven hundred dollars while earning over one hundred dollars a week. Still, there were signs of class resentment. In a holdover from the Depression years, drivers frequently asked for more than the metered rates for inconvenient trips. One driver noted, "Some of the boys I used to drive down to Wall Street about ten o'clock in the morning are using the subway now. Maybe it evens up in the long run." The actions of the ODT to decrease the amount of travel made such resentment common among drivers. By summer, the police commissioner acknowledged that cabdrivers were taking advantage of the situation, especially gouging servicemen. There were reports of fees nearly double the meter or charging groups by the individual.[6]

The failure of the TWU's strike and better pay during the war years meant less incentive to organize. Cabdrivers' weekly earnings jumped during the war to sixty-five to seventy dollars for the day shift and eighty to ninety dollars for the night shift.[7] One reason for higher wages was the difficulty of getting parts to repair old cabs and of buying new cabs. The wartime ODT decreed in 1942 that no new taxicabs could be built and banned cruising, the use of cabs for recreational trips, deliveries, and trips longer than thirty-five miles. The ODT also took hundreds of cabs off the streets and used them to transport Long Island aircraft workers to and from their plants. New York City's government added to the shortage by refusing to allow shared rides, because of concerns that other taxi passengers might insult female drivers and that sharing might lead to crime. Even when a powerful snowstorm disabled or intimidated hundreds of cabdrivers, and city residents waited in droves for cabs that never arrived, the city government resisted ride sharing. Democrats tried to make political headway against LaGuardia in the dispute over sharing, but their measure died in the state legislature in Albany. As a result, cabs stayed scarce, cruising virtually vanished, fares rose, and fleets and drivers earned more than ever.[8]

The shortage of male drivers made room for the entrance of women into the trade on a larger scale. Before World War II, only a handful of women took up hacking. By 1944, there were sixty-eight women licensed to drive. But, according to the Hack Bureau, only half had cars. The rest took out licenses and then got better-paying jobs as riveters. According to one female cabby who recorded her opinions, women took to the job easily. Ruth Sulzberger received her hack license after going through the same routine physical and fingerprinting exams as the fellows. Shortly thereafter, she took her new hack license and badge to the Parmelee garage and was sent out with "one of the company's green cabs." On the streets, Sulzberger encountered four kinds of passengers: the hurried type, the backseat driver, the quizzer, and the silent type. Most fares were of the first type and were more concerned with a fast trip than with their driver's sex. Sulzberger found the backseat drivers the most annoying and enjoyed the quizzers, who seemed fascinated by her opinions on the war, the economy, and New York City. She found little animosity from other drivers, who were "not as tough as they may appear, for the days of tough hacking are over." She did find that women were far more interested than men in her presence in the driver's seat. Many women seemed to pity her, though they also appeared less threatened by her driving skills.[9]

A second autobiography by a female cabby is Edith Martz Clark's *Confessions of a Girl Cab Driver*. Although Martz drove cab in Philadelphia, and later became a physician, her reminiscences are useful for understanding the experiences of women drivers in New York. Martz estimated that she was one of about three hundred female cabbies in Philadelphia. During her work, she met a woman who had driven during World War I and had loved the job. Martz found that many passengers were astonished to see her behind the wheel. A blind and drunken man told Martz that he was terrified of female drivers. When Martz picked up another fellow, he exclaimed: "I haven't been drinking that much—or have I?" Martz was warned frequently about criminal passengers. Female drivers were advised not to wear jewelry, though Martz usually wore her wedding band to fend off would-be lovers. She knew of one female driver who was lured into a barren place in New Jersey and escaped rape only by biting the assailant's thumb. Unwanted sexual approaches were common. One fare, cold from the weather, invited her into the back seat to warm him up. He then offered Martz a job delivering goods for him, which he promised would pay twice as much as hacking and would involve doing dictation "sitting in my lap, slowly." Another passenger asked her to marry him several minutes into the ride. Female passengers could be troubling as well. One asked Martz to come up to her apartment and smoke marijuana with her; another made an open lesbian invitation. Martz learned to drive slowly by police cars when she felt danger from her passengers. One strange fellow pretended to be a detective and had Martz drive him to a number of dark streets before jumping out and beating the fare. She learned that the fare had done the same thing to a few other hack men the same day.[10]

The *Taxi Weekly* interviewed several female cabbies who seem to have taken easily to their jobs. "Miss Alice M. Zeller" of Brooklyn boasted, "I know Brooklyn. Name any Brooklyn Street and number and I will figure out the least roundabout way to get there in a hurry." "Miss Lulu Kennedy" worked the night shift around Times Square and made it her business to know all the plays. She challenged her fares to simply give her the name of the play they were attending, needing no further direction. If the fares had forgotten the name of the show, she quizzed them about the characters until she could manage to get them to the right place. Mrs. Helen Hollander drove a cab because her husband was an invalid and "one of us has to work." She argued that the only trouble she faced as a cabby was with drunken young women who failed to pay. She would drive them quickly to a police station for arrest. Not every female cabby adapted as well. One woman who had trouble reading traffic lights started hacking and quit the same day.[11]

Solidarity across gender lines was shown in a poorly designed publicity stunt in 1944. A *New York Daily Mirror* advertisement for a magazine named *Modern Screen* showed Frank Sinatra punching out a cabdriver he believed was attacking little children. The *Taxi Age* blasted such "reprehensible fiction" and demanded a retraction from the newspaper. A similar protest came from Mrs. Ruby Phillips, one of the city's female cabbies. She denounced the stunt and stated that no cabdriver she knew would stoop to beat little children, as most were fine family men. An article on her noted that she was among the first female licensed airplane pilots and was famed throughout Europe.[12]

The image of women driving cabs, taking orders from and giving orders to fares, and ramming around the city amidst possibilities of romance was irresistible to Broadway producers and dramatists. Hollywood did not linger far behind. The character of Brunhilde "Hildy" Esterhazy, the sexually aggressive cabby of the 1944 hit Broadway production *On the Town*, satirized female cabbies. Hildy, after picking up a sailor, rejects his demands to go sightseeing and inveigles him to "come up to my place," singing an amusing ditty penned by Leonard Bernstein. The Hollywood production, with Betty Garrett in the role of Hildy and Frank Sinatra as the sailor, was released in 1949, one of six films during the 1940s that featured female cabdrivers.

Even before the stage version of *On the Town*, Universal Pictures produced a musical in 1943 called *Hi Ya! Sailor*, in which cabdriver Pat Rogers (Elyse Knox), helps a couple of sailors break into show business by finding a cigarette case belonging to a major chanteuse. Pat and one of the sailors marry at the end of the musical. Producers Releasing Corporation, a budget studio, put out *Danger! Women at Work* in 1943. In it, taxicab driver Pert (Mary Brian) gives her friend Terry advice on her recent inheritance of her uncle's truck and home. The two women then begin their own trucking business. In the 1944 Universal production *In Society*, cabdriver Elsie Hummerdingle (Marion Hutton) drives two plumbers, played by Abbott and Costello, out to Long Island to fix the pipes of a wealthy socialite. In a series of class reversals, the cabby and Abbott and Costello are mistakenly taken into high society, wreak havoc, rescue a rare painting from theft, and then clumsily destroy it. In the 1946 Warner Brothers production *Cinderella Jones*, Julie Bishop plays Camille, a cabdriver who enables the heroine to figure out her complicated love life. In all of these films, female cabdrivers play supportive roles, are often comedic figures, and in only two cases wind up in successful romances. In those two films, *On the Town* and *Danger! Women at Work,* the cabdrivers' masculine qualities were deemed suitable by their working-class lovers or husbands.[13]

Hollywood portrayed male cabbies largely as comedic figures. William Bendix starred in a series of films made by the Hal Roach Studio about the McGuerins, a family of Brooklyn cabdrivers. In *Brooklyn Orchid* (1942) the first of the trilogy, Tim McGuerin (Bendix, making his Hollywood debut) and his brother build up the Red Circle Cab Company, a fleet of over a thousand cabs. McGuerin may be a top cabby, but his wife Sadie (Gracie Bradley) offers nothing but grief. In this film and a sequel, *The McGuerins of Brooklyn* (1942), family feuds rather than the men's occupations drive the films. Shot on location at the Uplifters' Ranch in Santa Monica, California, the films created a comedic vision of a harassed, working-class cabdriver unable to satisfy his wife. A third episode, *Taxi, Mister!* (1943), provides a flashback to how Tim and Sadie first met. The series is important for its portrayal of the cabby as an everyman, beset by family woes, alienated from his work, and rarely finding camaraderie among his fellow workers.[14]

Bendix excelled at playing the little man who strived to get along with society and did not demand much in return. In *Guadalcanal Diary* (1943), Bendix amended his cabdriver narrative in the war theater in the South Pacific. His character, "Taxi" Potts, is an amiable sort who wants only to do his time safely and then return to Brooklyn to rejoin his wife and watch Dodgers baseball games. His plaintive statement is: "I'm no hero. I'm just a guy. I come out here because somebody had to come [but] I don't want no medals. I just want to go back home." His ordinariness is contagious among his fellow GIs of myriad ethnicities. They view women not just as sexual partners, but also as loving companions with whom they can start a family. Together they sing, "I want a girl, just like the girl that married dear old Dad."[15]

Genuine cabdrivers were tiring of the "canned casting" in Hollywood's portrayal of their jobs in the Bendix movies. In truth, Bendix's character, referred to in reviews as a "dumb but great-hearted cabbie," was offensive. One hack man collected dozens of clippings about cabbie heroism, generosity, and honesty to combat the negative portrayals in the films. He mentioned one elderly lady who watched him for ten minutes from the sidewalk near his hack stand, then came to ask if he was a safe driver. She told him that she had seen reckless drivers in Hollywood films.[16]

In a reprise of 1930s films, cabdrivers were portrayed in criminal situations in films in the 1940s. In part this was because Hollywood, in response to War Production Board curbs on set expenditures, forced film directors to use easily accessible props. More importantly, the trend toward film noir meant more attention to the urban working classes. Cabdrivers, like detectives, nightclub entertainers, and war veterans worked at night, alone possessing a real understanding of the anxieties and depravity of human behavior. As nocturnal people, cabdrivers saw and participated in corruption, greed, and violence. As lower-class workers, cabdrivers could not rise to the level of being important heroes or villains, but played accomplices or supporters. None of these roles allowed status elevation.[17] Cabdriver Steve Cavaroni (Paul Fix) murders a former accomplice in *Alias Boston Blackie* (1942). A cabdriver takes the murderer to the scene of his crime in *The Big Clock* (1948). A cabdriver is bribed to obtain information about one of his customers in *A Dangerous Profession* (1949). Spies disguised themselves as cabbies in *Dangerously They Live* (1941), *Madame Spy* (1942), and *Rio Rita* (1943). Gangsters also worked as cabbies to hide their identities: In *Johnny Eager* (1942), Robert Taylor drives a cab during the day, then dons evening clothes and runs a gambling business. He falls in love with a passenger, but before he can propose, the police shoot him.

One of the most interesting films of the 1940s was *Kilroy Was Here* (1947), in which Jackie Cooper returns to his job as a cabdriver after serving in the South Pacific. The storyline begins when Johnny Kilroy (Cooper) receives an acceptance letter to attend Benson College on the GI Bill. Along with his cabdriver pal, Pappy Collins (Jackie Coogan), Johnny clashes with the more privileged fraternity brothers. Even after the school discovers that he is the "real Kilroy" of the famous soldiers' slogan from World War II, "Kilroy was here," the fraternity brothers ostracize him when they realize he is a cabdriver and friends with many more. The brothers invite Kilroy and his friends to a dance. When the hack men arrive in shabby clothes, the frat boys publicly deny knowing them. Humiliated, Kilroy plans to leave school, until a friendly professor convinces him not to quit, and the student body applauds him. Rife with class tensions, despite the happy ending, the film indicates the growing distance between the middle class and cabdrivers.[18]

One problem was that there simply were not enough cabdrivers available. The *New York Times* reported that although there had been fewer cabs during the war, ridership had doubled since 1941; over seven hundred thousand New Yorkers a day took cabs. At least the taxis were improved. New Yorkers were excited when the Packard Federal Corporation, the New York representative of Packard taxis, rolled out the new post-war cabs. The new cabs featured room in the front for two passengers separated from the driver by a Plexiglas shell. A large backseat provided roomy comfort for three more people. Special defogger windows, passenger-operated radios, and fold-down seats made the Packard a special treat for fares. Despite these attractions, the Hack Bureau withheld approval, contending that the new cab was not as safe, that it lacked comfort features, and that the new doors were potentially dangerous. Within two weeks, Andrew Wallender, head of the Hack Bureau, banned the new Packard.[19]

The wartime shortage of cabs and drivers convinced many that taxi driving could be lucrative. As veterans returned from the war, Mayor LaGuardia quickly sought to amend the Haas Act so that 155 cabbies returning from the war could regain their medallions. Soon over sixteen hundred ex-soldiers applied for hack licenses.[20] The ODT removed special wartime restrictions on taxi driving in August 1945. Even though the post-war bonanzas for cabdrivers lasted only into the summer of 1946, a booming New York City economy gave the medallions a new luster. Their value soared from the initial price of five dollars in 1937 as medallions became a marketable commodity after World War II. By 1947, the permits cost $2,500 in a burgeoning black market. Owner-drivers defended the practice of gaining "bonus" profits on sales on medallions. The United Taxi Council, an owners' group, argued that the "cab business is a going business. It does not consist only of the equipment, but of the going equipment." The owner-drivers argued that to prevent the resale of "the going equipment is to destroy the value of the equipment itself, for normally there is little market in the vehicle unless it can be leased as a taxicab." By these comments, the owner-drivers established a position that they were independent businessmen with a franchise granted by the city. Although the owner-drivers generally opposed expansion of the number of medallions, it supported the Hack Bureau's desire to "revive" about 1,800 of the permits, provided that they were sold to war veterans and thus reduced unemployment among them.[21]

At the same time, the owners' group sought an increase in the fare rates, arguing that there had been no increase after 1931, that business had dropped 25 percent since the war, and that maintenance and fuel costs were unlikely to go down. Fleet owners declined to comment on the proposed increase, contending that any support for the measure would be misunderstood and that their primary concern was to introduce new cars to replace the worn-out wartime cabs. In an attempt to placate drivers, ownership tried paternalism. The owner of the Terminal System, himself a one-time cabby, created two six-thousand-dollar college scholarships for the children of his drivers. Doubtless, the cabbies were more interested in daily earnings, but their request for an increase had little support in the city government; in mid-1948 the cabbies asked for a 30 percent increase, stating that business was the worst since 1942. Despite city council efforts to curb profits on transfers of fleet and individual medallions, prices doubled again by 1950 to five thousand dollars. This increase occurred despite the failure of the cabdrivers to push successfully for higher fares.[22]

Fare increases soon become a source of political contention. Owner-drivers first demanded a fare increase in 1947. The following year, fleets and owner-drivers worked out a deal with the city government for an increase, but the bill failed when several of the fleets refused to guarantee pay rises for the drivers. This issue became the flash point in a series of negotiations between the city and the fleets over the next few years. One bill neared passage until the New York Post uncovered corrupt deals between Terminal Cab Company, city aldermen, and the police—an audit of the cab company's books revealed annual payments of $27,064 "for the cops." The ensuing uproar derailed a fare increase for the next two years.[23]

Cabbies also chafed under the rule of the Hack Bureau in the late 1940s. The bureau tried to keep a short leash on cabbie behavior, insisting, for example, that they accept long hauls to the outer boroughs, which cabbies considered unprofitable. Hack men considered the bureau's surveillance to be harassment. Members of the City Wide Taxi Workers Union, which was a local of the Transit Workers Union, gathered together to decry the "gestapo tactics" of the bureau. Despite the presence of police officers at the meeting, cabbies criticized shakedown methods of the hack inspectors.[24]

Their thirst to keep apace of New York's booming economy pushed cabdrivers to drive harder and faster. Lyonel Feininger's photographs of midtown Manhattan chronicle streets choked with private automobiles, buses, and an abundance of cabs. Right after the war, E. B. White wrote that New York had never been "so uncomfortable, so crowded, so tense." He observed that "taxis roll faster than they rolled ten years ago—and they were rolling fast then. Hack men used to drive with verve; now they sometimes seem to drive with desperation, toward the ultimate tip." Despite the cabbies' lament about the lack of business, White argued, "at certain hours on certain days it is almost impossible to find an empty taxi and there is a great deal of chasing around after them." Getting a cab became an urban skill: "You grab a handle and open the door, and find that another citizen is entering from the other side." More New Yorkers moved in the manner described by F. Scott Fitzgerald twenty years earlier. His portrait of Tom Buchanan in *The Great Gatsby* delineated walking in an "alert, aggressive way, his hands held out a little from his body as if to fight off interference." One can easily imagine such a person getting into a cab, and telling the driver his destination and to "step on it!"[25]

In 1950, after the price of a medallion had doubled, city officials and the Regional Office of Wage Stabilization finally enacted a fare increase with a provision that drivers receive a commission of 45 percent after a number of years of service. Despite the fare increase, postwar cabbies faced a decline in income. By 1949, the average hack man was making about sixty dollars for a six-day, sixty-hour week. Expenses were high, especially for independent drivers. A cab cost about three thousand dollars plus insurance, gasoline, mechanics' bills, and replacement parts. Federal tax guidelines allowed for a 100 percent depreciation of the cab in only two years. Cabdriver self-esteem was low. Asked what it takes to be a New York City cabdriver, one responded: "Well, first you got to live in New York City. Then you got to have a hole in your head." Drivers interviewed by the *New York Times* for a special feature on their work complained incessantly about headaches from carbon monoxide. Their relationship with passengers remained poor, stemming from years of being asked to do impossible and/or illegal moves with the cab. Fares would ask a driver about the quality of a restaurant and expect him to be "an oracle, a counselor, a philosopher, and an almanac."[26]

In a city where union labor predominated, the lack of any real organization among cabdrivers was unusual. Historian Joshua Freeman has chronicled how potent the union movement was in postwar New York City. In a city where small-scale manufacturing was the norm and large numbers of city workers toiled on the docks, in the garment district, or in burgeoning service industries, over a million New Yorkers, or about one-third of its working class, carried union cards. Workers developed specialized skills for particular industries, gained temporary jobs, and later secured employment through union halls. Closed-shop techniques, the goal of unions until the Taft-Hartley Act of 1947 outlawed them, guaranteed the power of unions to lift wages and control the gates to employment. These accomplishments dovetailed with the historic aims of cabdrivers, whether working for fleets or owner-drivers. Yet unionism remained an elusive target for cabbies.[27]

New York unions stayed close to their craft identity, a focus that succeeded in overcoming ethnic and racial lines or barriers constructed by the employees. As noted previously, industrial labor unions in the city promoted unity through a variety of cultural and economic institutions.[28] That unity was notably absent among cabbies. For taxi drivers, the principal union activity in the postwar period came externally from the United Mine Workers, who claimed in 1949 to have organized the bulk of the city's thirty-two thousand licensed drivers, though fewer than half of them were active. In March 1949, the UMW called for a strike if the fleets did not sign the contract and recognize the union. The UMW demanded a guaranteed five-day work week and pay of nine dollars for day drivers and eleven dollars for night drivers per nine-hour day.

Mayor Paul O'Dwyer quickly opened negotiations to avert a strike, but talks proved futile. Alarmed, O'Dwyer went on the radio and, in a voice filled with frustration, warned both sides that goon behavior would not be tolerated. In late March, fleet drivers voted to strike, and owner-drivers, fearing assaults, agreed to stay off the streets. Newspapers reported that John L. Lewis, head of the UMW, had imported three hundred "organizers," from West Virginia to enforce the strike. Over 3,250 extra policemen patrolled the streets, the largest show of force since the 1930s. The job action promised to be the largest since the pitched battles of that decade. By March 30, there were almost no cabs on the streets. Meanwhile, the UMW warned of scabs carrying guns. One UMW official, using barely disguised racial invective, claimed "guns were passed out last night in Harlem and other dangerous areas to scab drivers." The *New York Post* published a list of streets where police were stationed and recommended that motorists stick to them. Owner-drivers were told which avenues were unsafe for cruising, picking up, and dropping off passengers. In a clear sign of the city's sympathies, the mayor recommended that cabdrivers willing to work refuse any suspicious fares and drop off passengers only in spots close to a patrolman. Judges also restricted union activists from picketing fleet garages.[29]

Initially, the strike seemed effective. The *New York Times* reported that only about 8 percent of cabs were on the streets by April 2. Incidents included a beating in Astoria, Queens, stoning of cabs in Queens and Brooklyn, and a fight in Jamaica, Queens. There was practically no threat of violence in Manhattan, but the police made thirty-seven arrests there. Police arrested a union official for throwing rocks at a scab driver, and other union activists were detained on similar charges. Two men forced a scab to drive them to a deserted street in the Bronx where four others beat him with truncheons. Despite such intimidation, the strike stalled. On April 5, a director of the owner-drivers associations announced that 80 percent of the five thousand owner-drivers in his group were working. Fleet owners claimed that over seven thousand of their cabs were on the street. Police estimates suggested that about 2,300, or roughly 20 percent, of the city's cabs were rolling. The strike tapped into cabdriver anger. The *New York Post* interviewed a number of cabbies who claimed that they had been upset over abuses for years. They cited a lack of seniority in the job and the harsh competition from part-timers that resulted in kickback demands from garage dispatchers. Cabbies blamed the Hack Bureau, which one described as the "greatest autocracy in the world."[30]

The role of the owner-drivers was critical. Protected by the police and emboldened by the associations' announcements of the day before, nearly all of them returned to work by April 6. The Bell Association, a large fleet not organized by the union, ended its sympathy strike the same day. By April 7, the strike collapsed. Although A. D. Lewis, brother of John L. Lewis, blamed communists and Mayor O'Dwyer for the defeat of the union drivers, cabdrivers blamed the exclusive use of West Virginia operatives and, more importantly, Lewis's failure to provide adequate strike pay for the cabbies or to hold a state-sanctioned election to gain recognition for the union. Methods that the UMW used to organize miners elsewhere proved ineffective among New York's cabdrivers. Miners, though poorly paid, still had steady wages while not on strike; the union offered miners credit during strikes rather than risk bankruptcy by issuing huge sums during a job action. That method could not work in New York City. Most cabdrivers lived hand-to-mouth, making the lack of strike pay a critical problem. Unused to union methods, many wondered why the UMW did not use its $14 million treasury to back the strike. The UMW blundered by not reaching cabbies by mail when they stayed home during strikes. This error meant the union could not counteract the garage owners' red-baiting slurs and lurid descriptions of bankrupted miners. Finally, the UMW did not deal with the cabbies' genuine human grievances. There were too few discussions about the shape-up, the lack of vacation time, and the abuses of the Hack Bureau.[31]

If the UMW's efforts among New York City's cabdrivers remained marginal, cabbie desire to organize a union stayed strong. Even after the strike ended, several Bronx garages stayed out and demanded that the fleet owner not single out strike leaders and fire them. In addition, a number of cabbies in Brooklyn made overtures to the Teamsters Union to send speakers to a meeting. Initially, the Teamsters declined, but later they expressed more interest and soon became major players in the attempt to organize the taxi drivers.[32]

The strike, a job action that cabbies had used so effectively in the past, did not result in any positive results in the late 1940s. The blame cannot be placed fully on the clumsy efforts of the United Mine Workers. There was successful organization across craft lines. Nor was the city government that hostile, though it was plainly wary of the cabbies' violent past. Strikes, as Joshua Freeman has indicated, were a common method labor unions employed after World War II to consolidate or protect their gains.[33]

Why, then, could the cabbies not organize a successful union? The *New York Times,* surely an establishment voice, argued that cabbies were burned in previous attempts at organization. Undoubtedly, some segments of the economy, notably white-collar finance workers, had proved difficult to organize. But the TWU in particular had great success organizing unions of bus drivers, subway employees, and elevator engineers, achievements that stemmed from left-wing actions in the 1930s. The TWU represented many fleet drivers from 1937 until the mid-1940s, and remnants of its influence were still present later in the decade. The *Times,* echoing a common belief, argued that cabbies, once they left their garage, were their own bosses and that the trade tends to attract individualists, who like to go their own way. Yet in the past, fleet drivers at least had shown on numerous occasions the ability to strive together. Now prosperity and potential ownership of their vehicle and perhaps a medallion, pushed many cabdrivers into petite bourgeois ambitions, as opposed to the collective efforts of the 1930s.[34]

Each era had its own particular reasons why cabbies did not organize successfully or why economic and social conditions limited possibilities. In the late 1940s, reasons stemmed from decent pay for drivers, the power of owner-drivers, and the bitter taste of past failures. Polls taken at the time indicated that the prestige of the job was low; cabbies were classified along with gas station attendants and waitresses and just above migrant workers, newsboys, and scrubwomen. Cabdrivers, feeling left out of the city's strong new prosperity, blamed themselves. That sense of despair was particularly strong among fleet drivers.

Herman Spector, a former union organizer, an erstwhile poet, and a left-wing editor who became a cabby during the last ten years of his life, forcibly expressed such feelings of failure. In ferocious prose, Spector excoriated the souls of the hack men. He argued that underneath the lovable images of successful cabdrivers were the seething sensibilities of failure. He believed hacking revealed the worst elements of humanity: "Remember, people are poison." A Depression virtuoso, now stuck in hacking, Spector referred to himself as a "pork chop," a driver who was "harmless and pitiable." Spector saw himself as a "night-worker who sometimes has daymares . . . a rickshaw coolie." His persona reeked of failure: "Here I am in the gangster's hat, shiny-bottom shoes, wearing the torn and egg-stained jacket prescribed for all my tribe. A pencil is stuck behind my ear; my belt sags with the weight of a fully-loaded nickel clicker. I am obese, greasy, semi-literate." His cap, required by the hack inspector, was a badge of servitude.

Spector and his fares were natural enemies. Customers were a "whirring, mechanical noise, like a cheap toy's windup," repeating the same monotonous intonations: "You coulda made that light, Mac!" Eventually, Spector developed a tin ear and responded with similar banalities: "thanksalot" and "Watcherstep." Spector despised the "columnists, nightclub comics, YMHA intellectuals and gimlet-eyed cloakandsuiters," who found his temper laughable, his thoughts stale and vicious. They viewed him as "the lowest common denominator of Mob Man," a criminal who insulted old women, rolled lushes, cheated out-of-towners, and bragged about misdeeds to his confederates around a table in the Automat. Fares who found Spector and his kind dangerous complained to the police. Stuck beside his skull, illuminated in lights and protected with glassine,

were his name, hack number, and instructions for calling the police
in case of any trouble. Spector warned that drivers should beware of
the "dime-tipper, the skunk, the neurotic, the deadbeat. Beware of the
Bronxite, Harlemite, Jersey Jerk, Parevener."

Spector rejected any possibility of camaraderie with his fellow hack
men. He understood "the cabbie's lacerated soul." Cabdrivers only "stuck
together in heavy traffic." The rest of the time they suffered from "occupational loneliness and often wind up as blabber-mouths, exhibiting a
weak drooling volubility to passengers in which sense and nonsense are
inextricably linked. Among themselves in coffeepots, they become brag-
garts, washerwomen, or rowdies." To the suggestion that cabdrivers were
"rugged individualists," Spector mixed chuckles and sobs. The routine
cabby, he argued, "is the dullest conversationalist this side of Hell," with
no thoughts "higher than the pork-and-beans of his daily earnings."
Hackers were no more individualists than was "an unsugared Automat
doughnut." Had they more self-respect, he argued, they would not have
"allowed themselves to be "bulldozed, badgered, pre-judged, and slapped
around for tiny infractions of a thousand senseless rules of the Hack Bureau." Cabdrivers lacked any effective organization to protect themselves
to boost their earnings. If they seemed loudmouthed, it was only because
"you have to get tough sometimes, or lose all human values."

Most cabdrivers were, Spector claimed, "hounds." They could be easily discerned: "Despite the loudmouth brag, the wise guy snarl, the greasy
whine, what remains basic about the character of the hound Hackie is
his treachery and cowardice," beating other cabbies to fares by cutting
them off, demoralizing them with lies about high bookings, or denouncing "anyone who talks union or Liberal."

Cabdrivers joked about those who sought to conceal their lowness,
said Spector. He wrote sharply drawn character studies of his fellow hack
men. Cabbies who carried the *New York Times* were called "Professor."
One taxi driver who wore white shirts and smoked good cigars was
known as "Senator," or "Governor." Daily bookings created a pecking order. Someone who worked fourteen hours a day and earned more than
others was either a "hound" or a "groessa fadeena" (big earner), depending on one's viewpoint. "The Sheriff" was known for his fanatical aver-
sion to cursing. He revered his wife, whom he referred to as "My Lady."
His sons were "fine boys," and when one of his many grandsons had a
"bris," the Sheriff came to the garage loaded with cigars, five crates of
whiskey, and boxes of the best pound cake. Less cheerful was the dis-

patcher, whom Spector referred to as "Caligari." For a while, Spector bribed the dispatcher with packs of cigarettes; later, after tiring of his rasping voice and his foul tongue, Spector stopped giving handouts in hopes of better cabs.[35]

Spector's Dostoyevskian thoughts about his fellow cabbies may have been his alone. Most hack men marched to the drumbeat of history and believed the war years and their aftermath constituted a kind of golden period for cabbies. Their culture became almost synonymous with New York's popular culture. As the Depression virtuosos of the 1930s aged and newer cabbies entered the job, hacking took on an air of stability. Leafing through the pages of *Taxi Weekly*, the trade newspaper for owner-drivers, one finds stories on hacking during the early years and features on such luminaries as William Greenberg, known as Bill Green, "the Singing Cabbie." Other articles detailed how driver John Howard Faust sang his own compositions to his fares and was included in "Who's Who in American Poetry" and in the *Poetry Digest Annual Anthology of Verse* for 1945. The newspaper told of taxi events such as when over two thousand cabbies flocked to the Hotel Diplomat for the annual League of Mutual Taxi Owners (LOMTO) Dance. Big fleet owners' and cabbies' families danced until dawn. The periodical mentioned the achievement of the son of Terminal Garage driver Martin Wilner, who won a big scholarship to Columbia University.

Cabdrivers found themselves achieving moments of evanescent fame. Louis Klatzgow, a twenty-five-year veteran of hacking, won a month-long vacation in Chicago, Sun Valley, San Francisco, and Hollywood after being selected to appear on the hit radio show "This is Your Life." The producers of the show spent a month researching Klatzgow's life. Members of the staff rode in his cab for days, pretending to be tourists and pumping him for information. His wife was secretly interviewed. On the day of the show, the show arranged for Dorothy Sarnoff, the Metropolitan Opera star, to be one of his fares; she sang arias to him as they drove through Central Park. The producer of the show, Ralph Edwards, got into his cab after Sarnoff and directed him to go to the Waldorf Astoria. There he requested that Klatzgow help him carry his bags inside. A policeman volunteered to watch the cab. Inside the hotel, Klatzgow suddenly found himself in an auditorium in front of 1,500 people. Asked if he had ever heard of the show, he replied, "No!" Edwards then explained the format and told Klatzgow that he was this week's special guest. Edwards observed that Klatzgow was a big Brooklyn Dodgers baseball fan;

to surprise the cabby, the voices of the Dodger Quartet, featuring Bert Shotton, Jackie Robinson, Pee Wee Reese, and Preacher Roe, sang "Happy Birthday" to him. Edwards then reviewed a number of heroic incidents in Klatzgow's career and introduced people who had benefited from his kindness. A teenager who had been born in his taxi walked out on the stage. Dorothy Sarnoff reappeared. The finale was the presentation of the vacation through the western United States. The show, and by extension, its American public, viewed Klatzgow as a selfless, heroic, working-class icon who could enjoy baseball and the Metropolitan Opera.[36]

Klatzgow surely was overwhelmed by Dorothy Sarnoff's attentions. Most cabbies, however, worshipped beautiful women regardless of their talents. They preferred cheesecake images of women. The *Taxi Weekly* conducted contests for "Miss Taxicab." To honor Miss Taxicab of 1950, the city government proclaimed the week of October 22–28 to be "Taxi Week."

The public regarded cabdrivers as essential allies against danger. Newspapers ran stories that assured New Yorkers that in the event of an atomic bomb attack, cabdrivers' knowledge of city streets would help avoid traffic snarls. Such accounts alerted celebrities, who learned the value of an association with local cabdrivers. Actor Milton Berle served as guest host for "Your Night Out," a cab radio show. Comedian Red Skelton invited hundreds of cabdrivers to the premiere of his film, the *Yellow Cab Man* at the Capitol Theater in New York. Skelton invited cabbies on stage, showed them how to throw a baseball at a car windshield without breaking it, and generally won their approval with his slapstick efforts.[37]

New Yorkers recognized that cabbies created the first impressions that many visitors had of the city. An informal survey in 1948 contended that "the fellows who drive our taxis include a pretty fair cross-section of our metropolitan population." This segment of the populace was overwhelmingly male, the journalist noted, for the female cabbies of the war years had now virtually disappeared. Speaking to visitors, the writer learned that one woman was highly pleased at the polite service a cabby gave her from rail terminal to hotel and witnessed him carrying an invalid customer to the hotel elevator. Another tourist was shocked when a cabby stopped for a drink en route and left the meter running. A third consultant, a resident of the city, mentioned an ex-soldier who drove him aimlessly around town. Another cabby, though more competent, rattled on endlessly about the unfairness of the police and the Hack Bureau.

One last cabby had retired many years earlier to Florida, but came back for months at a time just to drive a taxi.

A similar study written a year later emphasized the international reputation of the talkative cabbies: "The cabdriver knows this and plays his role eagerly. Most passengers don't realize it, but the driver of a cab is putting on a very artful theatrical performance up there in the front seat." Because the driver is selling speed, he darts his way in and out of traffic, honks his horn incessantly, complains about private cars, and glowers at cops. While none of these tactics better time of arrival, the passenger buys an illusion and tips accordingly. Better cabbies know how to make a turn from the middle of the street without being caught, how to take the best streets, and how to deal with drunks. Cabdrivers sometimes astonished their passengers. When the French aviator and writer Antoine de Saint-Exupéry visited New York City for a second time in October of 1940, he and some companions decided to take a cab to Chinatown for bird's nest soup. Saint-Exupéry's English was limited, and when he stumbled through directions to the restaurant, the cabby turned around, laughed, and told him, "I know where you want to go. I took you there four years ago." It was the same driver who had recommended the restaurant to Saint-Exupéry in 1936, when the writer first visited the city.[38]

African American cabdrivers were relegated to uptown work in Harlem. Midtown was still rigidly segregated. But there were signs of tolerance among cabbies for African Americans that were part of the system. The *Taxi Weekly* published a front-page article and a full-page advertisement for the opening of the Caribbean Carnival in December of 1947. The ads featured Adolph Thenstead, an African American and the producer of the carnival, and hailed him as "one of your own," a "New York cab operator." Joining Thenstead were such Caribbean stars as the Duke of Iron, Josephine Premise, and Pearl Primus. As related in the *Taxicab Industry Monthly,* Thenstead became a model for African American success. His balls and celebrations became major events with stars "coming straight from the Apollo Theater" to give performances. Thenstead was a successful fleet owner. Starting from a single cab, he gradually built a small empire of sixty-five cabs that he called Jat Transportation Company, which he still owned at the time of his death in September 1964.[39]

African American novelist Julian Mayfield described relations in a small garage such as the one Thenstead operated. Dispatchers learned to covet good drivers and cajole them into better production. The dispatcher, Frank Devito, Mayfield wrote, ran a garage of about sixty cabs and 120 drivers. DeVito was a "chunky Italian who smoked and chewed cheap cigars and had ulcers." He nagged his men about booking averages, taking them into the office for quiet talks, asking them what was wrong and if they didn't prefer working with him rather than a larger garage which would treat them more impersonally. Often, the driver "worked harder and produced more money" after the talk. If he did not, "he came in one morning and found that his car had been given to someone else." Frank was especially aggrieved when a car went unused because a driver was late for his shift.[40]

African American–oriented films emphasized that black cabbies shared many of the virtues and vices of white drivers. The film *Girl in Room 20* portrayed a young African American woman new to New York City who takes a cab in a vain search to find relatives. At her destination she finds that her family is gone, and their home is now a brothel. Unlike the cabbies that acted as pimps in the 1920s, this time, the driver takes her to a hotel where theatrical people reside. Later, he prevents her from being robbed and is supportive of her eventual suitor, who marries her and takes her home to Texas.[41]

Hacking blurred ethnicity, melding a more uniform lower-middle-class character among taxi men. During the postwar period, a distinctive New York talk developed, a lower-middle-class argot derived from ethnic speech mixed with "a wise-guy quality" and based upon a presumption that New Yorkers had something to say about everything. Anyone who could not understand the rapid-fire clip in Spanish, Yiddish, Italian, or corrupt English was considered a rube. Travel writer Jan Morris found the cabbies' "insatiable appetite for conversation" indicative of their folk wisdom. Morris regarded the cabby as "immensely worldly-wise, priding himself on his insight into character and his inability to be surprised by anything." Folk wisdom poured from the front seat to the back: "What I say is, if a guy ain't true to what he thinks, that guy ain't worth thinking about," or "Like I say, there's no use working your ass off if the meaning of life's just passing you by." Morris listened carefully to the city's hack men, though she found that they occasionally repeated themselves and could be tiresome. Still, she felt inspired by James Maresca's observation, "Who knows what may happen? It's good just to dream in New York City, even though you're only a cab-driver."[42]

Writer John McNulty captured cabby talk in a short story, entitled

"The Lady Was a Bostonian, They Call Them," about Little Marty, who was "one of the hackies who plays the corner of Forty-Second Street and Second Avenue near the Shanty there." Little Marty had a way of "talking that he can pronounce capital letters." Describing a celebrity who was in his cab, Little Marty called him, "The Salmon King. You'd know there were capital letters on 'The Salmon King.'" Little Marty had the idea that "the slightest thing happens to him, it's important."[43]

Little Marty picked up a fare at three o'clock in the morning: "This lady is twenty-nine years of age—I didn't ask her but she told me her Life History, you might say. She's a Bostonian they call them." During the ride, "she explained the Situation." She wanted to have a drink with Little Marty although "I'm not the type guy drinks much anyway, especially whiskey, which is what you'd have to do, I figure, on a time like this." But Little Marty figured it would be all right to take her to a place on Third Avenue where the bartender and he both were graduates of St. Gabriel's Queens. When Little Marty and the woman arrived in the bar, he immediately went to "excuse myself and slip into the men's room and put water on my hair and plaster it down with my hands." It turned out the lady had a husband waiting for her in the hotel; the couple were in town for the dog shows. Little Marty was surprised she had a husband, and he was embarrassed in front of his friend the bartender when "this Lady Bostonian kept saying, 'This is quite a picturesque scene.'" Little Marty took the woman back to the cab, but had to find Sen-Sens to hide her drinking. At her hotel, she gave Little Marty a dollar-and-ten-cent tip on top of a ninety-cent fare. The Lady Bostonian ended the incident "with the doorman there listening and all, damn if she didn't say it again, 'It was quite a picturesque evening.' I scrammed out of there." Marty fled the bar knowing that the class condescension of his fare doomed any potential sexual liaison.[44]

Famed journalist Damon Runyon, who doubtless took thousands of cabs during his career, perceived the yawning chasm of class between cabbies and fares. In Runyon's short story "Pete Hankins," published in the 1946 collection *In Our Town*, Hankins is a virtuous cabby who believes that "honesty is the best policy." Hankins places a small plaque in his cab with that logo and preaches the message to his son. Hankins has four children, a situation that makes his fidelity to his beliefs difficult. One night a wealthy couple berates him, contending that he cheated them on the fare. In reality, his fare was higher because he took safer streets to their destination. The woman denounces Hankins as "ignorant." Later he notices that she left behind a purse containing two thousand dollars, a sum far more than his annual pay. Hankins searches for the couple in club after club before finally locating them. The couple shows no gratitude for his honesty; the woman eyes him suspiciously while she counts the money to see if any is missing. Hankins remarks to himself that they should at least have paid for the gas he used looking for them.[45]

Real cabbies often had lives as colorful as their fictional counterparts'. The life histories of individual owners may be found in the "Checker Family Album" series that ran in the *Taxi Weekly* in the late 1940s and early 1950s. The advertisements featured portraits of drivers with summaries of their lives. There were cabbies with extensive service. Edward J. Carroll started hacking in 1905, and "was there at the beginning when the first automobiles and meters were put into service." He became an owner-driver in 1920. A Checker driver, Carroll and his wife owned their own home in upper Manhattan, where they raised six children and now "enjoy 8 grandchildren." Angelo D'Angiolitto was described as a "philosopher, wit, raconteur, Checker cab owner since 1922 and now proud father of a 6 pound baby boy born March 10, 1951." Some mentioned previous lives as entertainers or sports figures. Harold Kreloff of Brooklyn had been driving for forty years after giving up a career in show business. Umberta Festa had been hacking since 1922 and had become an owner-driver in 1947. He now drove a "new model A-4 Checker." Festa had been an acrobat in the Keith and Loew's circuses before a pair of broken kneecaps forced his retirement. He and his wife, Maria, had two grown children: a son and a married daughter. Herbie Kronowitz of Coney Island was a "former leading middleweight boxing contender." He fought for eleven years and "retired at his peak one year ago as the 9th ranking middleweight." Now, at twenty-seven years of age, he was "one of the youngest Checker owner-drivers." He served three-and-a-half years in the Coast Guard during World War II. Anthony Caruso was also a war veteran and "one of the younger and newer Checker individuals." Caruso served in the U.S. Air Corps in China as a mechanic.[46]

As American society tilted to the right in the postwar period, owner-drivers rejected any overtures from unions, whom they considered left wing. When a new union organization, the City Wide Taxi Workers, strived to gain leverage among cabbies through criticism of the Hack Bureau, owner-drivers in particular avoided the local's left-wing politics. At times, the owner-drivers made public examples of their patriotic attitudes. The LOMTO, for example, organized to picket the Soviet delegate to the United Nations, Andrei A. Gromyko.[47] *New York Daily Mirror* columnist Robert Coleman saluted the patriotism of cabdrivers in an article entitled "America Rediscovered in a Cab Ride." In the article, Coleman described a cabby who "happened to be of the Jewish faith. He was born in Poland. He came to America to find freedom, opportunity to make a living and to establish an American family." Coleman continued by describing one of the driver's sons, who was serving in the New York National Guard, along with, "Negroes and whites, Methodists, Baptists, Presbyterians and Congregationalists. They are all Americans."[48]

During the 1940s, owner-drivers emerged as a major force in the taxi industry. As the medallion took on unexpected value, owning a cab became a stable, somewhat profitable enterprise. With the failure of unions to organize fleet owners, getting one's own cab seemed the best bet for any ambitious young taxi man. It created pride of ownership, freedom to set one's own work schedule, and a degree of prosperity. For such taxi men, driving a cab became a lifetime job.

5

The Creation of the Classic Cabby, 1950–1960

In the prosperous postwar era, New York City became a world capital of finance, the arts, and sports, and it also excelled in the power and visibility of its workers. Just as the New York Yankees were confident of winning every baseball title, as the New York cultural world felt an equality with Europe's, as New York rivaled London as the finance capital, so ordinary New Yorkers felt a new pride in their city and themselves. Jan Morris perceptively remarked that as New York's new status as a world city became apparent, being a citizen of it was "a bond beyond class." Few workers were so public with their self-regard or required to be more vocal in their opinions about the city and the world than were cabdrivers.[1]

Despite their loud public personas, hack men were in fact among the weakest of the city's workmen. In the 1950s, a period termed the era of "Big Labor" in New York City, cabdrivers were anomalous for their lack of political power. Industrial unions consolidated economic and political power in New York City. The city government doubled the hiring of municipal workers, many of whom were from the newly politically empowered Jewish and Italian communities. Working with a sympathetic mayor, Robert Wagner Sr., many of these workers organized effective unions and secured higher wages and improved benefits. During Wagner's mayoralty, unions accomplished significant feats by creating job security, health benefits, and good housing for their members. In contrast, cabbies were remarkably unsuccessful at unionization during the same period.[2] Cabdrivers' organizing slowed to a trickle after the failure of the United Mine Workers' efforts in the late 1940s. Thinly veiled racketeering undermined efforts by Local 102 of the United Automobile Workers (later renamed the Allied Industrial Workers to avoid confusion with the more famous union of automobile manufacturing workers). One Johnny Diogardi, who possessed a sizable criminal record and who was later indicted as a conspirator in the blinding of labor columnist Victor Riesel, was the major force in Local 102. Known for his penchant for seizing control of unions and extorting money from their members and from parent organizations, Diogardi and his local became so notorious that the American Federation of Labor made a pronounced effort in 1953 to banish the local. Diogardi was in prison at the time for accepting $11,200 for the sale of a dress factory that he owned with a secret proviso that the company would remain nonunion. The UAW had to bribe Diogardi with $26,000 to accept the revocation of his local's charter. The payment did not keep Diogardi out of taxi organizing.

In January 1956, Diogardi affiliated with the Teamsters Union, formed Local 826, and called a taxi strike to "show strength." The police department went on alert in preparation for a one-day work stoppage, an action that angered drivers. The Teamsters were able to attract about five thousand cabbies to a mass meeting. The drivers demanded seniority power during the daily shape-up, pay for waiting time during car breakdowns, a welfare program, paid vacations, and the right to park at rest stops for a half-hour lunch. That the cabbies were still seeking to fill such basic needs indicates how weak they were and how unrelenting the fleet owners were. The strike gained little for the cabbies. An initial one-day work stoppage was ineffective during sunlight hours, but gained greater strength after dark, when more drivers stayed off the streets. By the next day, fleet drivers ignored picket signs and worked. In frustration, the president of the local, William Nuchow, got into a street brawl with a nonstriking cabby and was arrested for assault. Nuchow also failed to convince owner-drivers to join the walkout. Independent owner-drivers denounced the union and refused to halt work in sympathy. Predictably, the *Taxi Weekly* denounced the left-wing leadership of the union. As late as 1960, Local 826 won the right to hold elections in sixty fleets; in the balloting, the local lost in fifty-seven of sixty garages. As the local only had two hundred members, this defeat was not surprising.[3]

An incident early in the 1950s indicates the low regard legitimate labor organizations had for the taxi men. Mike Quill, head of the Transport Workers Union, formerly the representatives of New York cabmen, was returning from a union meeting in Philadelphia with two associates. They got a cab at Penn Station and then, with deliberate vagueness, directed the cabby to drive near the Transport Hall on West Sixty-fourth Street. The cabby was immediately belligerent, shouting at other drivers, moaning about the lousy cab he was driving, and venting against bus drivers. Quill observed to the cabby that bus drivers were doing well because they had a strong union. As Quill recalled, "The driver exploded. The fucking union and that son of a bitch Quill, that no good gangster, lining his pockets with dues money from the workers, taking graft from the bosses, living like a king." Asked how he knew such things, the cabby retorted, "Because I know the bastard." He insisted that he knew Quill like "my own brother I know him." Indeed, the cabby assured his passengers, he remembered Quill from the Parmelee garage and had seen the union man take a payoff from the fleet owner. When the passengers inquired why Quill did not take a bribe in a hotel or someplace equally private, the cabby exclaimed, "that's what happened and that's why the men voted down his lousy union." When the cab reached Transport Hall, the cabby, plainly terrified and anxious that the passengers were union men, seemed to brace for a bullet in his head. When another of the passengers paid the fare, he told the cabby that Mike Quill had been in the taxi. Quill remarked that the next time the cabby told the story, he probably would add "Quill's goons threatened him with a gun because he was a witness to the payoff." In an indication of the little regard that the TWU leadership had for taxi men, Quill always called cabbies "the limping proletariat."[4]

In the 1950s, the big fleets, who remained all-powerful, opposed any sort of organization. The largest was Parmelee, which was controlled by Checker Cab Manufacturing Company. The National Cab Company operated over 1,600 cabs, followed by Wags Transport Company, owner of 607 cabs that were broken down for insurance reasons into over thirty different companies. In all, there were over eight hundred companies with about two hundred actual operators. All of the fleets used limited liability strategies to avoid major insurance charges that could bankrupt an entire corporation. Insurance costs alone amounted to more than $1,400 per cab each year, though owner-drivers paid less on the theory that they took greater care in driving. The equipment was expensive. New cars cost about $2,600 per Checker or $3,100 for a DeSoto Skyview, though fleets and groups of owner-drivers could hammer the price down to $2,900. Unlike private drivers, taxi men—fleet or individual—could not count on resale. In the early 1950s, taxis averaged about seventy thousand miles per year. Exhausted cabs could occasionally be sold overseas for two hundred dollars, but most were scrapped for twenty-five dollars for spare parts. Fleet owners pressured the city government to allow them to buy stock model autos, rather than purpose-built cars such as the Checker. The stock models were less comfortable for driver and passenger, but could be resold after eighteen months with a small profit for the fleet. The city government, spurred on by Checker and DeSoto, resisted such efforts for most of the decade.

The economics of the daily shifts favored the big fleets. Earnings totaled about forty-five dollars a day if a cab was used for two shifts, gasoline came to about four dollars per day, and total operating costs were about twenty dollars per cab each day. After subtracting the driver's earnings of $20.25, the fleets were left with an average of close to two dollars per cab per day. Because the big fleets could buy gasoline, cars, and parts in larger quantities, they were more solvent than smaller fleets, some of which fell into bankruptcy in the early 1950s. Owner-drivers were able to mitigate costs by joining associations that bargained for cheaper insurance, parts, and gasoline and hired their own repairmen.[5]

In his sarcastic comments, Mike Quill was speaking of fleet drivers. Owner-drivers did not participate in union organization. The 1950s was a period of higher incomes and lower costs for Americans in general. Cabdrivers may have wanted to emulate the comfortable livings enjoyed by middle-class Americans, but their circumstances allowed for only a smaller version of the "good life." A good illustration of this is the life of one driver profiled in *Taxicab Industry Monthly*. Driver George Poltzer earned about one hundred dollars per week, while his wife, Martha, worked in a dress shop near their home; together they earned about $7,880 per year after taxes. Their monthly budget of $650 included support for George's invalid sister and their teenager daughter and a two-year-old French poodle. A son, after a year of college, became a textile salesman in Manhattan and had two children. Poltzer claimed that most cabdrivers still inhabited the "$45 a month apartment they lived in twenty years ago." The Poltzers, however, saved and purchased a seven-room brick home for fifteen thousand dollars in Flushing, Queens. The down payment was $5,500, and monthly costs included $105 for taxes and mortgages, fourteen dollars for utilities, twenty-five dollars for heat, and two telephones for twenty-two dollars. Martha refinished the worn-out carpeting downstairs with vinyl for about eight hundred dollars. Their biggest costs of about $250 a month were for food for big family dinners. Clothing was a minor burden, about twenty-five dollars a month, because they shopped at discount and inexpensive stores. Martha explained, "George lives in slacks and sports shirts. I just wear skirts and blouses. From A & S, Klein's, Macy's." They bought a secondhand 1952 Oldsmobile and spent about fifteen dollars a month on gas and repairs. Charity for religious organizations, or to friends and relatives who needed money, cost another twenty-five dollars. Insurance came to about thirty dollars a month.

A big factor in monthly spending was the cost of raising a teenage daughter. The Poltzers did not stint on spending one hundred dollars per month on dental costs and an orthodontist to straighten the teeth of daughter Peggy, whose mother explained, "She's a young girl, and she has to have a nice appearance or it may affect her chances later on." Further benefits for Peggy were a one-hundred-dollar typewriter, a $125 portable television set, a ninety-dollar portable record player, and a forty-dollar portable radio. In 1957, the Poltzers sent Peggy to camp in the summertime, costing $650; another summer the whole family went away to a rented campsite for $720. The couple saved about two thousand dollars for Peggy's eventual marriage ceremony, though they hoped she would elope and thus simply receive the cash. College would be a big item, especially because "It's at least $2,000 for an out-of-town college, and, she, of course, wants to go out-of-town." Their nest egg was now about five thousand dollars.

Spending on the next generation and on homely pleasures required sacrifices. George and Martha decided that he would quit smoking in order to spend money each month on the poodle. As George worked five nights a week, travel was on the weekends and only to visit relatives and friends. George kept informed by reading four newspapers a day, plus such magazines as *Life, Reader's Digest*, and occasionally a book. But, generally, he found himself too tired to read more than a few stories. His wife credited George with being an exceptionally hard worker and for being smart enough to marry a good wife.[6]

Undoubtedly, Martha was an excellent household manager, and she surely made nearly all the decisions about expenditures, but the exacting details of her budget speak to a life always close to the edge, with a fall into the lower classes only an injury or illness away. The family put its future hopes in daughter Peggy and the middle-class dream of college and a good marriage, but the fate of her older brother, who had dropped out after only a year, was an indicator of the fragility of such desires.

George Poltzer undoubtedly made a private peace with his life. Still, he could not have been happy with the way that Hollywood chronicled the narrow prosperity cabdrivers maintained in the 1950s in *A Catered Affair* (1956), starring Ernest Borgnine as Tom Hurley and Bette Davis as his wife, Angie. Their life in the Bronx is tough. Tom's main ambition is to save enough to buy his own cab. Angie wants more, if only a refrigerator. The daughter of a humble painter and now the wife of another workingman, she is frustrated by their lack of cash. A crisis arises when Angie decides that her daughter's wedding must be catered, and the girl must wear a white satin gown. Tom's objection that such costs would deplete their savings is met with scorn. Angie proclaims that the wedding is a unique event that might help negotiate the coming disappointment of marriage and allow their daughter to have "a kind thought for her father and mother. You've never given her nothing." Matters turn worse when the daughter denounces them for having a loveless marriage; capping Tom's humiliation is the announcement that the parents of the prospective bridegroom are offering a year's free rent on a new apartment for the young couple. Tom can only respond angrily that every dime has been hard to come by and "I am sick and tired of being put up in front of my children as a penny-pinching miser." Eventually, Angie relents and keeps the family savings for a new cab. She tells her daughter that she will have to expect sacrifices, a message that, John Bodnar explains, comes from Hollywood's conviction that the ordinary person will gain little from their life struggles.[7]

For fleet drivers, the petite bourgeois comforts of the Poltzers seemed unattainable. For the ordinary fleet driver, women were not good partners, but objects of illusion and despair. In *My Flag Is Down,* the first of his two memoirs, cabby James Maresca revealed his obsession with women, believing that "it's the female characters that really give a hack driver some screwy moments." Maresca divided women into numerous categories, including "career girls that have missed out . . . there's something eating each one of them." Women who often ride in taxis "turn out to be characters," of several "different classes." First were female nightspot workers; second were women with obsessive personalities, including single-minded devotion to sailors, cops, bellhops, soda jerks, waiters, musicians, and even cabdrivers. Maresca distrusted bobby-soxers, whom he regarded as "tramps of the worst kind." He especially disliked upper-class girls who tried to get him to drive them for free, or teenagers who took rides to Coney Island, than told Maresca that if he did not let them go without paying, they would claim he tried to rape them.[8]

Women used Maresca as sounding boards for their life laments. One woman, a chorus girl who was preparing to marry a rich man she had never met, explained her entire situation. "Why was she telling him?" Maresca asked. The passenger replied, "'I live all alone in this damn town. I cannot sit in a trolley car and talk about all this to the motorman.'" Nor could she talk to the bus driver, and she didn't want to explain everything to her girlfriends. "'So I thought the best bet would be a cabdriver. You guys always know the answers, anyway.'" Maresca did not have the answers, however, and had difficulty managing a relationship. One night, he picked up his girlfriend and another man and watched with horror as she greedily kissed the man in the backseat.[9]

Maresca continued his saga in a second book, entitled *Mr. Taxicab,* which he published in 1958. Despite his fame and occasional hope for marriage, Maresca had not found happiness. He still distrusted women and regular relationships, which he regarded as difficult for the cabdriver. He commented, "I feel sorry for the married guys. One of them was telling me how he had not been able to take his little son to the park on Sunday for three months." The boy barely recognized "this strange man who was supposed to be his daddy." Maresca had no such problems, because "I'm still a lonely bachelor." The single life plus bad experiences from being "fooled by a dozen women, deceived by a dozen pals," had made Maresca into a philosopher. Like Diogenes, Maresca was a cynic, "especially as regards women." Maresca believed women were essentially deceptive, saying, "It's a glorious feeling when a girl runs her soft, tender fingers through your hair, and you can be sure that she loves you truly for that wonderful minute." But in the next, she will be doing the same in a "nice cozy corner with another guy." The only way to make a woman happy, he advised, was to grab her by the hand "and live with her in a cave."[10]

Despite his misogyny, Maresca tolerated homosexuals and transvestites. He got along with the latter, especially after one told Maresca, "I enjoy and love women just as you do." The man chatted with Maresca about his lifelong fascination with women's clothing and his successful life as an engineer. Maresca classified the transvestite as merely another New York "queer duck." Though he tolerated two women who necked in the back of the cab, his anger and disgust came out when they started quarreling. Later, one of the women told him that she was not gay herself, but that the other woman was dominating her. Maresca interpreted this as proof that gay love was not real.[11]

Perhaps apologizing for Maresca's ribald narratives, Edward Adler, author of a profile on cabbies and a cabdriver himself, argued that hack men were among the most literate New Yorkers. "We are on top of everything," he proclaimed, "because we're great readers and we're never very far from a newsstand and we always get the latest edition in our hands." Most read tabloids, "because time is money to me and print is big and there are lots of pictures." For others, the racing form and the *Morning Telegraph* are the main sources of current news. So in touch are they that "a number of cabbies can be seen hustling the town with transistor radios on hand." Drivers also picked up information from fares and read whatever magazines and books were left on the back seat.[12]

Observers began to describe cabmen as philosophers, comparing them with Socrates, who was a "great street talker in Athens." Cabbies, one writer proclaimed, included a large number of college graduates. "You could find guys who had been cowboys, guys who are part time actors, guys who write and sell television scripts." Meyer Berger, famed columnist for the *New York Times,* profiled another intellectually talented cabby, Albert Uswelk, who spoke French, German, Yiddish, Italian, and Bulgarian. Because of his linguistic abilities, United Nations staff looked for him to give tours to international dignitaries. On one occasion, Uswelk became embroiled with Andrei Vishinsky, the Russian ambassador to the United Nations. When Vishinsky rode in Uswelk's cab, the driver used his Bulgarian skills to speak to him. Uswelk noticed that Vishinsky was taking notes during their conversation. A few weeks later, he encountered the Russian again, near the U.N. This time, Uswelk's passengers were following a cab carrying the ambassador. Suddenly at a red light, several burly men got out of the first cab and came over to Uswelk, grabbed him from his taxi and yelled at him in Russian. Apparently, they were convinced he was a spy.[13]

Fiction writers plumbed the cultural manifestations of class divisions between the hack men and middle-class Americans. Richard Yates satirized James Maresca's sensational brand of taxi narrative in the short story "Builders" in his 1962 collection, *Eleven Kinds of Loneliness.* Based upon autobiographical material from the late 1940s, the story recounts how cabdriver Bernie Korman hires Bob Prentice, a hack writer, to write a book based upon the cabby's collection of hundreds of stories, all neatly organized on file cards. Prentice, whom Yates modeled after himself, meets the cabby at Korman's home, which is equipped with plastic-covered furniture, a sizable television set, and dozens of knickknacks on otherwise empty bookshelves. Clothing and cleanliness are class indicators. Yates describes Korman at home as a man "in his middle or late forties, a good deal shorter than me and much stockier, wearing an expensive looking pale blue shirt with the tails out. His head must have been half again the size of mine, with thinning black hair washed straight back, as if he's stood face-up in the shower, and his face was one of the most guileless and self-confident faces I've ever seen." Later, Prentice encounters Bernie in his cab and describes his work clothes as "a twill cap, a buttoned sweater, and one of those columnar change-making gadgets strapped to his waist." He noted the filth accumulated by a day's work. Bernie's fingers were "stained a shiny gray from handling other's people's coins and bills all day."

The two agree to work together. The book Bernie wants to write about his life is much different from Maresca's stories of "gangsters, and dames and sex and drinking and all that stuff." Over the next few months, Bob adapts stories from Bernie's collection of anecdotes and receives five dollars for each one. Prentice notes the cabby's tenuous ties with celebrities. Korman prides himself upon associations with a famous movie star, (whose character was based upon John Garfield), and an eminent psychologist, who was best known for insisting that the public buy television sets for their children's emotional development. In one excruciating scene, Bob and his wife, Joan, visit Korman and his wife, Rose, for dinner. Rose "turned out to be a quick, spike-heeled, girdled and bobby-pinned woman whose telephone operator's voice was chillingly expert at the social graces ("so nice to meet you; do come in please . . ."). Bob wants to write stories that are reminiscent of early Hemingway, but Bernie demands sentimentality. Placed among and working for the despised lower middle classes, Bob soon gets drunk and insults his hosts. He lampoons Bernie's philistine need for sappy narrative and wrecks his business relationship with the cabby. Later, Bernie informs him that a new writer is adapting his stories into comic strips. Bernie mentions that Rose had nearly died a few months before. Yates's uncanny sense of the petite bourgeoisie world of cabdrivers, their yearning for celebrity, and their mild pretense comes from his unique blend of an aristocratic awareness of class mixed with the sad reality of his own experience with poverty. At the close of the story, Bob acknowledges that the lives the cabby and his wife have constructed are more meaningful and substantial than those of the celebrities they admire or, for that matter, the lives of Bob and Joan, who divorce a year later. The story illuminates the social gaps between the middle-class writer and his petite bourgeoisie employer.[14]

Even more searing to the public perception of cabdrivers was J. D. Salinger's hilarious account of the taxi driver as autodidactic fool. In his classic 1952 novel, *The Catcher in the Rye*, Salinger narrates an exchange between Holden Caulfield and a dim cabdriver named Horwitz. Holden is riding through Central Park in Horwitz's cab, which is "a real old one that smelled like someone'd just tossed his cookies in it." Holden asks Horwitz if he knows what happens to the ducks in the Central Park lagoon during the wintertime. The question angers Horwitz, who switched the topic to the lake's fish, who, in his opinion, have it "tougher than the ducks." Horwitz explains to Holden that the fish "live right in the goddam ice, it's their nature . . . They get frozen in one position for the whole winter." Holden argues this absurd point by asking what the fish eat and is told, "Their bodies take in nutrients and all, right through the goddam seaweed and crap that's in the ice. They got their pores open all the time." Amused by this eccentric scientific explanation, Holden suggests they stop for a drink, but Horwitz angrily declines. Placed in one of the most important and widely read novels of the second half of the twentieth century, this scene had to influence public attitudes about hack men. It is indicative of the low regard young people had of the Depression virtuosos, whose minds perhaps seemed addled by millions of miles driven on the city's asphalt streets.[15]

Sadly, it appears that Salinger's tale was accurate or, at least, that some cabdrivers had begun to live down to its portrait of them. A few years after the appearance of Salinger's novel, a writer named Arthur J. Roth decided to learn what cabdrivers truly believed happened to the ducks in Central Park during the winter. He asked the same question that Holden had posed to Horwitz of cabdrivers he encountered. The first driver answered as if it was a normal question: "Where do you think they go? Where does everyone go inna wintertime? They go down to Florida, to Miami Beach, or someplace like that." Asked if the ducks took trains, the cabby did not rise to the bait: "They're ducks and they fly down. They take off every winter like the rest of the birds. Pigeons are the only bird that stays—but pigeons are pretty dumb." As the cab pulled up to the destination, the driver looked thoughtfully at Roth and asked, "You really wanna know where them ducks go?" Told yes, the cabby responded that there was a lake in Brooklyn: "Brooklyn's a hell of lot warmer in the winter. They got a lake there that don't freeze, ya know. They got it heated or something." The next cabby Roth asked about ducks pointed at his mug shot and license number and informed the writer, "Listen Mac, that license is for driving a cab, not to be no information booth, for Christ's sake," closely echoing Horwitz's impatience with Holden Caulfield. A third driver told Roth that the Central Park Zoo had a special house for the ducks. He assured Roth, "Don't worry, Buddy, they treat the ducks pretty well in this town . . . New York has the biggest duck menagerie in the world." What was the truth? Roth finally called the Department of Parks to get an official answer. To his surprise, a gruff voice told him that the department did not do anything about the ducks, did not own them, and cared less. Naturally wild, the ducks were now domesticated and waited for people to feed them. The sole, nominal effort to make the ducks comfortable was to keep a section of the lake ice-free when the remainder was frozen for ice-skating.[16]

Roth's informal survey bolstered Salinger's acerbic lampoon of the hack men. Apparently inured to nonsensical questions from their passengers, the taxi drivers Roth interviewed responded with absurd, erroneous information. The elitism in Salinger's portrait is clear. Horwitz was ignorant yet anxious to impress the upper-class teenager in the backseat with his knowledge of nature and city life. Roth's taxi drivers apparently knew nothing of Salinger's hugely popular novel and fell into a trap in which they, like Horwitz, came forth as unschooled loudmouths. Roth's article appeared in the trade magazine and is one of the very few critical pieces ever written about cabdrivers. Just for a moment, Roth gave genuine evidence of the taxi drivers' intellectual pathos and uncovered the hidden injuries of the class divide between drivers and passengers.

If New Yorkers increasingly viewed cabdrivers as affable fools, drivers in turn judged New Yorkers by the size of their tip. By the 1950s, tipping had become an institutionalized part of the taxi fare. Tips were now considered mandatory across the nation.[17] New Yorkers generally understood this and most tipped, regarding the gratuity as an incentive. Many were anxious about confrontations with taxi men, while a few saw tips as ameliorating the cabby's poor pay. Cabmen could increase tips by overcharging for storing luggage, driving fast or slow according to the wishes of the fare, or entertaining the customer with droll stories. Cabbies had their own rating systems for their customers. On top was the "sport," a

Gatsby-like character who tipped well and knew the score. Sports seldom complained or patronized the cabby and seemed the best customer to have in the backseat. The blowhard was a fake sport—a big talker and braggart who held out promises of good tips but never came through. An example of a fake sport might be the character of fast-talking publicist Sidney Falco, played by Tony Curtis in the award-winning film *The Sweet Smell of Success*. In the film, Falco uses taxis to shuttle around town or as negotiating sites for his intrigues. Rarely does he tip a driver. Businessmen were the staple of the cabby. Their habits were predictable; brisk, efficient, and disinterested in small talk, their tips were generally fair. They were the standard by which others were judged.

The lady shopper was as common as the businessman. Middle-aged, fashionably but unattractively dressed, she perched on the edge of her seat, watching the meter, convinced that she was being "taken for a ride." Her preferred tip was the dime, regardless of the length or cost of the ride. Annoyed, the driver often flipped the dime back at her, telling the woman she needed it more than he did. One arbiter of tipping advised women not to give in to disagreeable cabbies who try to make women feel guilty about not tipping enough. She warned that anything over 20 percent was damaging to the next passenger. On the other hand, she warned that cabmen regarded a tip of less than fifteen cents as grounds for murder. Poor tipping was also the practice of wealthy New Yorkers; for this type, the coins should be bounced in contempt over the roof of the car to land at their feet.[18]

The standardization of tips had a negative effect on wages. As fleet drivers became wholly dependent on the number of fares they could garner in a single day, cabdriver anxiety, or "cabbyitis," surfaced in the quest for better tips. New York cabbies became notoriously aggressive about tips, and customers responded accordingly. Writer Robert Ruark complained in 1957, "If they don't say thank you for the tip, I don't close the door when I get out." Visiting businessmen admitted that even if they did not tip cabdrivers at home, hack men in New York so intimidated them that they regularly handed out bigger tips.[19] When tips were in doubt, cabbies had other ways of adding to their wages. Of ambiguous character were the "live ones," visiting conventioneers, college students, and others seeking nighttime revelry and expecting the cabby to steer them, pronto. Often cabbies felt little remorse or guilt at padding the charges for such people. The live ones were often drunk, so adding to the fare in advance was advisable, because they often forget to pay or to tip. On rare occasions, the cabby encountered a celebrity—a movie star, politician, entertainer, or journalist—who listened carefully to the taxi man in hopes of gaining some folk wisdom that could be passed along in a newspaper column, nightclub act, or political speech. Some paid for the knowledge. One celebrity who traded on his reputation with cabbies was comedian Jack Benny. Renowned for his penurious attitudes, Benny often gave cabbies tips worth three times the fare to keep the cabbies from sneering: "He's as cheap as they say." Benny's punch line was a gloomy pronouncement delivered after the overtipping: "I'm not as rich as they say."[20]

Contact with celebrities made cabbies wonder about their own fame and fortune. James Maresca's success inspired other drivers, spurring columnist Hy Gardner to claim that since publication of *My Flag Is Down*, "I haven't run into a hackie who hasn't got similar literary aspirations." Gardner captured the lonely yearning of the cabdriver's quest in one anecdote. He stepped into a cab and asked the driver if he had written any books lately. No, the hack man replied, but he had a good story. One night recently, he had picked up a gentleman: "Y'know, kid, soup and fish, high hat, gloves—the works, a regular Adolph Menjou type." After a couple of quick tours of Central Park, the fare asked Harry, the driver, if he wanted to get his tuxedo and hit the town with him. Harry responded "Can't . . . Gotta hack till four in the morning. Besides I ain't got no tuxedo." The passenger then ordered him to go by a store on Eighth Avenue to rent a tux. After that the pair went to the Waldorf Astoria bar, followed by the Stork Club, where they smiled at celebrities and drank champagne. After that, they "hit everything in town worth hitting, night clubs, bars, met and danced with a couple of dolls." At the end of the night, the fare gave Harry a "double sawbuck," for his earnings. They spoke of life, and the fare conceded that he could only do such partying once a year. In fact, he admitted that he blew his entire vacation pay on such a night once a year. Harry admired him and asked what he did. "What do I do . . . The same as you do, Harry, I drive a hack."[21]

Gardner's story may have been apocryphal, but another cabby publicly displayed his hunger for fame. Cabdriver Stanley Berman became notorious in the early 1960s for successfully blending into a small crowd in the presidential box at the inaugural ball of John F. Kennedy. The *Taxi Weekly* printed a photograph that showed Berman seated amidst Ted and Robert Kennedy, Jacqueline Kennedy, and vice president Lyndon Johnson. Berman gained entrance to the ball when a journalist gave him a pass. On the floor, Berman claimed, celebrants mistook him for Robert

Kennedy, and he was "accidentally" pushed into the presidential box by the secret service. He sat there until the president-elect and his father, Joseph Kennedy, entered the reserved area. The pair eyed Berman with confusion until the older man approached the cabdriver and told him, "Sir, you are in my son's seat." Berman then graciously moved over a couple of places, sitting in a place intended for Robert Kennedy. For a while that ruse worked. Berman was able to get the autographs of the two Kennedys and even helped the new president untangle his legs from some television wires. When other luminaries arrived, however, the game was up, and the secret service abruptly ordered the cabby to leave the building in one minute or face arrest.

Berman had previously gained fame for walking up to Queen Elizabeth II as she regally sat at an official reception at the Waldorf Astoria and asking her for an autograph. Later Berman gate-crashed the inauguration of Governor Hughes of New Jersey; Berman inveigled himself into a seat right behind the governor-elect and was photographed looking over the new official's shoulder while he reviewed his speech as his predecessor introduced him. Berman reprised his stunts by interrupting the nationally televised 1962 Academy Awards ceremony in Hollywood. As actress Shelley Winters announced a winner, Berman walked out of the wings of the stage, grabbed the microphone, and gave a special Oscar to comedian Bob Hope. Hope wisecracked that the ceremony had a cabdriver but really needed a doorman. The *Los Angeles Times* declared Berman's intrusion as the most exciting moment in an otherwise dull Oscar ceremony. Berman stayed on in Los Angeles, basking in his fifteen minutes of fame, getting more attention in a gossip column a few days later along with his girlfriend, Evelyn. He claimed to have convinced her to gate-crash a nudist colony. Stanley also bragged that Jerry Lewis planned to do a movie about his exploits. Then it was back to New York and hacking. Berman claimed to have inveigled his way unasked and unwanted into over two thousand ceremonies. His massive collection of autographs supported his boast. He was spotted a few years after the Kennedy inaugural ball leading a protest at City Hall against attacks on cabbies. He died of a blood disorder at forty-one, survived only by his parents in Brooklyn.[22]

What can be made of this story? Is it simply the account of an eccentric gate-crasher? After all, Berman was but one of thirty thousand New York cabbies. He did not publicize his intrusion of the Kennedy ceremony until eight months after the event, but did so then because other cabbies in his garage refused to believe him when he bragged of his exploits. Berman had a photo of himself with the presidential family. Published first in the *New York Journal American*, the photo and accompanying story created a sensation. After the revelation, Berman basked in the glow of fame. The trade magazine, the *Taxicab Industry Monthly*, ran approving accounts of Berman's deception and used his story to make a political point about public perceptions of cabbies. Recently Jack Paar, host of an evening talk show, had made a number of disparaging comments about cabdrivers. At the inaugural ball, the magazine gloated, Paar only circulated on the dance floor, while Berman, the ordinary hack, sat among the most elite luminaries.

Of course, Paar was there legitimately, and Berman was kicked out after his ruse was uncovered. The cabby's penchant for gate-crashing and his brush with fame demonstrate the uneasy self-esteem common in the trade. Cabbies were often in the news, though only occasionally in flattering terms. They interacted frequently with important and famous people, but at the end of the day had little to show for it. Unlike factory workers, who shaped a community at the workplace and had few illusions about magical leaps up the social ladder, cabdrivers were often tempted by momentary contacts with the rich and notorious. Their highly public personas only worsened the confusion. Berman was simply acting out the fantasies many cabbies held about fame and fortune. He was possessed by class envy, desiring to assume the identity of a privileged person. His media attention only made him more zealous in his pursuit of fame.

Cabdrivers were acutely aware of their presentation in the media. While they could laugh at themselves, as their reaction to Red Skelton's film indicates, they were sensitive to negative portrayals. For example, the staff of *Taxi Weekly* reacted strongly to the 1953 Twentieth Century Fox film *Taxi*, starring Dan Dailey and Constance Smith. The newspaper accepted the portrait of Dailey's hack man as "human, kindly, and overall sympathetically drawn," but it objected to parts of the film in which Dailey cussed passengers, cheated them, and seemed unfamiliar with much of the city. The newspaper was also concerned about the film's "talky" qualities, spotty characterizations, and the implausible plot device of having a cabby drive a woman around aimlessly for hours, cheating her, and then falling in love with her. *Cue Magazine* agreed with the complaints, stating, "Cabby Dan Dailey is more unpleasant than any New York cabby I ever met."

The plot does include a number of scenes that slight cabbies. Ed Neilson (Dailey) deliberately takes a fare on a circuitous route, but the passenger informs Neilson that he used to live in New York and knows the best route, and stiffs him with a nickel tip. When Neilson meets the girl he will fall in love with at the immigration office, he becomes angry when she has only five dollars to pay for a $12.50 ride. Nonetheless, the film received generally good reviews and became a modest hit. Cabdrivers were disgruntled. A few years later, the *Taxi Weekly* ran a column comparing a taxi hero with the "phony concept of the 'gabby, greedy, unshaven bum of a cab driver'" that emanated from the "tortured minds of gossip columnists and radio-TV commentators with time hanging heavy on their hands." Later, cabdriver protest forced author Harry Golden to take back slurs against cabdrivers in his book *For Two Cents Plain*. Cabdriver protests also convinced Hugh Downs, producer of the Jack Parr Show, to apologize on the air for a joke that disparaged the honesty of New York cabbies. They also convinced entertainer Perry Como to ask forgiveness for a skit that satirized cabbies who cheated on fares. Cabbies blasted basketball coach Frank McGuire for joking that New York boys were flexible and agile athletes and had to be smart, as there were eighteen thousand cabdrivers trying to run over them every day. McGuire denied that he intended to slur hack men, claimed that one of his players was the son of a cabby, and offered to apologize for any misunderstanding.[23]

One of the biggest champions of cabbies was journalist Hy Gardner. In his guidebook to New York City, Gardner called the "average New York hackie [an] honest, hard-working, careful and skillful driver who's been doing this kind of work temporarily for twenty-seven years." Cabbies, Gardner remarked, worked twelve to fourteen hours a day to earn between $120 and $140 a week, including tips. Although he acknowledged that some were "belligerent wise-guys," he identified those with "little, gold bands pasted on the driver's license," as heroes, who received their commendations for helping cops catch criminals. However, when the police ticketed such cabbies, they lectured them, saying: "You! Ought to know better than these other guys."[24]

Gardner's favorite cab story was about a cabby who picked up a wealthy, lonely dowager about to embark on a world cruise. When the lady learned her driver was a bachelor, she invited him to drive his hack into the hold of the ship and sail to Europe with her. Upon arrival at Le Havre, they hauled the cab off the ship with the meter running, then drove to Paris,

Nice, Monte Carlo, and back through France to the channel and over to London, then to Rome, Berlin, and the Scandinavian countries. All the while the meter kept ticking. After a two-month, whirlwind tour, the pair returned to New York, where the generous passenger paid a fare of $12,457. "Now, Irving," she asked, "please take me to my home in Brooklyn." The hackie shouted, "Brooklyn? Sorry, lady, you'll have to get another cab. Every time, I go to Brooklyn, I have to come back to Manhattan empty."[25]

Hy Gardner cited an instance of a generous cabdriver. One rainy night, a young woman was headed uptown. When her cab stopped at a red light, she spotted a frail, elderly woman. The fare offered the other lady a lift and eventually took her home, which was a considerable distance out of the way. When taxi driver and lady arrived at her original destination, he refused to take the entire fare, telling his passenger, "I'd like to go 50–50 on the old lady."[26]

Reports of such decent-folk attitudes balanced visions of cabdrivers as self-taught fools. Generous cabdriver stories enchanted Americans who identified cabbies as the ultimate New Yorkers. Americans found heart in cabdriver slang talk. A good example of this fusion of Jewish and proletarian argot may be found in Wallace Markfield's satiric novel *To An Early Grave*, later made into the film *Bye, Bye Braverman*. In the novel, several Jewish friends driving into Manhattan to a friend's funeral get into a small bumper-scraper with a cabdriver. The cabby, eager to downplay the accident and get away without any responsibilities, first appeals cynically to the men by asking if they are Jewish and proclaiming, "And what's religion? Oi-oi-oi and singsong? Crap, that's crap." Better he argued, to be like his boss, who is Italian but "lets everyday be human brotherhood." The driver (he is never named) proclaims happiness because his wife's worry about cancer was just a scare, because "the next four and a half rooms in my building I absolutely get," and, finally, because "my Milton is gonna bellhop at Scaroon Manor. Where even a busboy comes home with fifteen, eighteen hundred." The driver's affability fails and the scene turns angry. The cabby calls the other driver a "putz" and claims that the men disrespect him because he drives a cab, despite "Eighty-eights I got in all my regents, except once." The driver asks "The Depression was my fault?" Soon, the men fight and bloody each others' noses. When the fisticuffs break up, the cabby tells the other man to see his lawyer, "Conif the Goniff," and "let him aggravate." One can imagine such a scene played out many times a day around the city.[27]

Gradually, the ethnic character of the trade shifted. There were more African American drivers after World War II. While much of America accepted the mild Amos of the famous radio and television series *Amos 'n' Andy* as the prototype of the black cabdriver, other portraits were more assertive. Jimmy Lee, a cabby character in Julian Mayfield's novel *The Hit,* told off his dispatcher. One reason for arguing with the man was that "part of the price of being a Negro was that he was never satisfied with the Fight he put up with for his dignity and pride." A second compelling reason was because he was "a hack man with a good record. He could get a job anywhere."[28]

James Maresca's misogyny aside, there were still as many female cabdrivers in the 1950s as there were during World War II. Mary-Elizabeth "Boo" Sherwood, from Salt Lake City, Utah, was one of eighty-two female cabbies in 1954 (there were 32,086 male hack men). Dissatisfied with office jobs that required she spend more money on clothes than she earned, Boo turned to hacking. She believed she made as much money as most men. Her favorite story was about a drunk who was three cents short on a fare, stumbled into his house, and returned with a steak as a tip. Betty Fishbein, the last of the wartime female cabbies, was still working in 1958 when the *Daily News* profiled her in its Sunday edition. Mrs. Fishbein had been a vaudeville and nightclub singer but started hacking because "show business was shot and I did not have training for anything else." Women also filled in when their cabdriver husbands were ill.[29]

As television became a more common form of transmitting ethnicity and class to the American audience, producers often created comedies with working-class scenarios. *The Honeymooners, Life of Riley,* and *The Goldbergs* are among the most famous. *Hey Jeannie,* starring the Scottish singer Jeannie Carson, featured her as the friend of Brooklyn cabdriver Al Murray. In one episode, Al decides to hide his taxi in a friend's garage so that he can take the day off to watch the Dodgers play at Ebbets Field. The fleet owner, sensing somehow that Murray is goofing off on his time, makes a pompous speech about how the taxicab is a public utility and Murray's brief absence "cuts into my profits." The boss's secretary, in an act of working-class solidarity, calls Jeannie to tell her that the owner is driving around looking for Al and the taxi. Jeannie then takes the taxi out of the garage and drives away looking for her friend. She is accustomed to driving on the left side of the street, and a police officer stops her for doing so. The cop is sympathetic to the immigrant woman turned temporary cabby. She gets to the ballpark in time to turn the cab over to her friend before the boss catches him. He, in turn, apologizes to the owner. The show, as George Lipsitz has demonstrated, is packed with working-class resentment. In it, women are seen as conductors of popular protest against the greed of the capitalist owner. At the same time, there is no change in class relations.[30]

Racial interactions between cabbies and fares were often strained. African American driver Jimmy Lee so resented being called "George" by one passenger that he pulled the cab to a sudden halt, dragged the man out of the back seat, and knocked him to the sidewalk. The issue heated up in 1953, when a passenger named Florence Silver complained to the Hack Bureau, the New York State Commission Against Discrimination, and the *Taxi Weekly* about a driver who told her that he would not stop for passengers on Central Park West until he ascertained that they were white. When she remonstrated with him that his attitude was undemocratic, he replied that he was thinking of his safety. Silver's letter to the *Taxi Weekly* provoked a flurry of responses. Herman Kurland wrote an angry letter asking Silver if she considered how many "cab-drivers were held up, in many cases, waylaid, stabbed, shot and in many cases beaten up . . . ?" Kurland insisted that black drivers did not want to work in Harlem, and that black passengers were decent tippers outside of Harlem, but bad within it. Kurland asserted that the "Negro doesn't need Ben Davis as its spiritual leader, as it has Booker T. Washington." In the next issue, a "Hackman's Wife" rhetorically asked Silver if she considered the safety of the husbands and fathers who hacked. She repeated the assertion that black drivers won't work in Harlem.[31]

Their place in American popular culture secured, cabdrivers still felt the cold sting of poverty in the 1950s. The close of the decade saw worsening economic relations for cabbies. Gas prices stayed high and the city government instituted a ten-cent per ride tax amidst reports that taxi fare rates in New York City were among the lowest in the nation. After a huge outcry by cabmen and fleet owners and denunciations from many journalists and entertainers, the dime tax was repealed in January 1960. Cabbies also coped with increased rumors of holdups and physical attacks. The Hack Bureau, in response to declining numbers of drivers, agreed to license part-timers. "Bootleggers," or non-medallion cabdrivers, were becoming a problem. The New York City Council passed a law in 1958 outlawing any illegal hack operators, but the issue remained prominent.[32]

The romantic image of the cabby so common in the first part of the decade seemed long past. One driver, the subject of a feature story in the *New York Times* in late 1960, informed the public that he and his brothers and a few sisters were "neither a rolling repository of colorful folk wisdom nor a Delphic sanctuary." Rather, as a sergeant at the Hack Bureau had recently lectured to new cabbies "Now it's a lonely job and a lot of you will tend to lip off on everything under the sun—but remember you're just an average hound in an average rig hounding down the buck like the rest of the slaves in town." The prosperity of the 1950s had benefited some cabdrivers but left the majority thinly positioned above poverty, just a day's wages away from being penniless.[33]

A principal cause of the loneliness of the taxi drivers was their glaring lack of organization. Since the collapse of the Teamsters' flawed drive in 1956, no union had stepped forward to challenge the anomie of the hack men. Owner-drivers continued to revel in their reputations as oracles of the street, but fleet drivers understood that without a union, they were at the mercy of tough-hearted owners who viewed them as expendable and servile. Cabdrivers in the next decade labored to defeat that perception by achieving a trade union.

6

Unionization and Its Discontents, 1960–1980

The 1960s represented a high point in cabdriver organization, with the creation in 1965 of a fully recognized local associated with the AFL-CIO. Cabdrivers united under the effective leadership of Harry Van Arsdale, a veteran labor man. Mayor Robert Wagner Sr. became the first mayor in decades to work sympathetically and supportively with taxi men's efforts to organize. Even after successful organization, powerful changes sweeping the industry undermined the potency of the union.

Successful union organization came only after years of struggle. Initial attempts at unionization in the early 1960s were not promising. The Teamsters Union again attempted to organize the cabdrivers, but could summon only nine hundred members while losing in elections at Terminal, National, and other large garages. Meanwhile, the city government contemplated a ten-cent fare increase. Medallion prices soared over twenty thousand dollars. The Hack Bureau rigorously prosecuted cabbies that overcharged fares.

Mayor Wagner returned in 1961 to the committee method of attempting to reform the taxi industry. His working groups, headed by former postmaster general James Farley, recognized that taxi rates in New York City were among the lowest of major cities in the country. The committee recommended a ten-cent increase in the initial charge and urged that the hike be used to create a medical insurance plan for drivers, with nearly half of the remainder of the increase going to the drivers. The fleet owners would get only a quarter of the rise in rates. Opposition came from the newspapers, particularly the *New York World-Telegram,* but the bill did finally pass. This achievement did not bring labor peace. As inflation cut into the value of the increase, fleet owners went back to the city government a year later, seeking another increase in order to curtail a rising union effort. The fleets asked the city government to grant an increase that would provide 45 percent directly to the drivers and 55 percent to a trust fund for health and other benefits.[1]

Taxi drivers strived to gain respect from the public. Companies found that cabbies could be good advertisers for their products. Hotel chains, radio stations, movies, and restaurants encouraged cabbies to flaunt their products in the taxis to their captive audiences. WHN radio station ran a contest that featured a "mystery location." Cabdrivers who tuned into the station, which was returning to a format of standards after a brief and unsuccessful playlist of rock and roll, could follow clues throughout the day. Winners who guessed the right spot and whose names were selected were rewarded with a transistor radio for themselves and a hair dryer for their wives.

Respect for cabdrivers rose to new heights in the early 1960s, a popularity that was useful in their struggle to raise fares. It also helped in times of trouble. Stories abounded of passengers aiding cabbies in distress, sympathizing with them about abusive customers, writing letters to fleet owners about good behavior, and rewarding them for returning lost items. During the major union drive in 1965, a helpful article in *Reader's Digest* listed the many ways cabbies helped policemen and performed acts of courage and charity. In response, Mayor Wagner proclaimed January 27, 1965 to be "Taxicab Day" and honored one hundred hack men at a testimonial dinner in the Hawaiian Room at the Hotel Lexington. A special salute went to cabbie Gustave Detmar, who had been on a ship in Pearl Harbor on December 7, 1941; he was honored for subduing an armed robber. Outside the hotel, friendly pickets reminded guests of the union drive.[2]

Still, cabbies learned that media attention had its perils. A hit television show, *East Side West Side,* bought a script from cabdriver Edward Adler and filmed most of the action inside the garage of Kroy Service in Long Island City. The fleet owner learned to his consternation that the television producers had replaced the sign of his garage, muffled his phones for the day, used lighting backdrops throughout the garage, and disrupted the shift changes completely. Lee Grant, the show's female lead, took over the office to use as her dressing room. When the pilot episode, entitled "Not Bad for Openers," ran on CBS, the industry periodical panned it and gave Adler a "severe rap on the knuckles for his un-friendly and unkind treatment of his former fellow hackies." The maga-zine defensively blamed Adler for "pushing himself into the big time and big dough by insulting and smearing the very same guys he may have swapped stories with over a mug of coffee at the local java joint." Adler portrayed the cabby as a "compulsive gambler, a cheat, a liar, a thief and a lazy bum to boot!" The magazine noted that Adler was holding on to his hack license because of the uncertainties of show business. In that case, the monthly asked, "Why is he biting the hand that feeds him?"[3]

Cabbies foiled media attempts to portray them as fools, even if the sub-ject was tipping. New York cabbies depended on tips. Unlike their Lon-don counterparts who considered higher fares the method to better prof-its, New York's hack men felt that higher fares might mean less pay and regarded tipping as the best means to better income, especially as tips could easily be hidden from the tax man. Gratuities were a reward for better service, although one cabby agreed that tipping bred servility, ex-claiming, "Mister, I will hold my cap out for a fifty cent tip."

Cabbies' dependence on tips was revealed in the experience of Allen Funt, the creator of the famed television show *Candid Camera*. The hit program filmed people's reactions to surprises. Funt first went to Lon-don, where he took a taxi and during the ride handed the cabby a card stating that while he would pay the fare, he refused to pay a tip. The Lon-doner reacted with aplomb: "That's up to you. If you want to tip me, all right. If not, that's your business." When Funt performed the same stunt in New York, he first asked a cabby the exact fare to a destination. When he heard the response that the cost depended on the traffic, Funt handed the cabby the card. The cabby glanced at it, told him, "Go find yourself another cab!" and walked away. Shortly after, the cabby returned and ex-plained to Funt, "Look, friend, don't show that card to a cabdriver or you will never get a taxi. If you don't want to give a tip, that's your business, but don't go around flashing that card." More than worried about the prospect of lost income, the cabdriver was simply asserting his dignity.[4]

Dignity was a real goal for taxi men who, after years of failed organ-izing and a public reputation that vacillated between comic and crimi-nal, had low self-esteem. A sociologist took a survey of over 250 fleet cab-drivers and union members who took part in a Cornell University School of Industrial and Labor Relations Program between 1964 and 1966. The academic learned that over half of the cabbies who responded to his questionnaire made between $85 and $115 per week for a nine-hour day, five days a week, or between two and three dollars per hour or roughly twenty dollars per day. The vast majority were veterans of ten years or more on the job and were more than fifty years old. At the time of union organization, these drivers lacked paid holidays, sick leaves, pensions, life insurance and, before December 1964, any hospitalization or medical insurance. Fleet owners regularly fought any attempts by drivers to receive New York State unemployment insurance; drivers could not achieve any seniority and had no special claims to the job. Fleet dispatches used the shape-up system, which encouraged favoritism, bribery, and shakedowns. Unsurprisingly, the survey determined that cabbies felt very low self-esteem and were beset by oppressive bosses and the Hack Bureau. One cabby described the job as a "disease" from which there was no recovery. They had internalized the "lousy" perceptions of taxi men found in the newspapers, films, and television. Perception of cabbies was indeed negative, as the job's prestige was lower than it had been in the late 1940s. Now cabbies ranked with coal miners and below farmhands. Because of the high costs of medallions, few ever expected to rise and become owner-drivers.[5]

Given their despairing attitudes, and following years of failed attempts, it seemed unlikely that a cabby union drive could be successful. In 1964, full-time fleet drivers formed a group called the Taxi Driver Alliance (TDA) and pondered how to attract good leadership to help them gain better wages and medical benefits. Understanding that previous efforts at unionization had collapsed in part because of drivers' suspicion of exploitation by racketeers or ideologues, cabbies turned to labor veteran Harry Van Arsdale, the head of the International Brotherhood of Electrical Workers (IBEW, the fourth largest union in the nation) and the Central Labor Council, with memberships of over a million workers. Van Arsdale was a significant supporter of Mayor Robert Wagner, who showed the greatest sympathy for cabdrivers of any mayor since La-Guardia decades before.[6]

The TDA met with Harry Van Arsdale on June 29, 1964. He agreed to head the new union drive if they gained the signatures of ten thousand cabbies. Over the next month, the TDA gathered thirteen thousand endorsements from the ranks of taxi men. Van Arsdale put money and experienced recruiters from the IBEW into the effort to recruit the cabdrivers. Shrewdly, Van Arsdale decided not to collect dues until the union achieved representation. Van Arsdale felt sympathy for the cabbies, whom he believed had been exploited. They in turn trusted him. Taxi drivers interviewed by sociologist Abraham Nash contended that Van Arsdale was a "great man" and a "power at the helm that would or could not be bought off." They regarded him as a "labor leader of fine reputation" and "a leader whom we could trust." One stated, "With a man of his stature, I felt we couldn't loose." According to Nash, cabdrivers felt that the qualities of honesty, dedication, confidence, trust, sincerity, strength, and certainty of success had been absent in previous organizing drives. They believed that Van Arsdale's honesty was the primary reason to support him. Assured by Van Arsdale's experience and encouraged by Wagner's backing, drivers quickly signed pledge cards.[7]

In addition to Van Arsdale's appeal, the efforts of the AFL-CIO New York City Central Labor Council, created in 1959 by the merger of the councils of two labor organizations, were critical. They provided the taxi organizers with a non–dues collecting organization, four borough business offices, lawyers and legal staff, funds, technical assistance, and educational opportunities through Cornell University's labor college. Within months the taxi union had a "key man" and a committee functioning in every garage. There were regular meetings and lists of cabbies willing and ready to respond to calls for demonstrations or picket lines whenever the union needed to confront intractable bosses.[8]

There was one major stumbling block, which plagued the union and trade for years. By the early 1960s, the number of part-time drivers nearly equaled that of full-time "steady men." Under a National Labor Relations ruling of 1960, part-timers had an equal vote with full-time drivers. Van Arsdale feared that the part-timers were anti-union and that an open National Labor Relations Board (NLRB) election would defeat his efforts. The NLRB, revised by the Taft-Hartley Act of 1947, allowed for open shops and restricted much union organization. Wagner, whose father, a U.S. Senator, wrote the Wagner Act that had created the NLRB, was in an awkward position. The mayor proposed a solution by which the city would sponsor the election and provide a "certificate to bargain" to the union. However, this new device did not give the union full power to bargain in labor-management relations. Uncertainty over the benefits of the new plan created disagreements and led to its collapse. Van Arsdale called a one-day "holiday" for cabdrivers, the first full work stoppage since 1949. The strike was nearly 100 percent effective. Drivers stayed home, partly because of threats of violence. In fact, over a hundred cabs were damaged and eighteen people arrested.[9]

Over the next few years, Mayor Wagner worked closely with cabdrivers, promoting fare increases, listening to their disputes with the Hack Bureau, and supporting a fare hike only if most of the money went to the drivers. After cabdrivers took an eighteen-hour holiday to remind New Yorkers of their value, Wagner made a surprise appearance at a meeting of the Taxi Drivers Organizing Committee on September 15, 1964 and voiced his approval of their efforts. Thousands of cabbies rallied on October 1 for the proposed union.[10]

Showing the rising strength of the union movement, over nine thousand drivers rallied in support of the union in a mass meeting at Madison Square Garden on March 25, 1965. Speaking at the rally were Van Arsdale, who received a loud call of support, Mayor Wagner, David Dubinsky, president of the International Ladies Garment Union and a famed national labor leader, and A. Philip Randolph, founder of the Brotherhood of Sleeping Car Porters and well-known in the civil rights movement. In addition to attracting this distinguished cast to the rally, Mayor Wagner appointed veteran labor negotiator Ted Kheel and former judge, Charles Murphy, to help the organizing drive and to check on complaints that the fleets were not paying the revenues derived from the last fare hike the year before.[11]

On May 1, 1965, the Kheel Committee recommended that full-time and part-time drivers, working at least three days a week, should be allowed to vote. Drivers in a Queens garage went on a wildcat strike after a dispatcher refused to assign cabs to union activists. Such fleet uncooperativeness hampered further negotiations until a frustrated Wagner ordered the city labor council to hold union elections on June 15 and 16. More than twelve thousand drivers voted, and the city government warned that if the drive was successful, the fleets would have a "moral obligation" to bargain with the new union. Infuriated, the fleets and representatives of the NLRB sought and gained a judicial injunction that impounded the ballots. In retaliation, the drivers went on strike on June 28. Nearly 100 percent of fleet drivers and about 20 percent of owner-drivers honored the strike call. Heavy police presence limited the amount of violence. Following the end of the strike on July 5, Van Arsdale reluctantly agreed to work with the NLRB, a shift that resulted in a new election being scheduled for July.[12]

A standoff at the Classic Cab Company in the Bronx during this strike demonstrated the value of Harry Van Arsdale's leadership. Michael Mann, regional director of the AFL-CIO, recalled how in the midst of tough negotiations, the owners of Classic Cab declared that they were ready to open the garage doors and send out scabs to work. Over two hundred cabbies milled around in front of the garage doors ready to battle the company and its scabs. About fifty or seventy-five uniformed police and innumerable plainclothes detectives were ready if any violence ensued. Present as well was a van filled with tactical or special policemen, who were used in "the real strong arm stuff." As tension thickened, the doors opened to roll out the cabs. Van Arsdale quickly ran into a mom-and-pop candy store, commandeered its telephone and called the mayor at home. Told that His Honor was ill, the union man told the mayor's aide that Harry Van Arsdale was calling. Mayor Wagner took the call; Van Arsdale apologized for bothering him, but warned that the situation at Classic Cab was about to become ugly. The cops were "more than rough," and Van Arsdale could not be responsible if a riot broke out. Wagner asked to speak to the police captain on duty. Mann, who had accompanied Van Arsdale, ran into the street, got the officer, and put him on the phone. Wagner talked with the captain and within a few minutes averted a potential street melee. The police left and the garage doors closed. Mann then understood why Van Arsdale had spent so much time working with city officials. In the past, the scabs would have gone out, the police would have used any means necessary to clear away the cabby protesters, and another union drive would have collapsed. Van Arsdale's contacts high in city government prevented such a fiasco.[13]

Under the new agreement between the fleet owners and the Taxi Drivers Organizing Committee, any driver who had worked twenty-six days in the past three months could vote, an improvement over the past ballot, which sought open voting regardless of time of service. Voting would be held on a fleet-by-fleet basis and with a ballot slot for the Teamsters Union. Over the next few weeks, drivers faced intimidation and reacted with a wildcat strike. Worried, Mayor Wagner appointed former mayor Anthony Impelliteri as "taxi czar" until the elections. The union earned recognition in two stages, initially on July 21 when thirty-seven garages approved it by an overwhelming percentage, and then again in December when the union was declared the winner in twenty-eight of forty-two garages. Despite persistent opposition from the fleets, who first tried to use a proposed fare increase to argue that the union was unnecessary, and then blamed Wagner, the NLRB, and Van Arsdale for any violent incidents and took all three to court to reverse the elections, the union's victory gave drivers much greater job security and protected them against daily quotas the fleets might impose.[14]

Hailed as a major labor victory, the union strived to create the kind of social welfare programs found in other unions. There were now pensions and educational programs, a credit union, and health benefits for full-timers. The union reached out to owner-drivers as well, offering health benefit programs that exceeded plans offered privately. The union strived to emulate the taxi culture featured in the *Taxi Weekly*, the newspaper of the owner-drivers. The *Taxi Drivers' Voice* filled columns with news from garages around the city, ran articles on veteran cabbies, showered praise on the children of cabbies who won union-endowed college scholarships, devoted stories to labor and taxi history, and called for political action. In keeping with the social democracy of trade unions, the *Voice* ran grief-stricken editorials about the murders of Martin Luther King Jr. and Robert Kennedy and urged cabbies to get out and vote for Hubert Humphrey for president in 1968. Humphrey received the cabdriver endorsement and returned a thankful telegram. Cabbies took part in their first Labor Day parade in 1968 and proudly marched by Humphrey and AFL-CIO President George Meaney.[15]

The union faced new challenges. Fares remained low, and negotiations continued for two years amidst constant threats of strikes before the city government raised the minimum charge a quarter to $1.35. To halt use of the off-duty sign by cabbies wanting to avoid picking up African Americans, the city instituted timing devices that prevented the driver from turning the light on and off at will. To counter the rising number of attacks on cabbies, the city government approved special hack licenses for off-duty policemen, who were allowed to carry their guns while driving. As fare disputes mixed with anger at Mayor John Lindsay over new regulations boiled over, cabbies staged wildcat strikes that opened the strength of the union to question. In the eyes of veteran labor organizers, the cabbies also expected too much too soon. Irving Stern, director of the United Food and Commercial Workers International Union, recalled that the taxi labor force was highly transient and lacked understanding of the patience demanded in collective bargaining. He remembered that many cabdrivers turned against Van Arsdale because they expected that "he would deliver at first blush a contract comparable to the benefits of perhaps the electrical workers that had 75 years of organization." He criticized the cabbies for wanting immediate results just because they had signed a union card.[16]

The union also faced challenges from younger drivers. Hacking suffered from the powerful generational tensions found in other working-class groups. Abrasions occurred between veteran cabbies and the new part-time drivers. As college students, hippies, and young radicals took up driving as a part-time job, they angrily resented the union's extraction of a dime per ride for the pension fund, which few of them ever expected to receive. Mayor Lindsay signed a law on May 27, 1969, lowering the minimum age for a hack license from 21 to 18. By mid-summer of 1969, over six hundred college students, many with shoulder-length hair, drove cabs. They discussed hairstyles, Vietnam, black politics, and marijuana use with their fares, some of whom greeted them with hostility and others with friendly sympathy. Fleet owners were delighted at the arrival of energetic, if casual, drivers. Stanley Wissak, who ran a large fleet garage, exulted over the long hours student cabbies would work: "Six religious nights a week this kid works. I need him, the public needs him— if they want a cab in the City of New York." The young drivers were unfamiliar with city geography; one told a reporter that he had to ask other cabbies for directions to Times Square. More liberal than veteran cabbies, the college students routinely picked up African Americans and partially alleviated a festering urban problem.[17]

Even if many only worked for a summer to save money for college, the hiring of part-timers and students created a clash of cultures.[18] In addition to contention over the dime pension contributions, students, hippies, and radicals became resentful of garage managements and of the union. Given the inequities of the union contract toward part-timers, the clash of cultures with older hack men, and the tough business ethics of fleet owners, working part time as a hack bred cynicism, an attitude that manifested for some in smoking marijuana on the job, or, equally worrisome to management, working off the meter. Part-timers soon learned to cut wires connecting the roof light to the meter so that the for-hire sign was no longer illuminated even while the meter was idle. The driver could then negotiate a price with a passenger. Because the public shared the driver's contempt for taxi management, many paid the bargain fare, which the driver pocketed. By 1973, fleet owners claimed to be losing more than three million dollars per year to cabbies who drove "stick up."[19]

The hippie cabdriver had eerie similarities to the Depression virtuoso. Often well-educated, filled with dreams and visions, some perhaps inspired by pot, hippie cabdrivers saw hacking as free of the constraints of the corporate world that they so despised. Ultimately, the hippie hack man had to face the bitter fact that most New Yorkers marched to the drumbeat of a career. Harry Chapin's 1975 international hit song "Taxi" captured the bittersweet quality of the hippie cabdriver. Situated in San Francisco, but applicable to conditions in New York, the song narrates a chance encounter between Harry, the cabby, and Sue, a long-ago love who had done well in life and was now a fare in his cab. Though Harry said she looked familiar, Sue initially rebuffed him, then looked at his license and gave him a sad smile of recognition. The cab, as so often happened, became a place where hardened surface emotions melted; Harry remembered how "she was gonna be an actress and I was gonna learn to fly." The momentary familiarity ended as Harry turned the cab into her driveway. Sue gave him a twenty-dollar bill for a $2.50 fare and told him "Harry, keep the change." Some men would have become angry, but Harry watched as Sue walked into her fancy home. The song closes by repeating the memory of her plans to be an actress, but adds that Harry is: "flying in my taxi . . . Taking tips and getting stoned."[20] Just as in the 1920s and 1930s the cabdriver may have shared a bootleg bottle of liquor with his customers, in the 1970s sharing a joint with a fare was common for hippie drivers and helped enliven the hours of relentless driving.

Although students and radicals received perhaps greater media attention, the stories of most ordinary cabbies reflected ethnic shifts in the trade during the decade. During the 1970 strike, the New York Times profiled what it considered to be the average fleet cabby. Sixto Ramos had become a cabbie earlier that year on the advice of an uncle who had been driving for twenty years. Born in Puerto Rico and formerly a factory worker, Ramos felt he had made the right move by going into hacking. His income of $150 per week plus his wife's $140 weekly check enabled his family benefit from cheap rent in an $84 a month apartment in Park Slope, Brooklyn. He had saved a few hundred dollars in anticipation of his wife's third pregnancy and sent money each week to his parents in Puerto Rico. He believed that hacking was ideal for now, but said he would not want to do it the rest of his life because "it's just too hard on the nerves."[21]

Female cabbies made a modest comeback in the mid-1960s. In 1965, 204 women held hack licenses, a tiny fraction of the forty-four thousand licensed hack drivers in the city. Female drivers evinced confidence that they knew the city as well as the men, but they were faced with constant questions about their personal lives. Ida Costa, who drove for three years in between stints as a cruise ship waitress, felt "tempted to write my own history and paste it up in the cab. Out of 40 passengers a night, maybe two or three won't ask why and how I got into this business." She found herself becoming an "unpaid psychiatrist" to the men who would get into her cab and "immediately open up with their troubles." Male cabbies seemed less bothered by their female counterparts. Ben "Redcap" Mack, a fifteen-year veteran of hacking, argued "there ought to be more women so we can get rid of the broken-down men in this business."22

Racial tensions resurfaced in the late 1960s. Fantasy met reality in a Hollywood adaptation of the 1950s novel *To An Early Grave*. Screenwriters transformed the Jewish cabdriver into an African American and cast the well-regarded actor Godfrey Cambridge in the part. In the movie, entitled *Bye, Bye Braverman*, Cambridge played the part with broad satire, performing as an intellectual but bigoted cabbie. It was ironic, then, when Cambridge experienced racial prejudice from a cabdriver in real life. On Christmas Day in 1969, he complained to the police department that a cabby unwilling to have him as a fare dragged him ten blocks with his arm caught in the window. Cambridge told the police that the driver, one William Schreiber, rolled up his window and took off at a speed that reached thirty miles an hour and tried to "knock me out against the other cars." The cabby told police that he thought the well-dressed Cambridge was a "holdup man . . . I've already been held up twice," and then refused to comment further. Cambridge, who in his nightclub act satirized taxi drivers who spurned blacks, said that he was "angry as hell." He said, "I'm tired of being emasculated by these guys who won't take me where I want to go."

Cambridge, who stated that he did not drink, had been at a dinner party with the actress Joan Fontaine and later had gone to several discotheques. He was escorting three white women home on the East Side, then planned to go to his own home on Central Park West. After three or four cabs passed him by, Cambridge pushed one of the women up front, telling her: "Honey, I need you for your whiteness." Cambridge then used his thirteen-dollar Tiffany cab whistle to imitate a doorman. When Schreiber stopped for the woman, Cambridge opened the back door, then Schreiber took off. As the cab dragged the actor down the street, going through red lights, Schreiber yelled at him: "I'm going to kill you." Only when another driver, a black man, forced the cab into a curb was Cambridge able to free himself. He suffered severe leg bruises and abrasions.

Cambridge, a former cabdriver himself, had once torn a cab door off its hinges when a cabby tried to close it on his wife's foot. That case had resulted in the driver's suspension for three days. About Schreiber, Cambridge contended, "I'm definitely going to bring this man to justice." It took the comedian four years until he settled a suit with the Pat Service Company and received twenty thousand dollars in damages. Cabdrivers had been cited frequently over the past few years for refusing service to black New Yorkers, an issue that played heavily in the debate over licensing gypsy cabs.[23]

Willie Morris, famed editor of *Harper's* magazine, noted the rise of racism among cabdrivers. A fan of taxis, Morris savored the "rides swift and furious and bumpy like ships riding the hardest waves, the dim facades of the nocturnal diners with shadowy figures out of Hopper, interminable traffic lights switching in metronomic cadence up the broad islands as far as the eye could see—going God knows where, only up and down Manhattan." While he believed that cabbies "ruled the town," he found many of them to be among the "meanest, sorriest creatures I had ever encountered, meaner than the worst Mississippi misanthrope."

Morris had a memorable exchange with a driver named O'Ryan. Writers Marshall Frady, James Dickey, and Morris were talking in the backseat of a cab. The driver, overhearing their southern accents, assumed they were colleagues in hate and launched into a racist diatribe, "the likes of which for vitriol I had never heard even in the Mississippi Delta." Frady listened to the blaring racism then leaned forward and drawled, "Mr. O'Ryan, if there's anything I can't stand it's an amateur bigot."[24]

Cabby discrimination against African Americans inspired public anger and intense city government scrutiny. Medallion cabdrivers became notorious for racism toward African Americans and Hispanics. As complaints arose, the city government intervened. On March 5, 1966, William Booth of the City Commission on Human Rights did nighttime surveillance of cabbies and watched as they passed up African American fares. As the number of reported robberies of drivers soared from 438 in 1963 to 3,208 in 1979, many drivers believed that the blame lay within the city's minority population. Cabdrivers reacted by avoiding black neighborhoods and refusing to pick up even middle-class African Americans. Not going to Harlem, the Bronx, or parts of Brooklyn kept down the costs of "deadheading" (returning to Manhattan without a fare), but racial prejudice was far more the reason for lack of yellow cab service in the outer boroughs and uptown Manhattan. In reaction, African Americans developed "gypsy" fleets, or non-medallion cabs, which proclaimed that they were "not Yellow. We go anywhere."

The number of non-medallion cabs exploded during the 1960s, growing from around three hundred in the entire city in 1961 to more than eight thousand in 1970 and then to forty thousand by 1979. City commissions studying the gypsy phenomenon urged better insurance regulation and briefly considered issuing more medallions, but that plan fell afoul of the vested interests of the individual owners.[25] Commissioner Booth, however, argued that the city should license the gypsy cabs in African American neighborhoods, because medallion cabdrivers were not doing the job.

The city council passed a bill on July 8, 1968 that prohibited non-medallion cabs from using typical cab colors of yellow, orange, red, or gold. Booth could not have been pleased with this initial response. The council ordered the doors on gypsy cabs inscribed with words stating that the vehicle was for hire only by radio and not when cruising. A later law, effective January 1, 1970, made yellow the official color of all medallion cabs, which were to be equipped with bullet-resistant dividers to protect the driver, and assigned undercover police to drive cabs. Gypsy drivers protested against these regulations by burning seven yellow cabs. Although Mayor John Lindsay called the bill unfair, he did little to stop it.[26]

Relations between cabdrivers and the African American populace of the city worsened in 1970 when cabbies blamed a spate of violence against hack men on black people. In the summer of 1970, in the midst of still more angry discussions about fare increases, the union and the Metropolitan Taxicab Board of Trade, an owner-driver organization, pleaded with the city for more protection during a series of armed robberies of cabbies. The city government continued to have police drive "dummy cabs" and also required cash lockboxes to be installed in all cabs.

There were clear distinctions between the handling of murder stories in the owner-driver and union newspapers. After the seventh murder of a cabdriver in 1968, Arthur Gore, publisher and editor of the *Taxi News,* charged that attacks on drivers could not solely be blamed on drug addicts and small-time hoodlums. Rather, Gore contended, "militants, through constant 'hate whitey' campaigns provoked direct assaults" that protected gypsy cabs in black neighborhoods. He claimed that such rhetoric "indirectly incited the 'highly emotional' or the 'feeble minded' to make wanton, vicious attacks." This was an apparent attack on Calvin Williams, who operated a sizable private livery service in Brooklyn and had spoken strongly against racism in the medallion system. Williams had been indicted in 1968 for the burning of several medallion cabs in Bedford Stuyvesant, Brooklyn; he later complained that he had accepted guilt to protect others. In contrast, the union newspaper ran sorrowful stories about the murders of a white and a black cabdriver rather than making thinly veiled racial slurs.

Amidst such inflammatory appeals, cabdriver anger over attacks by fares mixed with concerns about economic issues. After the murder of Hispanic cabdriver Benjamin Rivera, the union asked members to stage a twenty-four-hour walkout to commemorate his death and remind the public of the dangers of hacking. After a quick flurry of negotiations between the city, the fleets, and the union, an arbitrator prohibited a planned protest over the murder. The union had called for thousands of cabbies to attend a mass for Rivera at the Universal Funeral Home on Fifty-second Street and Lexington Avenue and then march behind the hearse across Fifty-first Street to St. Patrick's Cathedral. The arbitrator ruled that anything that extended beyond the one-hour mass was a work stoppage and illegal under the operating agreement between the union and the fleets.

About fifteen hundred cabbies marched down Fifth Avenue after the funeral. The taxi in which Rivera was slain was decorated with black crepe crosses, an American flag, and a large photo of the forty-year-old victim. Behind the cab came his coffin, also draped with an American flag and accompanied by six pallbearers. About one hundred cabs with their lights on followed the coffin. The turnout was smaller than the union forecast, and most of the city's 6,800 fleet and five thousand owner-drivers stayed on the streets. Those passing near the procession were greeted with shouts of "scab" and "get off the street" from the angry marchers.[27] In a poignant footnote to this incident, city authorities failed to locate any surviving relatives of Rivera's in the United States, the Caribbean, or Latin America and planned to bury him in a potter's field. After the union discerned that Rivera was a World War II veteran, it obtained permission to inter him at Pine Lawn National Cemetery in Farmingdale, Long Island.

As the agreement between the fleets and the union lapsed at the end of the year, the acrimony over the summer of violence capped by Rivera's death spilled over into fare disputes. Cabdrivers started charging "premiums" over the metered fare during busy times. Negotiations faltered in early December, and the union called for a strike. Almost seven thousand fleet cabs were idle. Some cabbies undercut the strike by soliciting fares in private cars, while gypsy drivers exploited the need for travel to the airports. Leonard De Champs, head of the Harlem chapter of the Congress of Racial Equality, called for the police and the city to allow gypsy drivers unrestricted access to midtown during the strike, a move that doubtless would have worsened tensions. For the meantime, New Yorkers seemed little affected by the strike, though members of the upper classes did find themselves forced to ride in buses and on the subway. Businesses along Fifth Avenue reported little loss of income from the strike. On December 21, cabbies approved a new contract and returned to work, though they warned that if the city council did not announce a fare increase soon, there would be another strike. The city government responded by demanding that cabdrivers improve long-haul service to the airports. Mayor Lindsay called for a new commission to regulate the industry.[28]

To regulate the taxi industry and to shield the mayor from further political disputes, on January 29, 1971, the New York City government announced plans for a Taxi and Limousine Commission; the city council met late into the next night before agreeing to the new commission and to a fare hike of 50 percent, both proposed by the mayor. His Honor signed a law creating the Taxi and Limousine Commission on March 2, 1971. The new commission was charged with power over the yellow medallion cabs and the non-medallion or gypsy cabs, although the latter were restricted from cruising. It admitted that non-medallion drivers currently earned as much as 70 percent of their income from cruising. The police department rarely issued citations for illegal cruising, and their lower rates and willingness to cover areas outside of lower Manhattan made gypsies profitable.[29]

Mayor Lindsay's drive for a Taxi and Limousine Commission received significant support from Calvin Williams, owner of the Black Pearl Company and newly elected New York State assemblyman from Brooklyn. In an interview, Williams objected to the term "gypsy" and noted that New York State licensed his association and drivers while the so-called gypsies were not licensed at all. He derided the fears of medallion cabdrivers who refused to pick up passengers in Harlem and other black residential areas, arguing that robberies and attacks on cabdrivers accounted for about 1 percent of crime in those neighborhoods. In a repeat of his earlier indictment for burning yellow cabs, Williams was indicted for attempting to bribe a gypsy cabdriver, Richard Ford, to drop charges against his son, Bradley Williams, for assault, robbery, and auto theft.[30]

The operating methods of the non-medallion fleets are noteworthy. There was one industry-wide association, the Brooklyn Private Car Association, which included forty-three private livery companies operating five thousand cars. The largest firm was Williams's Black Pearl, which worked primarily in Brooklyn and owned about one hundred cabs in 1969. Black Pearl and its competitors rented cabs on a daily basis, charging slightly more than fourteen dollars a day during the week and sixteen dollars for the whole weekend, from Friday through Sunday. The company supplied a dispatching service and the car, but not gasoline. This method, known as "horse hiring," was unique to the non-medallion cabs in 1970 but was adopted by medallion cabs within ten years.[31]

The Taxi and Limousine Commission solved few problems. More cabbies were murdered in their vehicles over the summer of 1972; gypsy cabdrivers fared worst. In a trend that continues to the present day, more of them were killed in robbery attempts than medallion drivers. The Taxi Workers Union and the Independent Taxi Owners, who rarely agreed on anything, joined forces in the spring of 1972 to fight the TLC's plan to regulate gypsy cabs. In the autumn, Black Pearl announced that it would not abide by TLC regulations that required removal of meters from company cabs. Williams denounced the TLC for racism in protecting the interests of the medallion system. Other critics charged that the TLC was ridden with corruption and patronage.[32]

The morass in the industry in the 1970s affected all sectors. The fleets were facing major problems. For decades, the fleets depended on low labor costs and inexpensive automobiles and maintenance, and created credit by mortgaging small groups of medallions to the hilt, a practice that also protected them from insurance liabilities. In the late 1960s, labor costs rose to nearly 60 percent of bookings, automobile and maintenance charges jumped, and banks lowered credit allotments after a series of disastrous insurance settlements. Moreover, rates did not rise for many years, making New York City's the cheapest taxi fare among large American cities. Inexpensive fares, poor labor relations, a uniform commission for days and nights, and the dangers of driving created a shortage of cabs and drivers, especially on holidays, weekends, and at night.[33]

Another sign of sagging profits were the cabs themselves. Long gone were the luxurious land yachts of the 1940s. Checkers remained the standard cabs of the 1960s, though with ample competition. In the early years of the decade, nearly four thousand Checkers rolled through the streets along with about 2,700 Fords, 2,600 Dodge cabs, 1,100 Studebakers, 1,000 Chevrolets, and an assortment of other vehicles. The DeSoto cab, plentiful in the 1930s, vanished by 1965. By the middle of the decade, however, Checker cabs lost more than three-quarters of their street presence as inexpensive Dodge cabs became dominant, followed by lower-grade model Fords.[34]

Costs remained high. An accounting firm assigned to evaluate daily costs estimated that necessary expenses including gasoline, tires, and the earnings of the drivers plus benefits meant that fleets made a profit of only about $562 per cab in 1966–1967. Fleet medallion values dropped precipitously from twenty thousand dollars in 1960 to ten thousand dollars in 1971. In contrast, private ownership attracted buyers as the price of medallions for individual drivers rose steadily in the 1960s, from about twenty thousand dollars in 1960 to twenty-eight thousand dollars ten years later. Even another fare increase of 17.5 percent enacted in October 1971 could not stem the losses of the big fleets.[35]

Pressured by such costs, fleets used the cheapest vehicles allowable. Unlike the sleek, comfortable cabs of the 1940s and 1950s, the Dodge cabs of the 1970s were cramped and uncomfortable, with thick Plexiglas barriers festooned with advertisements and warning stickers separating the front and back seats. New Yorkers complained in letters to the editors about dirty and unsafe cabs. Passengers vied for the larger Checker cabs, but they were disappearing from the streets. There were attempts to dress up cabs. One company named Helen Maintenance used Checker cabs with green and white checked vinyl-covered seats and matching interior walls. Helen Maintenance went so far as to paint the seatbelts blue with an occasional white cloud and song birds. Pop art collector and taxi entrepreneur Robert Scull operated a taxi company known as Scull's Angels that offered larger, roomier cabs and gave out free breakfasts in the morning rush hour, although the egg wrappers, plastic spoons, and juice cartons only added to the squalor in the rear seats.[36]

Most 1970s cabs were slightly modified passenger automobiles. Designed for appearance rather than function, these cars were low and difficult to enter or exit, particularly for elderly people or people with disabilities. *Time* magazine described cab interiors as featuring "the world's sleaziest cigarette butts and paper cups on the floor, dirty windows, leprous upholstery, chewed gum and sticky candy wrappers on ripped seats, and jagged metal protrusions waiting to savage the clothing of entering or departing passengers." The backseat was so uncomfortable that a journalist argued that fares were forced into a "paralytic yoga position, fists clenched into the white-knuckles mode, knees to the chin, eyes glazed or glued shut, bones a-rattle, teeth a-grit." Contact with the driver came through a slot in the Plexiglas "contrived to pass money and cigar smoke back." The writer joked that the brief attempt to use the serviceable and comfortable London taxi in New York failed because hack men "rejected them when they discovered that the passengers enjoyed the ride."[37]

In a vain-glorious attempt to change such a civic disgrace, the Museum of Modern Art organized an exhibition in 1976 entitled *The Taxi Project: Realistic Solutions for Today.* The museum invited a number of automobile manufacturers to submit designs for better taxis. Co-sponsors of the exhibit included the Taxi and Limousine Commission and the New York City Taxicab Drivers' Union (Local 3036, CIO). Volkswagen and Volvo submitted designs, as did the American Machine and Foundry Company, which proposed a steam-powered auto. The presentations were excellent, the public admired the innovative cabs, celebrities were photographed in the prototypes, and plans to implement them into the fleets of the city went nowhere. Arthur Gore of the *Taxi Weekly* commented caustically, "The exhibition is a showcase that doesn't make much sense at all. It's like planning for a future for an industry that has terminal cancer." Al Kanner of the Independent Taxi Owners Council, representing 4,900 owner-drivers, argued that European cars could not take the abuse of New York City streets. Low-slung Dodges and Chevrolets remained the staple taxis of the era.[38]

Matching the decline of the cab were the problems of the union. The drivers' union, which had promised so much to the trade a decade before, faced worsening obstacles. Part-timers suspected that Van Arsdale's initial election was tainted. Dissidents formed the Rank and File Coalition in the spring of 1971, accused Van Arsdale of rigging elections, and strived to oust him from office. The coalition issued a monthly paper, satirically named the *Hot Seat* after the wired mechanism in the backseat of a cab that automatically started the meter in response to pressure. The *Hot Seat* opined in 1972, "In the past the union has been able to manipulate us, because we were disorganized. In the strike three years ago, they were able to call off the strike without getting what we wanted. But if we can unite, then they won't be able to do that this year." The *Hot Seat* blamed drivers' use of "riding on the arm" (not turning on the meter) as the reason why unity was impossible. At the same time, editors of the *Hot Seat* decided the union was going to help management identify cabbies that drove "stick up," and in so doing the union would become a part of the fleet owner's "rat squad."

The Rank and File Coalition touched upon the cabbies' deep distrust of Van Arsdale and anger over the union's decision to offer benefits only to full-timers, thus cutting out half of the drivers, all of whom paid into the pension fund. Because the union received membership dues and pension contributions through automatic withdrawals of a dime per ride from a constantly shifting and transient clientele, part-timers felt powerless and alienated. Union officials circulating through the garages to temper discontent answered such grievances with the general response: "You're trying to destroy the union." Van Arsdale, who took a very positive view of the cabdrivers and their abilities to become good trade unionists, finally resigned in 1977, stated in his farewell speech that unity was everything and keeping the union strong was essential.[39]

In some ways, the Rank and File Coalition mirrored the frustrations and anger found in cabdrivers of the late 1940s. One driver talked about how he had enjoyed working in Harlem, taking black people to church on Sundays, and even went uptown to work because the pace was easier than midtown. Then one night an African American robbed him. The driver began to feel more racist and to sour on black passengers. Another Rank and File member noted that few African Americans were involved in the meetings and that one night a member stated that he was glad cabbies passed up black customers because it made it easier for whites to get rides. Everyone laughed.[40]

Years later, after the Rank and File Coalition had disbanded, members regrouped to discuss its history and importance. One key issue discussed was the "gypsy cab" controversy. In an article that surveyed the coalition's history, the writer recalled how worsening poverty in black neighborhoods had sparked crime, especially against cabdrivers. Worried taxi men passed up black fares. As a result, entrepreneurs established gypsy fleets to service African American neighborhoods neglected by "yellow," medallion cabs. Fleet owners and the union, the writer claimed, railed against gypsy cabs and used inflammatory newspaper articles to instigate racial fears. Non-medallion "gypsy" cabdrivers were so alienated that they ignored calls from the Taxi and Limousine Commission to accept governance and gain legal recognition. In hindsight, the Rank and File veterans realized that they had failed to support the gypsy movement against fleet owners and the union, whom they regarded as natural enemies. There were too few African American drivers in the coalition, and their voices were not heard. Looking back at articles in the *Hot Seat,* the coalition veterans realized that they had not dealt with race issues in a systematic way, but were too concerned with class analysis. Their criticism of working-class racism, moreover, had been elitist; a true alliance could have been made with the gypsy drivers. While the union, they felt, was openly racist, they in turn had been overly cautious and had missed a major opportunity for true working-class unity.[41]

Rather than analyze their own racial anxieties, the Rank and File concentrated on pocketbook issues. In a major statement about the ails of the occupation, the Rank and File Coalition pointed out that the union was denying pensions even to those full-timers who had worked for decades. To qualify for a pension, a driver had to have worked twenty-five consecutive years and be sixty-five years old; this ruled out many who took leave for any period in the past. Even those who received the pension were hardly satisfied with the sixty-five to one hundred dollar monthly payments. Retirees who wanted to work to get by but still receive their pension were allowed to work only in the taxi business and only on Sundays and holidays, traditionally the slowest days of the year. The coalition blamed the union for not pushing management to improve the quality of the cabs, which it referred to as "moving death traps," stemming from management use of "deferred maintenance" that resulted in bad brakes, untuned engines, slipping transmissions, useless shock absorbers, inadequate wipers, faulty steering columns, and bald tires. Breakdowns resulted in hours of wasted time until the arrival of repairmen. The coalition pointed out the innumerable physical problems cabbies suffered, including constant "headaches, backaches, bladder and kidney troubles, and lung problems." Carbon monoxide poisoning was a major worry, but the union, according to the coalition, had done no research on the problem. The coalition accused the union of "top-down management" and argued that it had become a sell-out to management. They believed that only by a return to socialist grassroots organization could the plight of hacking be improved.[42]

These disputes resulted in a special election on November 15, 1971. The union won, but the election delayed approval of a contract agreed upon the year before until December 1972. Van Arsdale won reelection narrowly in November 1974 and, perhaps sensing that his power was waning, resigned from his presidency the following year and from the union council in 1977. With his departure, cabdrivers lost their best connection to the city government. With Van Arsdale gone, the hack men had no one who could persuasively argue their interests.[43]

The public image of drivers suffered in the early 1970s because of a few who overcharged tourists at the airports. A group of cabbies banded together to refund a Parisian secretary who was badly overcharged for a trip from Kennedy Airport to the city. The hack men also helped hunt the thief who had bilked her. Passengers complained that younger drivers had no idea where they were going, or, worse, routinely ignored red lights and became menaces to pedestrians. State senator Carl McCall had a cabby arrested for refusing to take him to Harlem; the driver was suspended for five days. Sadly, violence against cabbies continued. Bruce Scher, a recent graduate of Lehman College, was murdered in his cab just two days after starting the job in the summer of 1976. A few weeks after the discovery of his body, two young men, one only thirteen years of age, were arrested for the crime. At the end of this terrible year in New York history, an off-duty transit policeman moonlighting as a cabby was murdered in Queens.[44]

There were some better moments. Owner-driver Michael Konaplanik returned $33,000 worth of rare coins left in his cab. Konaplanik, who had a $13,000 mortgage on his medallion and a $6,000 mortgage on the cab, brought the little box containing rare eighteenth century coins to their owner, who had even gone through hypnosis in an attempt to recall the taxi identification number. Konaplanik was greeted with cheers and a $3,000 reward for his honesty. That was a better reception than he got a few years earlier, when he brought back a portfolio of airline tickets and payroll checks to a New York company that didn't even bother to say thank you. Other cabbies were cited for returning the notes of a famous Russian poet, briefcases, and travelers' checks.[45]

The new Taxi and Limousine Commission, which relieved City Hall of its responsibility for labor negotiations, lost a key court decision that legalized creation of mini-fleets. These were tiny corporations of a few cars owned cooperatively by drivers, who were not eligible for union membership. Every new mini-fleet represented three lost union members. The union was ineffective in attempts to stem the rise of mini-fleets or to mitigate their advantages by limiting double-shifts used by owners of the mini-fleets. Between 1973 and 1980, membership in the union slipped from twenty-five thousand members to about seven thousand dues-paying members. Moreover, banks were eager to finance mini-fleets as if they were individual medallions, thus creating a new market, which lifted the value of the city permits to new heights. By 1979, over two-thirds of fleet medallions were held by mini-fleets. During the 1970s, more than 4,700 fleet medallions were converted to mini-fleet ownership, leaving only 2,100 cabs in the fleets. This massive sell-off meant that the fleets were no longer major forces in the industry.[46]

Now owners of their taxis and medallions and drivers of mini-fleets earned more, reduced costs of maintenance and repair through more careful driving, and reduced "dead time," or empty cruising. Mini-fleet drivers could easily avoid taxes by underreporting their income, or "skimming," which analysts believed came to as much as 50 percent of actual bookings. Masters of their own record-keeping, mini-fleet drivers booked fewer rides per day than fleet cabs, an indication that of either skimming or refusal to "double-shift" the car, a practice that curbed maintenance costs but made taxis harder to find in the evening or night. Mini-fleet cabs were far more likely to use radios that curtailed cruising but, again, this left fewer cabs available for hire on the streets. Radios also increased the use of cabs as delivery services. Taxi men would pick up letters, packages, equipment, and medical items and, unaccompanied by a passenger, charge the same for the service. Cabbies were even delivering items in buildings, leaving their hacks in no-parking zones, and making deliveries to far-flung destinations in the suburbs. In so doing, cabbies were undercutting messenger package companies that hired unskilled workers who used public transit for their work.[47]

Underreporting of income and costs was endemic in the taxi industry. Fleets operated within a maze of internal corporations composed of individual cabs to protect the fleet from burdens of insurance and taxation. Perhaps more troubling to the general public was the tendency of mini-fleets to respond only to radio calls and ignore the outstretched hands of fares along the streets and avenues. Cabs with radios could pick and choose customers, something illegal under hack regulations; they often tacked on "reservation fees," illegal charges to confirm pickups. Frequent customers not surprisingly got better and more friendly service, including on-time arrivals and cabs available during rush hour. Although city regulations barred favoritism, radio dispatchers even sustained unlisted phone numbers, "golden lines," which broadcast the addresses of special customers across the city.[48]

Mini-fleets and radio cabs brought back a phenomenon absent since at least the 1930s: the hack stand hoodlum, a driver who parked at hotel stands and refused any passengers except those going to the airports. As one veteran cabby described such characters: "Honey, if you ain't carrying a suitcase, unless you whisper 'Pan Am' in their ear, they ain't going to look up from the racing form." An old cabby, which was in the business for thirty-three years, described how he dropped a fare off at a fancy hotel then decided to wait in the hack stand. The doorman told him to clear out; the cabby refused and waited about twenty minutes. During that time, the doorman came out with several suitcase-toting fares and gave them all to other cabs behind him. The hackie realized that "if I ain't paid my dues to the doorman or who the hell ever, honey, I'll sit there as long as Methuselah." The journalist who recorded this wisdom found out its essential truths a few days later at a hack stand serving the airport. She hopped into a taxi and told the driver to go to Kennedy Airport. Although the meter read about twenty dollars (in 1980), the driver insisted on twenty-five bucks plus tolls in advance. When she protested and decided to take another cab, he informed her that any cab would be the same price. She started to copy down his name when he "covered his hack license with a hairy hand, ordered her out of the cab," and told her she would "be very sorry if she did not leave right away."

Less heavy-handed but still authoritarian methods were in play at hack stands near Wall Street. There, elite Peugeot cabs lined up for pre-arranged rides for brokers. Unlike ordinary cabbies that had to cruise endlessly around the city, these cabs charged extra and saved cash on gasoline. Novelist Tom Wolfe captured the smugness of cabbies and fares. Sherman McCoy, protagonist of *The Bonfire of the Vanities,* describes how the "taxis lined up every day to take the young Masters of the Universe down to Wall Street. It was a ten-dollar ride each morning, but what was that to a Master of the Universe." McCoy's father always took the subway as a matter of principal. Despite graffiti, muggings, and murders, McCoy Sr. was not going to be driven off the subway. His son, in contrast, sought insulation from the masses by riding down to his job in a sleek new cab driven by a savvy veteran who shared his view of the world. The smugness and cynicism of pre-arranged cab rides pleased Sherman McCoy and made him feel au courant. After all, he reasoned, "If you could go breezing down the FDR Drive in a taxi, then why file into the trenches of the urban wars?" Gradually, their methods crept into practice when the Taxi and Limousine Commission ordained flat fees to the airports. Nonetheless, the practice of reserving cabs for Wall Street workers still irritated ordinary New York residents into the early twenty-first century.[49]

Notwithstanding the immense problems facing the cab industry, intellectuals retained their fascination with cabs and cabbies. Willie Morris sympathetically blamed the driver's hate mongering on the job, which required that he scratch and snarl "through the city's teeming entrails." Morris admired how cabdrivers felt themselves on a par with celebrities and regarded their familiarity with the famous as "imperviousness." The most casual encounters produced a "chemical blend of practiced cynicism and good-natured amusement. One driver, morose and silent throughout the trip, stopping at a traffic light, noticed the actor Jack Lemmon walking before the cab. The cabby erupted, "Hi Jacko, babe, how ya doing, Jacko! Give 'em hell, Jacko!" Lemmon removed his hat and made a deep exaggerated bow. Another driver jostled a sleepy Willie Morris from a fast-moving nap by roaring "Donny, sweetheart! Back in town where you belong, aincha, Donny? Sock it to 'em, babe," at a highly pleased Don Ameche, who gave the cabby a "brisk military salute."[50]

Artists and filmmakers remained absorbed by cabdrivers. One artist who understood the chaotic, restless nature of hacking was the abstract expressionist Al Held, who painted his giant murals *Taxi Suites* in 1959. Held envisioned his works, which were inspired by a "vision" of taxicabs on the streets of New York, as a reconciliation of modernism and primitivism and of energy and geometry. Less tilted toward the patterns of the streets themselves, Held's work was more concerned with the energetic gesture of New York City traffic. While the murals have geometric qualities, Held used a primitivist approach to depict "forms in the making"—taxis inexorably roaming the streets, creating experience, color, and image.[51]

The artist most enamored of cabbies was perhaps Red Grooms, whose giant assemblages of New York street life invariably included a cigar-smoking driver leaning out of a yellow cab. Cabs were prominent in his Ruckus Manhattan exhibitions, which presented a fantastic, pop-art rendition of the city's streets and people. His colorful 1976 drawing *Times Square in the Rain* showed the crossroads packed with dozens of taxis. Grooms included a giant replica cab in his show at the Burlington House in New York in 1982, and in 1992, he installed another immense papier-mâché cab in the new waiting room of Grand Central Station.

Patrons entered the cab to be greeted with a massive bellow from the cabby. Perhaps his most popular format was a widely-distributed three-dimensional paper taxi.[52]

The late 1970s hit television show *Taxi* captured the countercultural quality of hacking. Inspired by a 1975 article by Mark Jacobson entitled "Night-Shifting for the Hip Fleet," *Taxi* was set at the famous Dover Garage at the corner of Hudson and Charles Street in the West Village. The article shouted that "Hooverville" economic conditions pushed everyone into hacking and described how college professors, priests, Eastern European disc jockeys, musicians, sculptors, actors, and writers could be found "shaping up" for the evening shift. After Jacobson's article appeared, MTM Productions optioned his ideas for a television program about Dover's hackies. The superlative cast, which included Tony Danza, Marilu Henner, Judd Hirsch, Randall Carver, Jeff Conaway, Danny DeVito, and Andy Kaufman, was ethnic and urban. Hirsch headed the crew in his role as Alex, a middle-aged career hack with worldly wisdom and experience. Most of the skits take place inside the garage that Louis de Palma (De Vito), the dispatcher, controls with vicious humor and insane antics. As with Odets's play *Waiting for Lefty* forty years earlier, all the hack men, except perhaps Alex, are fallen or aspiring entertainers or professionals. Each has their small triumphs and larger disappointments. Alex once encounters his long-lost daughter, who insists that they cannot be related because her mother had always told her that her father owned a ranch.

In another episode that demonstrates icy class cruelties, Elaine (Henner) gets a rude fare who tells her to shut up and accuses her of running up the fare. A would-be art gallery designer, she is invited to a fancy party. She invites Alex to accompany her on the condition that neither admit that they drive cabs. At the party, Alex pretends to make a living extinguishing oil-well fires and impresses a pretty blonde. Then Elaine encounters her surly afternoon cab customer, gets angry with him, and announces to the well-coiffed assemblage that she and Alex are really cabdrivers. The blonde then dumps Alex, telling him that he is garbage, and spits on his shoes. He gets drunk and leaves in a foul mood. Later, Elaine calls him to tell him that the art crowd had actually admired her for holding two jobs and that the rude fare had given her a retroactive sizable tip. Alex is mollified only by his friendship with Elaine, one that lasts throughout the series. For him, any entrée into the elite classes will end in disaster.[53]

Taxi Driver, Martin Scorsese's 1976 epic, is one of the darkest Hollywood films ever made and a pivotal film about cabdrivers. The story of Travis Bickle, played by Robert De Niro, details the sociopath rage of an ex-marine turned cabby. The film has a superb bluesy score by Bernard Herrmann, which captures Bickle's loneliness, and uncommon cinematography of New York streets and characters. Most of the film concerns Bickle's obsession with Betsy, a beautiful blonde (Cybil Shepherd) whose class, education, and interests elevates her far above her cabdriver admirer. In marked contrast to the dashing romance of James Cagney's cabdriver in *Taxi,* made over forty years earlier, Bickle's courtship of Betsy involves taking her to a pornographic movie on a disastrous first date punctuated when Betsy jumps into a cab leaving a dejected Bickle on the sidewalk. Rejected, Bickle turns his murderous wrath toward a planned assassination of a presidential candidate. Barely escaping arrest by the secret service, Bickle rams his cab downtown to shoot a pimp who has ensnared a teenage girl, played by Jodie Foster. Bickle is not arrested for murder but becomes a popular hero in the tabloids for saving the adolescent. In a last, gorgeously photographed scene, Bickle and Betsy are reunited as fare and cabdriver before he drops her off at her destination. This scene enunciates the vast social gulf between the two and the impossibility of a romantic ending between a middle-class woman and a depraved cabdriver.[54]

Taxi Driver, as befits its exalted status in American film history, has received countless amounts of critical commentary. Recently, John Bodnar and James Sanders perceptively argued that Bickle represents the angry, young proletarian hero for whom only violence makes sense. Others argue that the film represents the city as a "desolate battleground traversed by human monsters on the very margins of sanity."[55] Seldom do these critics focus on Travis Bickle as a cabdriver. As James Sanders observes, Bickle rarely picks up a fare who is not sex-crazed. Scorsese mixes in innumerable pathological fares, including a personal cameo in which he plays a racist cuckold. Sanders emphasizes that the film "is no documentary." Yet there are fine scenes in the Fifty-seventh Street Garage where Bickle is hired, shapes up, and turns in his cab. Bickle meets other cabbies at the Belmore Cafeteria, the cabby's diner of choice during this era. The film, admittedly, is more about Bickle's personal demons than about hacking. Even so, reviews linked Bickle with genuine cabdrivers. Vincent Canby of the *New York Times* described him as "every paranoid driver you've ever met on your wildest nightmare ride."[56]

Despite the paucity of documentary evidence, *Taxi Driver* is a pivotal

representation of hacking. Filmed during a scorching New York summer, the film depicts a city of dirt and immorality, which Bickle promises to cleanse with blood. During an important transition period for the
trade, Bickle also represents the angry, threatened white driver, who is
aware that the older, segregated world of hacking is declining and that
African Americans and immigrants are encroaching on his racial pre-
serve. In one scene at the Belmore, the camera follows Bickle's suspicious
gaze toward a table of black pimps who stare impassively at him. Bickle's
anger is out of step with the 1970s' narrative of racial liberalism, and his
racism makes him appear to be an outsider, a loser. Even though racial
integration is now in decline in New York City and in the United States
generally, Bickle remains a pathological character.

What *Taxi Driver* does for the first time is to create a cinematic and
eventually public perception of the cabdriver as an outsider. As screen-
writer Paul Schrader argues, the taxi driver is a symbol of urban marginality, someone who is invisible to his fellow men, who is "acknowledged
briefly when the passenger enters the cab and then consigned to limbo,
to nonexistence." Drivers from earlier eras might challenge Schrader, but
the film announced new social perceptions of cabdrivers. A hack man
might be disturbed as Bickle is, or nonwhite and foreign, as would soon
be the case, but always outside the boundaries of American society. Once
American heroes, or lovable fools, cabdrivers were now outcasts.[57]

In the 1960s and 1970s, taxi drivers finally attained a stable union that
offered medical benefits and pensions to some but ultimately dissatisfied
young drivers who might have made a career in hacking, but instead
worked for years as bitter part-timers. The job remained low paying because of inflation, despite six fare increases between 1968 and 1981. The
unified power of the union was belied by the major changes in the industry. As fleets sold off medallions to mini-fleets, cabdrivers' pay per
shift stagnated in the 1970s and never regained the glamorous levels of
the early 1940s. One industry analyst has claimed that, adjusted for
inflation, cabdrivers' annual income was less in 2003 than it was in 1929,
just before the crash. The grinding poverty and alienation of cabbies was
reflected in their images in television shows and films. Even larger
changes were just ahead.[58]

Hack Man. Photograph by Alice Austen. Austen's late-nineteenth-century image captured the sturdy working-class quality of the city's hack men. Courtesy of the Staten Island Historical Society.

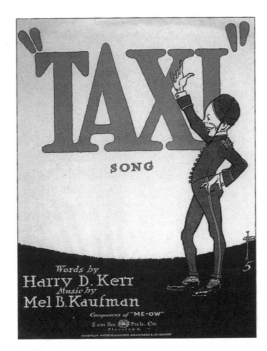

"Taxi," sheet music. By the mid-1910s, songwriters proclaimed the romance of a ride in a taxi for young lovers. Courtesy of Nancy Groce.

John Sloan's painting *The Lafayette.* 1927. Sloan's street scene portrays a doorman flagging a taxi for a prosperous couple. Gift of the Friends of John Sloan, 1928 (28:18). Photograph, all rights reserved. The Metropolitan Museum of Art.

Harold Lloyd as a cabdriver in Russell Holman's 1928 film *Speedy,* in which Babe Ruth played a terrified passenger (London: Reader's Library Publishing Company, 1929). Speedy's manic driving and motor mouth epitomized the new public persona of the New York City cabby. Collection of the author. Reproduced with permission of the Wisconsin Center for Film and Theater Research.

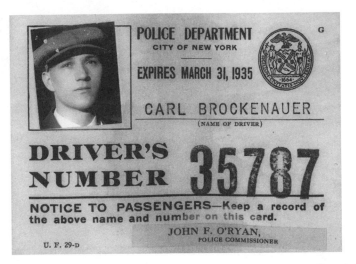

Public hack license for Carl Brockenaur, 1934. Since the 1920s, all taxi drivers have had to display this plastic-covered photo with their license number. Collection of the author.

Publicity still of James Cagney in *Taxi* (Warner Brothers, 1932). Cagney's breezy, confident persona epitomized the Hollywood ideal of the New York taxicab driver. Courtesy of the Wisconsin Center for Film and Theater Research.

Weegee, *In the Cab.* Weegee's classic noir photograph takes us inside the taxi's combination of the banal and the ominous as the driver sees a fare under the streetlight. Courtesy of Ubu Gallery, New York, and Galerie Berinson, Berlin.

DeSoto SkyView taxi. Along with the Checker, one of the most comfortable cabs for passengers. Collection of the author.

Female cabdrivers, World War II. As thousands of hack men went off to war, women filled their places as never before or since. Collection of the author.

One of the many racy postcards from the mid-twentieth century that suggest sexual possibilities in the cab, but not for the driver. Collection of the author.

"Sailor and Lady Cab Driver," from playbill for *On the Town,* by Leonard Bernstein. Brunhilde "Hilde" Esterhazy is the sexually aggressive taxi driver in the famous Leonard Bernstein–Jerome Robbins musical. Collection of the author.

Ted Croner, *Taxi, New York Night,* 1949. Croner's New York School photography depicts the taxi as a ghostly machine rushing through the night. Courtesy of Howard Greenberg Gallery, New York City.

Checker Motors advertisement. The beloved Checker, now a part of New York nostalgia, but in 1950s the standard issue taxi. Collection of the author.

Album cover, *The New York City Taxi Driver*, 1959. Filled with stories, opinions, and sometimes half-baked knowledge, the 1950s taxi driver became an icon. Collection of the author.

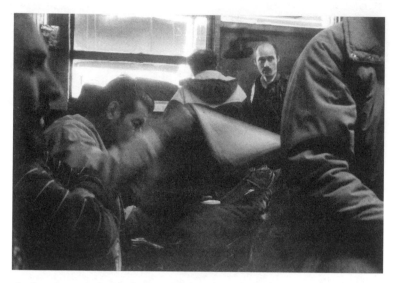

Long before he gets behind the wheel, the fleet driver must wait in a drafty, unheated room hoping to get a taxi. "Shaping Up, Inside the Driver's Room." Ambrose Clancy and Peter M. Donahoe, *The Night Line: A Memoir of Work* (New York: New Amsterdam Books, 1990). Courtesy of Peter Donahoe.

To stem boredom on the job, taxi drivers have become adept at mental arithmetic and can often tell to the dime how much they have made that night. "Jonathan, Driving and Counting." Ambrose Clancy and Peter M. Donahoe, *The Night Line: A Memoir of Work* (New York: New Amsterdam Books, 1990). Courtesy of Peter Donahoe.

7

The Lease Driver and Proletarian,
1980–2006

In the last two decades of the twentieth century, cab driving in New York City experienced momentous changes. Most important was the decline of native-born drivers and their replacement with waves of new immigrants from Russia, Africa, Asia, and, predominately, from India and Pakistan. More than had ever been the case in earlier periods, hacking became an entry-level position for immigrants hoping to gain part of an American dream. A major innovation in 1979 in the regulation of hacking hampered those hopes and cast many of these new Americans into a status as an international proletariat.

That change was in legalization of daily leasing of cabs, historically known as "horse hiring." On February 15, 1979, when only 2,400 cabs operated in unionized fleets, the Taxi and Limousine Commission made the most significant regulatory change since enactment of the Haas Act in 1937 by permitting daily leasing of cabs. Fleet owners could now rent out cars for an insured income while shifting the costs of gasoline to the drivers—after their outlay, drivers kept whatever money they earned. Gradually, attracted by higher wages from leasing or pushed by management, drivers dropped union membership in favor of the new system. Whether the union was complicit in allowing the new lease law to pass or, more likely, had no power to stop it, the new legislation doomed the traditional guild. In the future, only grassroots efforts could succeed in attracting cabbies who had become alienated from the union. Leasing also meant fewer part-time drivers, as the cost of daily rentals eliminated occasional driving.[1]

The lease law radically transformed the taxi industry. As older drivers who worked on the commission system were forced to convert to leasing, gains from decades of collective bargaining disappeared. The union held on until 1997, though it operated as a shell of an organization. Leasing cabs was an obvious attraction to fleet owners because the method insured daily receipts, removed the costs of gasoline, and negated losses from cabbies riding off the meter. The city government helped with the fifth rate increase in a decade in February 1980; accompanying the new rate was a special fifty-cent surcharge per ride for night work.[2]

Leasing took some time to sink in with cabdrivers. Drivers were now known as "independent contractors" and paid daily for use of the cab, gasoline, and repairs, plus noxious daily lease fees. Cabbies working as independent contractors paid the union fifteen dollars a month for dues plus a two-dollar-a-day "lease permit" fee, even though the union's powers were eviscerated by the new system. Older, experienced cabbies disliked leasing because it demanded more of them and negated any personal ties between fleet and drivers. As one driver commented, "under leasing we work more hours, make less money and are under more stress from the company and ticket enforcement agencies." Fleet owners and dispatchers regularly harassed older drivers about low bookings and pressured them to change from commission pay to leasing. Leasing meant that drivers could no longer accumulate a company pension plan and lost any sense of a stake in their work. Other losses were personal. Cabdrivers now had to stay out later to make money, a practice the family men among them argued caused troubles with their wives. Many cabbies resigned themselves to the new organization, but others responded by smashing taxi windshields and slashing tires when management abused them. Rather than becoming a career choice, taxi drivers now saw the job only as a temporary means to an end, something to do until something better came along. That meant the driver population was constantly turning over and bringing in newer, less experienced, and less knowledgeable workers.[3]

In the mid-1980s, leasing took hold as the dominant relationship between fleets and drivers. Younger, newer cabbies accepted leasing and were attracted to its fast earnings and low level of responsibility. One close study of leasing identifies supporters of leasing among female cabbies and unmarried male cabbies. Strangely, married cabbies with wives who were unemployed favored leasing. More logically, the remaining part-time drivers with little commitment to the job preferred leasing.

Cabbies with more experience resented leasing and longed for the return of the commission system. Whether a driver supported the leasing system or not, there were some aspects of it which were irritating for almost all of them. A number of fees upset the drivers. Initially, drivers forked over a two-hundred-dollar deposit to the company, returnable only forty-five days after leaving the job. Daily leasing fees were fifty dollars in the mid-1980s for a day shift and seventy dollars for the night. In the early 1990s, lease fees rose about 20 percent to sixty-one dollars for a Sunday morning shift and eighty-six dollars for a car on Friday night. By 1993, cabdriver and writer Iva Pekarkova reported that those fees were an "angel's song of the past," as a sharp increase in insurance costs sent prices per shift as high as $110 per night. The fleet and the union tacked on extra fees. Drivers had to pay for gasoline. No matter how full the gas tank was, drivers were charged for a full tank, which in 1992 cost over fifteen dollars a day. Drivers resented paying a two-dollar-a-day "lease permit" to the union in addition to monthly dues. Drivers were held accountable for lateness and even older commission drivers were fired if they were late several times. One cabby successfully sued for thousands of dollars of lost income after Dover Garage, the setting for the television show, *Taxi*, fired him for lateness. Fleets charged fees of twenty dollars an hour for taxis returned late, but only paid five dollars an hour for time spent with a broken-down vehicle. If a driver did not notify the company forty-eight hours in advance to cancel a booking, the full fee for the shift was deducted from their deposit. Frequent clerical negligence and mistakes were rarely corrected, leading to acrimony between driver and fleet. Drivers had to pay their own taxes and social security fees.[4]

Leasing also introduced a middleman, known as the broker, who handled affairs and rented medallions from owner-drivers, subcontracting cars and permits to drivers. In place since the mid-1970s, medallion brokering came into its own with the Lease Act of 1979. The first company to broker medallions was a fleet controlled by the Murstein family, which had been in business since 1937. Now, only the market limited the amount an owner could extract from daily rentals of his medallion. As older drivers and small fleets left the industry, brokers were positioned to make cash on sales and purchases. Gradually, brokerage firms consolidated management of medallions from a variety of owners. Brokers routinely paid medallion owners around three hundred dollars per month, plus an additional one hundred dollars a month for insurance, and $250 a week from the drivers without any further responsibilities. Often lease drivers purchased a car from the brokers, who acted as salesmen and bank. This practice opened lease drivers to exploitation. A cab, particularly near the end of its use, could cost substantial amounts in maintenance with little resale value. If a medallion was sold or lost, the driver would own a useless car. A single missed payment could cause forfeiture of the loan. Crooked accounting procedures by brokerage firms created more problems for the drivers, whose work schedules rarely allowed time to contest unfair practices.

Rather than creating independence, leasing became a means by which medallion owners, car companies, and brokers extracted cash from vulnerable drivers.[5] As a result, fewer cabdrivers actually owned their medallions, and the percentage of owners slipped from the 42 percent minimum mandated by law in 1937 to less than 30 percent at the end of century. Although this percentage was illegal under the Haas Act of 1937, no attempt was made to reform the situation. The organization of individual owners and mini-fleets by broker created entities that were remarkably similar to the old fleets. Mini-fleets as constituted in the 1970s disappeared by the end of the next decade. The remaining fleets, owner-drivers, and mini-fleet operators all employed cabbies known as independent contractors, who were doomed to a kind of wage slavery.[6]

Contentious issues continued from the 1970s. The New York Police Department stationed detectives pretending to be naive visitors at the airport to stop fare gouging of tourists. The city government, in response to reports that cabbies did not know the city geography, required in 1981 that all drivers carry detailed maps of New York. Later it opened a school for cabbies to teach them the city and took them for rides around town on tour buses. It instituted dress codes that forbade t-shirts and required sleeves and trousers or skirts that reached at least to mid-thigh and were without holes. Violent assaults and murders of cabbies occurred with sad regularity. Ownership of a medallion remained a largely white privilege. Editorials decried the small numbers of African Americans able to procure loans to purchase medallions.[7]

One improvement from the 1970s was the shift toward larger, heavy-duty cabs. The beloved Checker cab went out of production and the last remnants gradually disappeared from the streets. As late as 2006, one retired cabby drove a Checker around town, picking up customers and not charging, though he accepted tips eagerly and often was paid far more than the normal fare.[8] Working cabdrivers used tougher, stronger automobiles at the end of the twentieth century. A few Dodges and Plymouths remained in the 1980s along with tiny number of Checkers, including ones used largely for nostalgia. The Chevrolet Caprice and the Ford Crown Victoria were the industry workhorses, accounting for nearly all cabs in the 1990s. Chevrolet ended production of the Caprice in 1994, and since then the Crown Vic has become the universal New York taxi. The Caprice and Crown Victoria cabs were often used police cars adapted for use as cabs; overall, few cabbies bought new cars, and most drove their used cars longer. Most individually owned cabs had body-on-frame construction to endure the city's streets and to stretch the cab's lifetime over three hundred thousand miles, with an average annual use of over 63,300 miles.

Most owner-driver cabs used large V-8 engines, but fleets, believing that big engines caused accidents, preferred smaller four-cylinder engines. It was a rare cab that passed an initial annual inspection. Bad breaks, excessive emissions, and such serious structural defects as deteriorated ball joints and cracked chassis and motor mounts meant frequent returns to the body shop before the cab could pass inspection standards. Passengers might be unaware of many of these problems except for poor suspension systems that caused uncomfortable rides.

Passengers could not help but notice the barrage of stickers blistering off the cab divider, advising them about their Passenger Bill of Rights. For several years, the TLC mandated that cabs play recorded messages from celebrities reminding passengers to use their seatbelts. Tolerated to a degree, these messages did not meet the disapproval universally given to the video advertisements briefly installed in the passenger area of cabs. New Yorkers generally accepted the ads and zipper messages perched on the roof of the cabs, but refused to accept tiny screens blaring recorded messages. On this issue, cabbies and passengers overwhelmingly agreed, and the video ads and "talking taxi" announcements were removed.[9]

Crown Victoria cabs have continued to dominate the New York taxi industry into the twenty-first century. There were few alternatives. In the first years of the new century, Toyota, Honda, and Isuzu minivans were being used as cabs, as were about sixteen Ford Explorers. Owner-drivers and brokers resisted calls to use the spacious, distinctive, and far more expensive specialty cabs used in London on the grounds that "our goal here is to keep the taxi as democratic as possible." The clear preference for an inexpensive if dull cab such as the Crown Vic so exasperated a group of architects, designers, and urban planners that they called for a newly designed New York City taxi. This was the first such venture since cabbies ignored the Museum of Modern Art's prototypes in the 1970s. Paul Goldberger, an eminent architectural critic, recalled that designers and museum curators enthused about the 1976 exhibition but that taxi executives, fleet owners, and city regulators dismissed it, and drivers, perhaps annoyed at what they perceived to be the show's elitism, picketed it. In 2005, the planners envisioned cabs with digital maps, better vacancy indicators, sunroofs, sliding doors, better access for wheelchair users, and front seats that faced the rear of the cab. An additional plan to award cheaper medallions to cabs using hybrid motors became entangled bureaucratically. Other schemes included using cell phones to hail cabs, more hack stands, and rest stops with amenities for drivers. The Taxi and Limousine Commission gave cautious approval for the plans, provided that there were none for changing the cab color from yellow. The TLC commissioner contended, "If you took the yellow off the cab, I don't think it would be a cab anymore," forgetting the multi-hued taxis before 1970.[10]

Despite their numbers, there was a popular belief that there were not enough taxis available. Humorist Russell Baker recalled the famous dictum that you can always get a cab until you need one. Mayor Edward Koch sought to remedy the situation by doubling the number of medallions, the cost of which had soared to over one hundred thousand dollars. In part, Koch and Gorman Gilbert, the head of the Taxi and Limousine Commission and author of a highly regarded book on the taxi industry, contended that an increase in the numbers of medallions would alleviate the chronic problem of service refusals. In a harsh letter of January 13, 1987, Donald Stoppelmann, the president of the owner-drivers' organization the Metropolitan Taxi Board of Trade, wrote Gilbert that the members of the association were "stunned and dismayed" by the prospect of more medallions. Anxious that increasing the number of medallions might lower the value of established permits, Stoppelmann argued that the reasons for service refusals were "economic rather than racial" and that more cabs would only clog the streets. The failure lay with problems in mass transit. Stoppelmann reminded Gilbert that nowhere in the United States had increasing the numbers of taxis meant better service to outlying areas. He forecast that more "taxis stalled in immovable traffic jams cannot service their riders." When Koch tried to tie the plan to issue new medallions to a fare increase, he was answered by a massive taxi blockade. Non-medallion drivers also backed up traffic to protest a plan to give the TLC new powers to govern them and apply higher fees. If the union could no longer muster much energy, and fleet drivers were chafing under the new leasing system, owner-drivers remained politically powerful enough to halt any new plans for additional medallions.[11]

Fulfillment of Koch's plan took another decade and a half. His original idea floundered in part because the additional four hundred cabs would cause more air pollution. Not until the city government ran into a fiscal crunch in the early 1990s did it gain state legislative approval to auction the new medallions. The city of New York sold the medallions in three sets of auctions in 1996 and 1997 for record high prices that produced $85 million for the city treasury. Buyers liked the idea of "clean" medallions that had no previous owners or liens. Another set of medallions went on auction in early 2004. A total of nine hundred medallions were sold between 2004 and 2006. A few of them were designated for auction to bidders who promised to use wheelchair accessible cabs. The first vendue of medallions brought record prices of $344,400 for corporate licenses and $292,600 for individual medallions, raising over $96.8 million for the city treasury.[12]

Riding a cab remained inexpensive in New York. Cabbies complained that fares remained low even after the fifth increase since 1971 was enacted in April of 1980; the new rate lifted the cost of the average short haul to $1.80 and a 2.5-mile ride to $3.20. The Taxi and Limousine Commission allowed the fare increase because it recognized sizable increases in the costs of gas, insurance, and workman's compensation. Under the lease system, of course, those costs now resided with the driver. The TLC also required that mini-fleets operate twenty-four hours a day, with full insurance. In return, the owner could lease his cab for the second shift, thus introducing the new system into the universe of owner-drivers. New Yorkers, as the commission predicted, took the increase in stride. A locksmith commented that the only good conversations he had each day were with cabbies. A doorman acknowledged that "everything else was going up, why not cab fares?" New Yorkers got a short reprieve when the TLC postponed the increase to April.[13]

The average taxi fare in New York City remained the fourth lowest in the thirteen largest American cities in the 1980s. When the transit fare in New York City rose from thirty cents in 1970 to seventy-five cents in 1980, it became more than one-third the price of a short-haul taxi ride. That meant that when three passengers rode in a taxi, the fare per person was cheaper than taking the subway or bus. While the fare remained low, the transition to leasing pushed the value of a medallion higher to $68,000 in March 1980. Leasing allowed guaranteed profits for medallion owners. One reason the TLC postponed the fare increase was that it had become concerned about controversial economic methods in the industry. The commission argued that three different kinds of accounting existed: that done by fleets, by older owner-drivers, and by new owner-drivers. Since the TLC mandated second-shift leasing, thus accrediting the once illicit system of horse hiring, newer owners, under the pressure of medallion mortgages, did not report substantial amounts of income from leasing or from their own bookings. Ben Goldberg, president of the Taxi Drivers and Allied Workers Union, charged that only thirty of 4,700 mini-fleet drivers filed reports about second shifts. The power of the union was so greatly reduced that when it called a strike in 1983, few drivers observed it. The TLC also discovered that many newer owners had paid excessive and unfair "hacking up charges" when taking out loans for their permits, and paid sky-high interest rates of up to 24 percent per year, because as banks often considered new taxi drivers to be risks, medallion-seekers had to resort to private loans with extortionate interest rates. The need for a new fare rate was clearer to such drivers than to older drivers or to garage owners.[14]

Soaring operating costs for insurance, taxes, and gasoline and a tenfold increase in the motor vehicle tax meant harder times for the owner-drivers in the late 1980s. Between 1987 and 1989 alone, operating costs rose more than 20 percent for individual drivers.[15]

Making matters worse was the introduction of a new kind of limousine service that responded only to radio calls in midtown Manhattan and the airports and offered better quality cars and competitive rates. First initiated in 1982, these radio limousines quickly cut into lucrative airport trips and longer hauls in the city for medallion drivers. By 1987, there were over six thousand so-called black cabs for more affluent and corporate New Yorkers. In the early 1990s, the numbers of luxury cars available for radio calls increased to eight thousand, and by 2004 to almost ten thousand. Rather than be ruined by the "black cars," many medallion drivers adapted by driving them while leasing out their own yellow medallion cabs.[16]

Nor were working conditions any better. Fleet drivers still had to wait in filthy garages for the next shift. Iva Pekarkova described this experience in her memoir, *Gimme the Money.* Pekarkova actually liked the garage where she worked yet described waiting in a shape-up, avoiding the dispatcher's "pawings at her rear end," while other hackies "shivering with cold, stomped on a rainbowy oil slick, getting the soles of their boots covered with it, and sharing the horrors of the last night with each other in several languages. Thick clouds of yellow fog wafted from the garage," where a mechanic was touching up the color of the cabs. The fog settled on everything. Then there were the cab breakdowns. Even new cars, and the one she drove was hardly new, broke down every two or three weeks, and then "returns to the garage in a less than glamorous manner, hooked up nose down to the rear end of a tow truck." Drivers had to wait while the garage sent someone out to rescue them and the cab, a driver who lost money and time but still relished the opportunity to escape from the "blurry Yellow of your mundane job."[17]

As working conditions and competition for fares worsened, cabdrivers took out their grievances in public. The habits of cabbies bothered many. Pedestrians, especially those who were foreign visitors, complained bitterly about the dangerous behavior of cabdrivers. Xiao Qian, a Chinese writer visiting New York in the early 1980s, described the terrors of seeking breakfast: "Every morning, trembling with fear, we had to cross the street, which was under the tyrannical control of taxicabs—they drove as if they had gone mad and were determined to run over everyone." Poor quality of service also provoked public outcry. A story about a cabby who refused to pick up a blind woman and her seeing-eye dog scandalized New Yorkers. British actress Victoria Tennent was taken for a lengthy ride by a cabby that did not know where he was going; nor did any other cabby he asked. Travelers had to use ingenuity to get a taxi at rush hour.[18]

Getting a cab at any time required urban wisdom. Cabdriver-novelist Iva Pekarkova ably described the varied means by which fares summoned a taxi: "The uppity-mellow lifting of the left arms of little Madison Avenue ladies whose right hand is *holding* a leash with a choking lap-sized dog. The well-practiced wave of the stockbrokers. The supplicant, soft arm of musicians," hiding behind large instruments they know won't fit into the cab. She observed "the windmill of arms, legs, umbrellas, and heads of confused tourists." Experienced drivers could tell the difference between the assured arms of fares below Ninety-sixth Street in Manhattan with the frantic lifts up and down of pedestrians hoping to get rides to Harlem or the other boroughs.

Later, writer Colson Whitehead described the talents necessary to get a cab in the rain. He wrote that the availability of cabs shrinks "as thin fingers tilt and quiver at the edges of traffic. The bastard one block up-river gets it before you can stick a hand out, just as you are someone else's bastard one block downriver." People eager and impatient to get home calculate "the super-computer of cab-catching," including the time of day, the direction and force of the wind, sun spots . . . all important considerations in the acquisition of a cab." One woman lacked such instinctive, urbane knowledge: "She hailed it because she thought it was empty, but it speeds by with smug fares in the backseat who do not even notice her." Once ensconced in the backseat, all it took was a little cab fare in the pocket to "become royalty."[19]

Most rides were mundane. A study released by the city in 1982 indicated that the typical cab rider was a thirty-five-year-old white woman who earned $27,500 a year, lived in Manhattan below Ninety-sixth Street, and was very uncomfortable taking mass transit. A few days after the report was issued, a woman wrote the New York Times and commented that although taxi service was incompetent (she mentioned one driver who had never heard of Grand Central Station), taking a cab was still preferable to waiting for the bus or being jammed inside the subway.[20] Even celebrities took cabs. Andy Warhol's diaries reveal his daily use of cabs in the 1980s. His tax lawyer advised him to keep track of all cab fares during his daily jaunts around the city. Between night crawling, gallery openings, flea-market shopping, and trips down to his Factory, Warhol took about six cabs a day and regularly spent twenty dollars or more daily on them.[21]

One woman who transported the typical cab customer was cabby Bernice Kanner, who provided a nice description of a day's fares. In order, from 5:30 a.m. on, her customers included a grants officer from North Carolina on the way to LaGuardia Airport, a cook headed back to Manhattan to his restaurant, a consultant on child-support laws on his way to Grand Central for a train to Albany, an ad salesman for Business Week, a Yonkers man who worked for NYNEX and wanted a fast ride to the World Trade Center, a woman who discussed perfume with her, a real estate investor for Citicorp, a French man who ran the import trade for Remy Martin cognac, an elderly lawyer, and more than forty others during the day. Kanner found that businesswomen were the worst tippers. By the end of the day, she crawled exhausted back to the garage, stopping on the way to fill up the car's gas tank. At the garage she turned in her trip sheet and paid seventy-five dollars for the lease fee.[22]

Kanner was part of the new generation of hackers. The army of cab-drivers was changing quickly. Christine Oxenberg identified three types of cabdrivers during the transitional 1980s: the professional, the intellectual, and the immigrant. The professional, who drove for his entire adult life, accepted hacking as his life and aspired to no other job. Such drivers prided themselves in moving slowly but surely to a destination. The professional never imposed conversation on an unwilling fare, instead gauging what subjects were appropriate and "likely to increase the tip." Nothing phased the professional. Oxenberg witnessed one driver hit a stumbling drunk, sending the man twenty feet into the air. The driver shrugged his shoulders and commented, "When you're driving thirty years, this kind of thing is likely to happen sooner or later." The professional was often disdainful of customers. One told a story of the penurious entertainer Bob Hope. Hope dismissed the driver's conversation and told him not to expect a tip. Hope told the hack man that if he tipped, it would cost about twenty-three thousand dollars a year. At the end of the ride, the driver told Hope that he had planned to ask for an autograph but that because the actor had such a lousy personality, the ride was free. Hope dropped a dollar bill on the front seat, and the driver chased and threw the money at the fleeing actor.

A number of veteran cabbies were still working in the 1990s, some of whom had distinctive characteristics. Eli Resnick, the Candy Man, covered his cab with plastic flowers and handed out candy to smiling passengers. The Zipper Man plastered the dashboard of his cab with zippers, while the cab of Santa Claus was festooned with ribbons year around. Mad Pat was a Harvard graduate who had worked out the streets of the city to a science and was able to get passengers to their destination faster and safer than any other hack man. There were erstwhile celebrities behind the wheel, such as Larry Levenson, one-time owner of Plato's Retreat, a famous sex emporium from the early 1970s. Hacking still attracted younger men, who longed for the freedom it allegedly offered. Ira Eisenstein was a thirty-six-year-old accountant-auditor for a major accounting firm who had worked for the federal government for nine years before that and wondered if life was passing him by. One day, he took a cab in terrible traffic. The driver told him that after he finished this trip, he was going to the gym. Asked how he could do that, the driver responded that he could do as he pleased, because he owned the cab. Impressed, Eisenstein quit his accounting job, bought a medallion and a cab, and started hacking. He worked the morning shift and some of the theater crowd in the afternoon, enjoying his clean taxi and a nice stereo. He admitted that hacking might not be the end-all, but for now it was "living well."[23]

Writer Donald Westlake captured the cynical battles between fares and professional hackies in a poem entitled "Taxi Dance" that appeared in the *New York Times* in the late summer of 1980. It scored the paltry "ten cents a tenth," "six-hour shifts" that cabbies endured while getting somewhat even by "triple-charging the greenhorn," who never knew the difference.

> Sometimes I think the only de-gree
> You know could be the Nth;
> All you need is the chutzpah
> Come on, big boy, ten cents a tenth[24]

The laments went on for nine stanzas.

By the mid-1980s, leasing changed the ethnic composition of hacking. Immigrants now dominated the job. A visitor to the Taxi Driver Institute learned that about one-third of the students were white, about the same number were African American, 17 percent were Hispanic, and 13 percent were Asian. Nearly three-quarters were born outside of the United States. College-educated cabbies accounted for about 14 percent of the total; 9 percent had some graduate education. Less than half of the rest had graduated from high school. Despite the best efforts of the Taxi Institute, many of the newcomer cabbies could barely speak English, qualities that made nostalgic riders who lamented, "What ever happened to the old-school cabby who knew how to get around this city?"[25]

By the late 1980s, cabdrivers came from more than eighty different nationalities. Many of them owned medallions. Scholars have determined that immigrants arriving since the Hart-Cellar Act of 1965 tended to come to America with more education and money. They were able to either take loans or pool cash for medallions. One group that did this successfully was Russian Jews, who made up much of the immigrant taxi workforce of the 1980s. Some worked close to their community in Brighton Beach, while others believed that "in Taxi is the university of all mankind," and traveled across the city. In some ways Russian Jews resembled the "Depression virtuosos" of the 1930s. Like the 1930s drivers, Russian Jews faced downward mobility, unable to get work appropriate to their education and skills because American authorities did not recognize their professional licenses and experiences. Language also proved to be a barrier. Max, forty-nine, previously was a lawyer in Moscow. Differences between the American and Russian legal systems and language difficulties forced him to drive a cab. He acknowledged his fate: "It's not what I would call an intellectually challenging existence, but I support my family very well. That's what America is all about, isn't it?" For older men such as Max, accustomed to making a living but too old to start again at the bottom, cab driving was an entrepreneurial avenue to social mobility. It was cheap and easy to get into and offered a work environment free of bosses. Typically, a group of Russian men pooled their money to lease cabs, created mutual savings funds to buy medallions, and split shifts so that the cabs were working twenty-four hours a day.[26]

Hack language in the 1990s added a few terms to the earlier cabby argot. Foreigners at the airport were termed "suckers"; a "bid" was a good place to find suckers. A "chump" was a passenger who requested that the cabby wait while he ran off to make a phone call, then failed to return. Someone who was "big time" was a rider (passenger) who asked the driver to change a fifty-dollar bill. The driver's response would be "Hey (excuse me)! You gotta be from Jersey!" Some terms easily passed through the decades. A "pound" was five dollars plus tip. To "shell out" to a dispatcher was to bribe him. An old term with a new meaning was "hack bureau," now used for the Taxi and Limousine Commission.[27]

By the mid-1990s, transnational and immigrant workers from the Punjabi districts of India and Pakistan increasingly dominated cab driving. Pushed into migration to the United States by the Green Revolution, which encouraged large-scale industrial agriculture at the expense of small farmers who then lost their livelihood, and by energetic government efforts to export unemployed young men, Punjabis flocked to New York to drive taxis. They followed a pattern of chain migration, in which pioneers, after having experienced the new country and job, recommended that friends and relatives follow them. The transition was relatively easy, because hacking was part of India and Pakistan's urban culture. Hack men played significant roles in the huge Indian cinema industry. In *Taxi Driver,* a 1954 film noir starring Dev Anand and directed by his brother, Chetan, the cabdriver protagonist rescues a young woman from mobsters and helps her in a singing career. The female heroine also learns the tough culture of India's cabdrivers. The film climaxes in a shootout between cabdrivers and the mob.[28]

In the mid-1990s, the number of Indians, Pakistanis, and Bangladeshis applying for taxi licenses in New York City soared from 10 percent in

1984 to 43 percent in 1991. The percentage of American-born drivers fell from 20 to 10.5 percent in this period. Drivers from the subcontinent congregated at new restaurants on Lexington Avenue in the Thirties.[29] Better education, job prospects, moves to the suburbs, and supportive government policies all meant that native-born Americans, especially whites, were less likely to work as cabdrivers. African Americans and Puerto Ricans who gained work and political leverage in the public sector avoided hacking, leaving the job to newly arrived legal and undocumented immigrants. Taxi and Limousine Commission policies required that applicants show a temporary work permit only once, so renewal applications might allow immigrants with lapsed visas to drive cabs.[30]

A primary reason that native-born Americans avoided hacking was the introduction of the lease system. Under the commission system and union efforts of the late 1960s, regular fleet cabbies could count on a weekly paycheck, some job security, paid vacations, and other benefits. Now classified as independent contractors, cabdrivers lost those amenities. Citing the low pay and working conditions, native-born drivers largely quit hacking. Newer Punjabi immigrants in the late 1980s and 1990s, on the other hand, arrived in New York City with fewer resources than their better-educated counterparts who had come a decade or two earlier. Lacking an education at an urban, English-speaking school in India or Pakistan or other salable skills, Punjabi men used a network of family, social, and economic networks to get into hacking. Friends helped newcomers get temporary jobs until their hack licenses were approved. Garage owners learned to accept new applicants based upon personal referrals from other Punjabis. Although some garage owners demanded road tests to ascertain driving skills, others were content just to insure that shifts were filled. As historian Biju Mathew notes, hacking was one of the few jobs in the world in which a laborer understood that he might have less at the end of the day than when he started in the morning. That uncertainty was a primary reason for the constant turnover in the business.[31]

As Asian drivers came to dominate the trade, its argot changed. Urdu and Punjabi terms came into common use. In Punjabi, *chotta* (small) meant LaGuardia Airport, while *badda* (big) denoted JFK. *Babba* (old man) was the slang term for Lincoln Center. For the Broadway musical "Cats," drivers referred to *billi*. When considering actions against nonstriking drivers, taxi men talked of *chakka* jams, or purposely giving themselves flat tires in the middle of the road to immobilize traffic. Foods such as rotis and kabobs, while common to streetwise people in the city, became identified with taxi men when the *New York Times* published a story on their favorite delicatessens.[32]

The trend toward non-American drivers accelerated in the early twenty-first century. Taxi and Limousine Commission records for 2004 indicate that over 90 percent of medallion drivers were foreign-born. Pakistan, Bangladesh, and India contributed over 38 percent of medallion drivers, and the former Soviet Union over 10 percent. Muslim nations, including the three mentioned above plus Egypt and Morocco, accounted for more than 50 percent of newly hired medallion drivers in 2002–2004. People of African descent from Haiti, Ghana, and Nigeria amounted to over 8.5 percent of drivers, the largest black population ever among yellow cab drivers.[33]

With some exceptions, the newer immigrant cabbies were better educated than those in the past. Although statistician Bruce Schaller does not break down figures on education by city, he found that nationally over 40 percent of taxi drivers had attended at least a few years of college and 14 percent had college diplomas. Such figures doubtless had less to do with the attractiveness of the job than with the scarcity of better paying, more prestigious positions. Certainly, the average national wage of almost $27,000 for cabbies placed them substantially behind mail carriers, clerical workers, truck drivers, bus drivers, messengers, prison guards, and laborers in the last census. Cabdrivers were also older than before, with an average age of slightly over forty-two years in New York City, and although most worked over forty hours a week, few considered themselves full-time drivers.[34]

Women began to return to hacking in the 1990s, though their percentage remained only 2.5 of all taxi and limo drivers in 2004. Among them was the Czech writer Iva Pekarkova. After arriving in the United States in the mid-1980s, Pekarkova was "a mediocre social worker in the South Bronx, a lousy waitress, and a catastrophic bartender." Becoming a "pretty decent cabdriver," Iva found that she had to answer the same questions continually. So she authored a little booklet entitled "The Book of Iva in 'Q and A.'" In the small Xeroxed pamphlet, Pekarkova denied being afraid of driving at night and wrote that she liked the customers who taught her about the city and life, even though she "seldom had a chance to hear someone's whole life story. The distances are too short, the traffic not heavy enough. New York's too small." Pekarkova detailed the travails of night driving, including being robbed, and rec-ommended that cabdrivers not fight to keep their money from bandits. She later wrote an excellent novel, *Truck Stop Rainbows*, about a woman's one-night stands with truck drivers in Eastern Europe.[35]

Cabby Bernice Kanner penned a good description of the new qualifi-cations to become a hackie. She applied for a license at the Susan Main-tenance Company. The garage took her notarized application, ran a li-cense check, and sent her on to the Department of Motor Vehicle where she upgraded her common driver's permit to a chauffeur's license. After the new license arrived in the mail, Kanner collected her business certi-ficate, a certified medical examination, certified copy of her social secu-rity card, and certified checks for thirty dollars (the Taxi and Limousine Commission fee), and thirteen dollars (the fingerprint check), and took them down to the commission. After she waited for hours past her scheduled appointment, a clerk in a Miller beer baseball cap gleefully noted that her doctor had not filled in the date of his medical license. She had to hurry back so that she would not lose her place in line to take the last English test of the day. After surmounting that hurdle, she convinced another clerk to accept her duplicate social security card and had to give another new photos with better lighting. Then she waited an hour to an-swer inane questions about the addresses of major attractions and about basic English. Still, she noted that 20 percent of the applicants fail the test. After waiting four weeks for her hack license, she finally reported to work.[36]

Kanner's dispatcher advised her to stash bills of different amounts so that thieves would not get everything. The dispatcher told her to bring twenty dollars in change, a driver's license, change holder, street atlas of the five boroughs, the *Official New York Taxi Driver's Guide,* and a novel for slow times. A sign of the changed position of the lease driver, the dis-patcher's wise advice was to drive carefully, cruise one side of the avenues and not bolt across lanes, check every car for dents before taking it out, and make sure the mechanic signed the trip sheet after checking the car's fluids.[37]

Kanner attended the Taxi Driver Institute, which the Taxi and Limou-sine Commission operated on lower Fifth Avenue. There she listened as a moonlighting junior high school teacher taught his multinational stu-dents about the average length of a ride (nine to eleven minutes) and told of rules restricting recommendations of restaurants, forbidding storage of baseball bats as weapons, and detailing how to answer simple questions in several languages. Students learned that passengers had the right to control the radio and air conditioning. Enforcing these rules were the various kinds of police in the city and over 170 hack inspectors and tunnel authority officers. Drivers did not have to pick up anyone who was drunk or obviously deranged but had to take any "normal" person anywhere in the five boroughs. Most people, the instructor advised, would not bother to report violations, but people with disabilities who had complaints about accessibility were the most likely to follow through. After listening to such profiling, the students watched a movie about cabdriver methods of cheating customers. Because of the costs of insurance rates for drivers, the instructor argued, "half of you will be out of business in six months, and 80 percent will quit by the end of the first year." Such cumbersome entrance qualifications, doubtful advice, and pessimistic conclusions could discourage the most determined applicant.[38]

Kanner was one of many writers to recount experiences driving a cab. In contrast to the cabbie memoirs of early eras, hack writers of the 1990s concentrated largely on money. Vladimir Lobas related how another cabby told him: "Get this into your thick skull . . . A cabby's got to think about just one thing: how to make money. One hundred bucks. Every single day." Throughout Lobas's memoir, cabbies are obsessed with airport calls, long-distance fares, and avoiding short hauls that lose money. Rather than worry about women in the backseat as James Maresca had done, Lobas spent much of his time cultivating relationships with doormen at various hotels, trying to figure out the best tips. He finally hit upon a method by which he offered to exchange bills for the weighty coins that doormen found burdensome. Lobas would give a doorman a five-dollar bill, then refuse any change over three dollars, essentially bribing the doorman two dollars in an attempt to be assigned the next "Kennedy" that came out of the hotel.[39]

Immigrants and older cabdrivers shared a common propensity for the intellectual life. A few cabdrivers could match wits with the best. One driver Christine Oxenberg interviewed told of an exciting ride from Kennedy Airport with G. B. M. Anscombe, who was Ludwig Wittgenstein's literary executrix and Regius Professor of Philosophy at Cambridge University. The driver discussed a lecture Anscombe had delivered at Barnard College. The cabby told her that he was unable to follow part of her lecture; the professor explained that was because she spoke from a prepared text and left out a page. Honored by her presence, the hackie offered to give her the ride for free; the distinguished scholar accepted his kind offer and explained that, in fact, she had forgotten her purse.[40]

There were other incandescent moments. Denise Levertov recalled the golden days when cabbies and intellectuals found common ground in her poem, "Poet Power." "Riding by taxi, Brooklyn to Queens," she asks her apparently Hispanic driver if he is Mexican. An exile from Uruguay, he replies. She says that the only Uruguayan she has met is the writer Mario Benedetti. The driver suddenly lets go of the steering wheel and exclaims with delight:

> Mario Benedetti!!!
> There are
> Hallelujahs in his voice—
> We execute a perfect
> Figure 8 on the shining highway
> And rise aloft, above the traffic, flying
> All the rest of way in the blue sky. azul, azul![41]

Not all cabbies could recognize the names of poets. Christine Oxenberg asked numerous celebrities about their favorite memories of cabdrivers. Douglas Fairbanks Jr. recalled that one cabby kept looking back at him in the rearview mirror and finally exclaimed: "I've got it! I've got it. You used to pitch for the Yankees, right?" Songwriter Sammy Cahn recalled getting into a cab and calling the driver Joe. When the hack man asked him his name in return, the writer replied, "I'm Sammy Cahn." The driver, not believing him, asked another cabby in the hack line if his passenger was Sammy Cahn. The other cabby looked at him and contemptuously, said "He's fullashit!" and walked away. Cahn then told his driver to pull up next to the other one and ask him if he would bet his medallion about the dispute. Now concerned, the second driver looked up and said, "He's Sammy Cahn." Writer Alistair Forbes noticed his driver's name was Giuseppe Verdi. When Forbes asked the driver about music, the cabdriver turned around and snarled, "Don't give me any more crap about my name. Every goddamn passenger tells me the same thing every goddamn day. And you know what, I hate music." Another driver showed artist Keith Haring a drawing of his he had in the back and asked him if it was real. Haring told him it was a fake and gave him a real one.[42]

Cabdrivers with artistic hopes and talents abounded. One called "the Photographer" took Polaroid snapshots of customers as they entered the cab, then charged for the awkward images. There were at least three more serious photographers among cabdrivers. David Bradford worked as an art director in the advertising department of Saks Fifth Avenue. He had "a good job, regular hours, two-hour lunches, holidays, social status," but ultimately gave up the position for more independence. After an initial stint as a bicycle messenger, Bradford settled into hacking. A fare sold him a sophisticated camera, and over the next twelve years or so, Bradshaw shot images of the streets, crowds, workers, and his passengers. He received commissions for his pictures from the *New York Times* and the *New Yorker Magazine* and became internationally known for his images. In particular, Bradshaw likes the element of chance in taxi photography and the advice he receives from fares. One man told Bradford not to take pictures of New York using color photography, because "New York is only colorful on the surface. In reality the city is black-and-white." Bradford reflected, "I simply can't imagine ever not being a New York taxi-driver."[43]

Cabdriver culture became more self-conscious in the late twentieth century. Hack man Michael Higgins operated a small media empire that included a newspaper, television program, and radio show all named *Taxi Talk*. Ryan Weideman took a different approach to photography. A long-time cabdriver, Weideman installed a strobe light in the upper-left-hand corner of his cab and used it to capture images of himself and his customers, or simply the fares themselves. Weideman made a number of iconic images over the years, including classic shots of poet Allen Ginsberg paying his fare with a poem and a telling image of a family in the backseat floating dollar bills in the air, with Weideman's stoic face in the front. In Weideman's cab appeared punk rockers, Rastafarians, movie stars, transvestites, gay men, couples carrying three-foot sandwiches, and a myriad of other celebrities, characters, and ordinary people. Weideman published a collection of these images in 1991 that helped him win a Guggenheim Fellowship the following year. Weideman used the award to travel around the nation taking formal portraits of dozens of cabdrivers in many cities. His work received a major gallery showing in 2002.[44]

The 1990 collaboration of two cabdrivers in the book *The Night Line* used a more documentary style. Friends in the same garage, Ambrose Clancy, a writer, and Peter M. Donahoe, a photographer, recorded images of cabbies shaping up, the interior of the garage, shift changes, cashing up, and many images of cabs working the streets. The book includes candid shots of cabbies counting cash as they drive, accidents, and line jumping at the airports—all daily aspects of the cabdriver's world. Clancy contributed tales of hacking.[45]

There were readings by hack poets, featuring "the Cabby Prince." More serious was Mark Allan, a self-proclaimed metaphysical poet. For Allan, metaphysics could be applied to the variables of poetry and of hacking—whether to turn or go straight, whether to head for the hotels uptown or the bars downtown. Allan self-published a book of poems in 1985 entitled *Cool Algonquin,* about a lost love he had for a dancer from Queens.[46] Hacking had its own historian as well. Bobby Lowich, the owner of the last Checker cab in town, retired from driving so "he could spend his time doing what he loves most, which is driving a cab." Lowich preferred to cruise aimlessly around town, picking up friends and enjoying public admiration for his Checker. He considered himself a historian of hacking and was working on a study of Morris Markin, the founder of the Checker Cab Company and former owner of one of the largest fleets in New York City. Another cabby practiced feats with numbers in his cab, figuring the day of the week of their birthdays and other important occasions for his fares.[47]

Other authors emphasized the humor in cab driving. Jim Pietsch published two volumes of cabdriver joke books in the late 1980s. Pietsch began hacking in 1984 while trying to survive as a musician in New York. As a lover of humor, he began asking fares and other cabbies if they had heard any good jokes lately. Most hadn't, but gradually Pietsch collected enough for a first volume, which included many of his own creations. That effort led to work as a cartoonist and co-writer of an hour-long television special on cabby jokes. Pietsch got his break when he and a fare exchanged jokes one night; the passenger turned out to be an editor for a major commercial press.

Pietsch's jokes often had to do with his career as a musician. An example: "What do you call a drummer without a girlfriend?" Answer: "Homeless." Others combined music and sex. "What do a bass solo and premature ejaculation have in common?" Answer: "You can feel both coming and there's nothing you can do about it." But most had simply to do with sex and with cabdriver thoughts about the battle of the sexes. In one, a man asks his wife what she wants for her birthday. She replies: "A divorce." The man responds, "Gee, I wasn't planning on spending that much." Others make fun of ethnicity. A guy goes up to a Jewish man and asks, "Why do you Jews always answer a question with another question?" The Jewish guy replies: "Why shouldn't we?" Most of the jokes Pietsch heard were salacious, and so in 2005 he published a third volume, *The New York City Cab Driver's Book of Dirty Jokes*. As Pietsch explained, "The funniest jokes are, let's face it, usually the dirty ones." James Maresca, the taxi driver, memoirist, and misogynist of the 1950s, would agree.[48]

Risa Mickenberg's 1996 book *Taxi Driver Wisdom* combined humor and philosophy. Mickenberg guaranteed that all sayings in the book came from New York City cabdrivers. Among them are such comments on the meaning of life: "You must have something to care about. Otherwise you are empty," and "We are all born poor." On culpability, one driver contributed: "Democracy is only because everyone wants to share the blame." Ultimately, however: "You have no one to blame but yourself and everyone has you to blame, too." [49]

New Yorkers strived to commemorate their cabbies. One work of art created unexpected problems. In April 1996, the city installed a statue of a man hailing a taxi at the corner of Forty-eighth Street and Park Avenue. The piece was entitled "Taxi" and was sculpted by J. Seward Johnson. Within a few weeks, the city had to move the statue back away from the street because cabdrivers competing for the fare were getting into accident after accident.[50]

Representations of cabdrivers in film reflected their marginal, alienated status. There were traditional cabdriver success stories such as the Sylvester Stallone vehicle *Rhinestone* (1984) and the comedy *Taxi* (2004), which featured Queen Latifah, the rap star, as a female cabby. The most enduring image of the traditional cabdriver appears in the cartoon hit, *Who Framed Roger Rabbit?* (1988). Jim Jarmusch's charming *Night on Earth* (1991) includes five cabdriver sagas from around the world. In the New York segment, an Eastern European immigrant is so inept at driving a taxi that his fare, played brilliantly by Giancarlo Esposito, takes over the wheel. The fare is grateful to the driver for being willing to take him out to Brooklyn, a plot device that turns on the familiar problem of New York cabdrivers refusing fares to blacks, especially those going to the outer boroughs. The 1994 comedy *My Life's in Turnaround* chronicles the efforts of a young cabdriver to improve his life by approaching beautiful and hopelessly unavailable female fares. Even Hollywood cabbies are fringe characters. Bruce Willis's cabdriver character in the futuristic *Fifth Element* (1997) is little more than a homeless drifter. Mel Gibson's cabby character in *Conspiracy Theory* (1997) is tormented by visions of vast intrigues against society. That he is eventually right about one conspiracy does not take away from the cabby's portrayal as a self-taught, deluded sociopath. Cable television did little to improve the reputation of cabbies. A late-night favorite was HBO's *Taxicab Confessions,* in which passengers recounted tales of sexual escapades in the backseats of taxis. After the television run, the concept transferred to the Internet, where it continued as a pornographic site.[51]

Documentaries contained sympathetic portraits of immigrant cabbies, a well-meaning device that only accentuated their marginality. *Taxi Vala* (1994), made by Vivek Renjou Bald, looked squarely at the fate of Punjabi cabbies in New York. Michael Moore's documentary series *TV Nation* (1994–1995), examined racial profiling by New York cabbies. Moore filmed the well-known African American actor Yaphet Koto standing on one corner and Louis Bruno, a white convicted felon and accused murderer, nearby. Time after time, cabs passed by Koto and picked up Bruno. When questioned, the cabbies invariably argued that they had not seen Koto, and they were shocked when presented with a "Wanted" poster for the white man. A more sympathetic view of cabdrivers can be found in the Public Broadcasting Service documentary *Taxi Dreams* (2001). This film follows six cabbies, all but one of whom are lease drivers, on their nightly shifts as they try to learn the city and eke out a subsistence wage. The taxi men range from the uninitiated who allow fares to drive the cab to their destination to an old hand with two decades of hacking under his belt. He has saved enough to buy a house and a car and to give money to a school for girls in his hometown in Virginia. Another driver, who had been a teacher in his native Ghana, now has driven a cab in New York for a decade and a half. He has saved enough to bring his wife and children to New York, having seen them only three times in over ten years. For the director, Gianfranco Norelli, the film is about assimilation the hard way by driving a cab.[52]

In the 1990s, their union neutered by lease laws, cabdrivers sought new ways to organize. Working across ethnic barriers, hack men and left-wing activists attempted to improve the lot of lease and fleet drivers in 1993. Biju Mathew of the Taxi Workers Alliance noted how "drivers from other communities—Haitians, West Africans, Iranians—came forward to take on leadership positions" in the taxi reform movement. Ethnicity, Mathew explained, was directly confronted, revealing a clear understanding on the part of union leaders that cultural problems might arise. In fact, the cultural diversity allowed the union to benefit from organizing skills many cabbies had honed in resistance movements in their home countries, such as the Haitian struggles against Duvalier. Yet the

Lease Drivers' Coalition, as they were initially known, had to combat traditional problems in organizing cabbies. In the 1990s, high turnover, lack of a stable worksite, and few models for organizing across ethnic, racial, and national lines resembled difficulties cabdriver unions had faced in earlier eras.

It took several years, but eventually, thanks to the assiduous efforts of Mathew and the extraordinary leader Bhairavi Desai, the movement, now renamed the Taxi Workers Alliance, led drivers into three successful strikes in 1998. As a rare female activist among the virtually all-male taxi men, Desai learned that a woman could gain acceptance by becoming the "female ear" to the lives and struggles of the immigrant taxi men. Her status as a college graduate provided a degree of legitimacy even as it indicated a class difference. The men also prided themselves on protecting such female leaders. Desai learned about dedicated activism from Leo Lazarus, a veteran of the cab wars of the 1950s and 1960s. The alliance leaders worked hard to organize the drivers, many of whom were contacted on CB radios, using innumerable languages. On May 13, May 21, and July 1, over twenty-four thousand drivers clogged the city streets to protest conditions in the industry. Chief among their complaints were draconian rules promulgated by Mayor Rudolph Giuliani. These rules included sizable fines of up to one thousand dollars for drivers for rude behavior, smoking, and speeding. Once ticketed, taxi men found themselves guilty until proven innocent, which was a tough challenge. The public was excluded from the hearings, in which conviction rates were nearly unanimous. Drivers were also anxious about poor work conditions and pay, which barely kept pace with leasing and gasoline costs. Giuliani proved a particularly implacable foe of drivers, even going so far as to allow livery cars and vans to encroach upon the taxi industry. Later, after four hundred drivers marched across the Queensborough Bridge, Giuliani ordered the police to restrict them from Manhattan.[53]

The city government's reaction to the strike was indicative of the outsider quality of cabdrivers in the late twentieth century. Rather than portrayed as a labor dispute, as Joshua Freeman notes, the strike was seen as a struggle between forces of law and order and anarchy from the third world. In a reference that later became even more loaded, the police commissioner characterized the taxi drivers who clogged the streets in protest of burdensome regulations as "terrorists." Mayor Giuliani made conflicting statements about the strike. During the one-day walkout, Giuliani blithely proclaimed, "One day without cabs improved the quality of life."

His press secretary echoed this observation, saying, "Overall, it was a very pleasant day in New York." Two days after the strike, Giuliani issued an emergency executive order, good for sixty days, that allowed livery cabs to pick up passengers on the streets and the airports, because "open violations of the laws and regulations of the City of New York by owners and/or drivers of medallion taxicabs . . . are creating an imminent threat to the delivery of a necessary service," in the city. He noted that the situation was most severe at the airports. Giuliani's threat to use livery drivers as replacements for striking cabbies was eventually overturned by the courts, but not before Giuliani inflamed anger and provoked protests that irritated New Yorkers and allowed police repression. Sagely, Desai counseled drivers not to stage any demonstrations but to stay at home, thus avoiding any charges of "open violations of the law." While cabdrivers involved in the organizing efforts listened to Desai, others voted with their feet. As city harassment of cabbies increased, turnover soared to over 50 percent in less than five years. Garage owners who in the past had supported the Taxi and Limousine Commission's crackdowns, now complained that good drivers were leaving the industry because of the burdens of petty but expensive tickets.[54]

Racial profiling damaged the reputation of cabdrivers in the late twentieth century. African Americans in particular were infuriated by the refusal of hack men to pick them up. A TLC study in the late 1980s chronicled how white drivers routinely refused to provide service to blacks. Mayor Edward Koch threatened owner-drivers with fines if racial profiling continued. A number of well-known blacks attested that the problem did not cease. Philosopher and Princeton professor Cornel West fumed for an hour at a street corner as cab after cab passed him up. West concluded that such humiliations demonstrated the continued truth of W. E. B. Du Bois's famous dictum that the color line was the major problem of the twentieth century. Other well-known African Americans stepped forth to complain. Manning Marable, a professor of history at Columbia University, recounted how he nearly died of a high fever while trying to go by cab to a hospital only to have taxi after taxi pass him by. Former mayor of New York City David Dinkins told reporters he was rejected by cabbies. William H. Booth, former head of the New York City Commission on Human Rights, cited the Dinkins case and demanded that damages be paid. Broadway producer Geoffrey Holder observed that cabdrivers did not stop for him because they presumed he was going to Harlem. Journalist Jill Nelson asserted that "for a vast number of black

New Yorkers, hailing a taxi is a minor trauma, a humiliating experience that can make you murderously angry." One black professional told her, "In my life, the racism of cab drivers is about the only overt racism I feel, and it makes me want to take out a gun and shoot the tires out." Nelson took revenge on cabbies who ignored her by reporting their medallion numbers regularly to the hack commission and then showing up for their hearings. She claimed a high rate of convictions and urged other black New Yorkers to follow suit, providing all the methods of complaining to the commission in her article. She concluded her article by noting that a few cabbies on Forty-second Street and Eighth Avenue were looking for trouble: "Watch out medallion numbers 4D84 and 4H71, here I come."[55]

The issue of cabdriver racism toward African American passengers boiled over late in the 1990s. After years of complaints by ordinary and celebrated black New Yorkers, Danny Glover, a famous movie star, became enraged when cabbies whooshed past him and his daughters one evening in early November 1999. Finally, one driver stopped but refused to let Glover, who had a problem with a bad hip, sit in the roomier front seat. Angered, Glover decided to file protest with the Taxi and Limousine Commission against such treatment. Glover's fame ensured that his complaint received ample attention.

Glover's case was hardly unusual. As the commission's director of investigations had explained to Jill Nelson, understaffing meant inadequate inspections. Passengers making initial complaints failed to show up for the hearing in about one-third of the cases. As the story of discrimination against Glover spread, the issue quickly became politicized. Within a few days, state senator David Paterson and the Reverend Al Sharpton announced they were filing a class-action suit against the commission for condoning racism. A group of black police officers, 100 Blacks in Law Enforcement, launched a campaign to persuade the department to give more attention to the problem. Ordinary black New Yorkers talked to reporters about the deep hurts caused by such cabbie bias. Soon Mayor Rudolph Giuliani announced a sting operation called Operation Refusal that used inspectors and undercover police officers to entrap drivers who practiced racial profiling of fares. Guilty drivers were fined and threatened with loss of their licenses and their cars. Glover's lawyer criticized Giuliani for using a "Band-Aid approach" and argued that cabbies needed sensitivity training to correct distorted views of African Americans "rooted in the social stratification of their native countries." Other New Yorkers, aware of Giuliani's penchant for picking on poorer workers, cynically ascribed his plans as preparation for a run for the U.S. Senate the next year.[56]

Glover's ordeal occurred as part of a social trend. Service refusals rose during the prosperous 1990s after a decline in the late 1980s. There were changes in popular attitudes. Passengers who filed refusal complaints with the Taxi and Limousine Commission believed that economic considerations outranked racial prejudice as reasons for service refusals. Still, drivers told passengers that they did not want to deadhead back (come back empty) from an outer-borough destination or wanted to avoid being stuck on a bridge or in a tunnel during rush hours. Some believed that a trip uptown would be more profitable than a fare's desired destination downtown. Studies indicated that nonwhite complainants believed that money was at the bottom of service refusals, rather than race. The implications were that during difficult economic times, drivers will go anywhere, but during flush periods, drivers are choosy about whom they pick up and where they go. Another illustration of this was the amount of cruising miles, or mileage operated without passengers. During the 1990s, cruising mileage dropped by 15 percent; in the recession of the early years of the twenty-first century, cruising mileage increased, and the number of passenger complaints dropped.[57]

Cabbies resented Giuliani's sting operation. One Haitian-American driver stated, "There are two things you have to make sure of as a taxi driver; that you are safe and that you get paid." The cabby admitted that he profiled potential fares, did not pick up "customers who looked threatening" and felt, unfortunately, that "the problem is often with my people, with black people." Dave Pollock, the head of the League of Mutual Taxi Owners, blasted Giuliani for singling out cabbies for criticism. He and other taxi leaders felt that Giuliani had been too harsh on cabbies in recent years, contending that the city's tough enforcement of all taxi rules on driver conduct had doubled the number of disciplinary hearings for cabbies to over eighty thousand a year, or about two a year for every active driver. The publisher of *Taxi Talk*, a trade newspaper, claimed, "You are being nickled and dimed to death by the city!"[58]

The controversy spawned a debate about race and color in New York City. Glover and his lawyer claimed that immigrant cabbies suffered from prejudices originating in their home countries. Bhairavi Desai, the staff director of the Taxi Workers Alliance, which now consisted of over two thousand mostly Indian and Pakistani lease drivers, added that the "racist images flow throughout the world. The global impact of American movies, television, and rap music meant that immigrants arrived in the U.S. with deeply flawed attitudes about race. Sociologist Arvind Rajagopal of New York University concurred that South Asians tried to enhance their social status by differentiating themselves from American blacks and adhering to the values of white people. Jack Tchen, director of the Asian-Pacific Program at NYU, contended that Indians too often accepted a "model minority" stereotype, which was "effectively used by right-wing conservatives against Latinos and African Americans." Desai asked for understanding of the enormous economic burdens drivers faced daily and advocated sensitivity training on race. Other commentators contended that the drivers needed better assurances of safety in the streets, crime-detection equipment, and guaranteed wages.[59]

Former mayor Ed Koch, in a thoughtful editorial, spoke of how he argued with a Jewish driver in the early 1970s about picking up blacks. Koch, then a young congressman, told the driver: "I see by your name (on the license) that you are Jewish. After all the discrimination we have suffered, how can you say you wouldn't pick him up?" The driver stopped the car with a jolt, turned towards Koch, and said: "With my rear end, you want to be a nice guy?" During the controversy about Danny Glover's difficulties with a cabby, Koch talked to a Ghanaian driver on the way to LaGuardia Airport. The driver told him that he regularly rejected other blacks because he believed they would take him to Harlem and then not pay. Koch retorted: "No matter, if you can't abide by the law, get out of the business. Yes, life is unfair."[60]

The debate stemming from the Glover incident continued over the next several weeks, and in emotionally charged hearings, cabbies and passengers confronted each other. One driver, who had hacked since 1972, described how when he arrived in the United States, his heroes were Pelé, the soccer player, and Muhammad Ali, the boxer. Now, he said, the other drivers told him not to pick up black people. In a similar vein, Vladimir Lobas recalled harsh advice an older cabby gave him about picking up African Americans: "Remember: a black person should never be in your cab. You'll come to a bad end." When Lobas protested that his recent black passenger had a disability, the other driver responded: "That's none of your business. A cripple can take a gypsy cab to Harlem quite comfortably."[61]

The police crackdown initially seemed to spark some positive results. Over the next two years, the police department pursued cabdrivers who illegally refused to pick up African Americans. However, their methods were often arbitrary and in themselves discriminatory. The police often suspended the cabdrivers' licenses on the spot, instead of giving out summonses that allowed them to drive until conviction at a hearing. Lower court decisions terminated this summary justice, but in early 2004, a state appellate court permitted quick revocations. Even so, the Taxi and Limousine Commission claimed, their tougher policies caused the numbers of complaints and license revocations to plunge sharply to nearly zero, indicating that the worst offenders had been weeded out of hacking.[62]

Cases sometimes did reveal racial bias, but on other occasions, drivers with cars defective for myriad problems who were made anxious by Giuliani's Quality of Life campaign faced an unwelcome choice of risking exorbitant tickets or heading back to the garage for minor repairs and cleaning. At times, undercover agents accused drivers who used their off-duty signs to avoid unwanted fares of racial profiling of customers. Hack men believed that court proceedings were predetermined verdicts used to convict cabbies of violation or used records of past violations over the previous decades to decide guilt. Despite warnings from higher courts and lawsuits from the Taxi Drivers Alliance, the TLC continued abusive practices of summonses and pro forma hearings to harass drivers. What had begun as reform of social attitudes devolved into oppression of impoverished drivers.[63]

If anything, the Glover incident paradoxically pointed to the worsening status of nonwhite drivers in the city. Lacking any political power outside of the brave organizing efforts of the Taxi Drivers Alliance, disliked by the mayor, and receiving an increasing number of racial taunts and attacks, Indian and Pakistani cabdrivers found themselves identifying more with African Americans than with their wealthier, suburban countrypeople or with white Americans generally. While class was a very important social barometer in New York, race was always a factor. Nancy Foner argues that Puerto Ricans, Haitians, and other Caribbean immigrants to the city often came with limited experience in racial tension and seemingly well equipped with good educations and some savings. Because of their race, however, they found limited opportunity in New York except in hacking.[64]

Service refusals by cabdrivers inspired academic studies to determine how much racial bias was a factor. One study compared taxi men's techniques in war-torn Belfast, Ireland with those used by livery drivers in the economically worst sections of New York City. The implicit thesis of the study was that conditions in New York's most troubled neighborhoods were comparable to those of a war zone. Although New York drivers said they trusted in luck and God to protect them, many screened passengers by their appearance and dress, and many refused to pick up young men on the basis of skin color. Even livery drivers working in primarily black sections of New York discriminated against African Americans when color combined with other factors. Economist Glen Lourie argued that demographic odds doomed cabdrivers and young blacks into a cycle of stigma. Lourie contended that respectable, law-abiding black males, trying to get home late at night but wary of rejection, avoided cabs in favor of rides from friends, livery services, or mass transit. As a result, the likelihood increased that the only black males hailing cabs late at night were thugs intent on robbing the driver. Cabdrivers in turn became less willing to take a chance on the honesty of the person flagging them. In this cycle of stigma, young blacks regarded cabdrivers as racist while taxi men impugned black males. Such social typecasting was even intra-racial. One black journalist writing for the *New York Times* recalled discriminating against African Americans when driving a cab in the 1970s, arguing that a mistake might cost him his life. Drivers worried about violent holdups took the precaution of having some money to hand over rather than being empty-handed, which might be construed as a refusal to cooperate with a mugger.[65]

The terrorist attacks on the World Trade Center on September 11, 2001 adversely affected cabdrivers. In addition to experiencing the huge social trauma experienced by all New Yorkers, especially those who lost loved ones in the attacks, cabdrivers, most of whom already barely scraped by, immediately lost virtually all of their business as the Manhattan central business district and the airports shut down. Even after much of the city reopened within weeks of the tragedy, downtown stayed mainly closed for months. The city's economy reeled generally, but impoverished New Yorkers were hit the hardest. Cabdrivers faced declining nighttime business as tourists stayed away from such neighborhoods as Chinatown, Tribeca, and Soho. Cabdrivers were not given the financial succor received by many New Yorkers from the Federal Emergency Management Agency (FEMA). Despite business declines of as much as 20 percent clearly resulting from the attack, and in one case, a driver whose cab was crushed by the collapse of the towers, cabbies were refused any consideration for federal aid and were not even allowed to fill out applications. The Taxi Drivers Alliance called for a meeting in March 2003. Over three to four thousand drivers filled a Hunter College auditorium. The meeting jolted FEMA officials into action. Within weeks, in a significant victory for the Taxi Drivers Alliance, FEMA reopened the application process and even held clinics at the airports to help drivers apply for funds. Eventually, over two thousand cabdrivers took part.

FEMA assistance did not answer all of the cabbies' problems. Business losses and the steady demands from brokers meant, in Biju Mathew's estimate, that cabbies received only five hundred dollars a week, while brokers and garage owners took one thousand dollars weekly from each cab. Cabdrivers told stories of evictions from apartments and fears that the U.S. Immigration and Naturalization Service was detaining and deporting Muslims on spurious grounds. As members of the poorest and least protected class of New Yorkers, Muslim lease drivers felt the brunt of nativist feelings in the aftermath of 9/11.[66]

Still, their success at receiving federal aid inspired the Taxi Drivers Alliance to continue organizing, this time to push for fare increases using data detailing how little each driver earned by leasing cabs. Cabbies threatened to strike. New Yorkers, according to Mathew, generally agreed that a fare increase was reasonable, provided that the increase went entirely to the drivers. The TLC and the alliance's negotiations stalled over the issue of a lease cap, or the amount any broker, garage, or private owner could charge for a daily lease. Intensive bargaining later produced a result that caused cabdriver jubilation. In early 2004, the Taxi and Limousine Commission voted to raise fares by an average of 26 percent, the first increase in eight years. The increase in the lease cap was held to 8 percent, the new fares eliminated the night surcharge, a loss that Bhairavi Desai argued would cut down the number of drivers willing to work overtime. It was also unclear how much lease caps would increase, though the commission had circulated a proposal for an increase of fifty dollars per week.[67]

The alliance's triumph in negotiations with the Taxi and Limousine Commission was more than economic. During a period in which businesses and city governments seemed poised to curb wages and benefits for semi-skilled workers, the alliance had created a cultural and political unity unseen in hacking since the 1960s. Still, there was much to accomplish. Inflation would soon erode the fare increase. Historically, fare increases were infrequent and politically charged. The alliance was unable, or at least had not tried, to repeal the Lease Act of 1979, which now kept taxi men barely above survival levels. Unlike the 1960s, when New

Yorkers evinced powerful sympathies for the taxi drivers, alienation was now the rule. The alliance's membership indicated the full transformation of the hacking profession from native-born Americans to immigrants and sojourners who had limited ties to New York City. As the comments of Mayor Giuliani indicated, older immigrant groups in New York who now had become acculturated and politically powerful regarded the taxi men as outsiders. Hacking seemed less a rung on the ladder to success than a means of basic subsistence and of assistance to relatives far distant.

Epilogue

In early 2006, my wife and I hopped into a taxi and briefly gave the driver our destination. As the cab meandered through the streets, I noticed that the cabby was talking softly in Urdu into a cell phone mouthpiece. A quick glance at his license indicated that he was South Asian. Knowing that cabdrivers took advantage of cheap long distance calling rates to stay in touch with their families far away, I asked him if he was talking to someone outside of the country. The driver was polite and answered yes; he was having an argument with his wife. Where was she? She and the family lived in a village outside of Lahore, Pakistan. I marveled at how, in contrast to the voluble hack men of the previous centuries, cabdrivers now talked to family members across the world while losing contact with the people in the backseat. I did not find it offensive, though New Yorkers have sometimes expressed worries that taxi drivers are dangerously indifferent to their passengers.[1]

In his evocative study of lease drivers, Biju Mathew has argued that "family" is becoming an abstraction for the thousands of South Asian men who make up most of today's taxi force in New York City. According to Mathew, South Asian cabbies go home infrequently because of job demands, international security, and visa hassles. As a result, family becomes a distant memory, known only through conversations on cell phones and by the stipends sent home regularly. Continuing a pattern repeated by immigrants throughout American history, South Asian drivers are sent off by their families to eke out a lonely existence living in dormitories and eating at delicatessens in New York City, while the family waits for the money order across the world.[2]

Hacking a taxi in New York has always been a lonely job. The cabdriver, as we have seen, is often a distant father and husband, working long hours for decades to help pay for their family's dreams. In the past, taxi men routinely solved their loneliness by making speeches to their passengers. Now, with racial divides becoming sharper in the aftermath of the terrorist attacks of September 11, 2001 and the military disaster in Iraq, there seems far less contact between the taxi driver and his patrons. In the movie *Taxi Driver,* Travis Bickle utters the famous question: "You talking to me?" Now that no longer seems to apply. A proposal to eliminate the partition between driver and passenger met with little enthusiasm. Taxi men may be talking to friends or family in languages unfamiliar to the largely Anglophone public they serve. Rather than becoming Americans, contemporary cabdrivers are like the other service workers washed around the world to satisfy the needs of a rich population that has little attachment to or interest in them.[3]

Taxi men have changed in ways beyond culture. Data reported by the Taxi and Limousine Commission in 2004 show how much leasing transformed labor conditions within the industry. Owner-drivers accounted for 29 percent of all taxicabs, the lowest percentage ever, and down from 37 percent in 1982. Forty-four percent of taxis were leased to drivers on a long-term basis, primarily by large leasing agents (brokers) or from fleets. This percentage was a marked increase from 19 percent ten years earlier. Another 27 percent of cabs were leased daily by shift, down from 40 percent in 1992. Medallion prices increased to $247,000 for individual licenses and $283,000 for fleet permits. An auction of three hundred new medallions in April 2004 lifted prices to a record $292,000 for individual licenses and $344,000 for corporations. Despite a hefty fare increase in May 2004 that lifted the average ride to over ten dollars including tips and surcharges, taxi use stayed strong. The number of cabdrivers has steadied over the past decade at around forty thousand licenses, though the number of new drivers tends to increase only during deteriorating economic conditions. Full-timers account for only about 40 percent of all drivers, and nearly 30 percent drive intermittently.[4]

Although the Crown Victoria remains the standard cab, newer models include minivans and sports utility vehicles. Plans for new, improved taxis remain just plans.[5] For the first time in nearly seventy years, taxi men no longer revere the medallion. Angry lease drivers blame it as the source of their troubles. With the lease system, the possession of the permit means that owners no longer have to drive a cab. Rather, by working with a broker, they can secure a steady income without even being in the city. It is little surprise that one angry driver told Mathew the "medallion is the root cause of out problems." More than ever, the new generation of drivers is alienated from the past.

The Taxi Workers Alliance is the most important labor organization for taxi men in forty years. It achieved substantial gains in pay, if not always in benefits. As with all taxi unions, it needs staying power. Bhairavi Desai is a courageous, dedicated, honest leader but will need ample help in creating a true union organization. The alliance offers hope because it reaches out across national, racial, and gender divides. It has adapted quickly to new challenges, such as the fight against global positioning devices that track the driver rather than give geographical information.[6]

As South Asian, Haitian, African, Russian, and other nationals work at their jobs, they change the city in ways we can only dimly anticipate. The image of New York City as a great melting pot seems less viable as gaps in class and income grow. Still, the human element of taxi men prevails. New people, new Americans and New Yorkers will come from their experiences. The language of cabdrivers is now more Urdu than Yiddish; someday more New Yorkers will understand it. There may be less talking in the cab, but cabdrivers will always find a way to tell their own stories, whether on the Internet, in books, or in songs.

Appendix

DATA TABLES

TABLE 1
THE GROWTH OF TAXI AND LIVERY INDUSTRIES, 1907–2004

Year	Total Taxi and Livery[a]	Taxicabs	Car Services	Black Cars	Limousines	"Gypsy Cabs"
1907	65	65				
1912	2,800	2,800				
1923	15,000	15,000				
1931	21,000	21,000				
1933	15,500	15,500				
1934	14,000	14,000				
1937	13,595	13,595				
During WWII	7,500	7,500				
1947	11,414	11,414				
1964	14,300	11,787	2,500			
1966	15,800	11,787	4,000			
1971	21,100	11,787	9,300			4,400
1973	25,500	11,787	13,700			
1983	34,200	11,787	21,300	1,080		14,000
May 1996		11,920				
Oct. 1996		12,053				
Sept. 1997		12,187				
2000	54,000	12,187	30,800	11,000	3,100	
2002	50,900	12,187	27,400	11,300	4,500	
2004	47,900	12,487	25,500	9,900	3,600	

Sources: Gorman Gilbert and Robert E. Samuels, *The Taxicab: An Urban Transportation Survivor* (Chapel Hill: University of North Carolina Press, 1982); Edward G. Rogoff, "Theories of Economic Regulation Tested on the Case of the New York City Taxicab Industry" (Ph.D. diss., Columbia University, 1980); *New York Times,* 20 March 1949; Bruce Schaller, *The New York City Taxicab Fact Book,* 3rd ed. (New York: Schaller Consulting, 2004).

Note: Car services refers to for-hire vehicles serving neighborhoods around the city, primarily on a cash basis. *Black cars* refers to executive sedans primarily charging corporate accounts. Limousines charge by the hour and seat up to nine passengers. "Gypsy cabs" refers to vehicles not licensed to work for-hire or to pick up street hails.

Car service and "gypsy cab" figures are estimates for 1964–1983.

Car service, black car, and limousine figures in 1992 and 2000–2004 reflect the number of licensed vehicles. The shift to biannual licensing has somewhat inflated the number of licensed FHVs in 2000–2004 as compared with earlier years, as a larger number of licenses are no longer used but had not yet officially expired.

[a]Includes medallion taxicab, car services, and black cars. Does not include "gypsy cabs" or limousines.

Table 2

MEDALLION PRICES AND TRANSFER VOLUMES, 1947–2003

Year	Average Price		Number of Transfers	
	Individual	Corporate	Individual	Corporate
1947	$2,500	$2,500		
1950	5,000	5,000		
1952	7,500	7,500		
1959	19,500	20,000		
1960	20,825	19,450		
1962	22,000	23,400		
1964	26,000	34,145	290	
1965	26,000	30,000	610	
1966	25,000	19,000	390	
1968	27,000	16,000	490	
1969	24,500	n/a	650	
1970	28,000	14,000	670	
1971	25,000	10,000	430	
1972	26,000	12,000	580	
1973	30,000	17,000	600	
1974	30,000	17,000	590	
1975	35,000	22,000	570	
1976	42,000	24,000	800	
1977	55,000	33,000	680	
1978	63,000	52,000	810	
1979	67,000	53,000	830	
1980	60,000	50,000	700	
1981	60,000	50,000	n/a	
1982	57,500	49,300	697	637
1983	68,600	57,900	723	648
1984	75,900	66,200	795	796
1985	84,900	79,000	641	703
1986	101,600	92,900	660	778
1987	108,700	94,600	527	567
1988	129,700	121,500	532	646
1989	139,100	141,400	418	408
1990	128,400	135,700	374	272
1991	126,067	130,360	357	443
1992	128,577	143,199	281	407
1993	137,196	170,200	256	248
1994	$155,633	$214,221	232	164

(Table 2 continued)

Year	Average Price		Number of Transfers	
	Individual	Corporate	Individual	Corporate
1995	169,750	219,958	194	187
1996	176,333	207,292	264	267
1997	199,875	236,500	205	203
1998	229,000	277,318	155	215
1999	212,917	269,500	178	111
2000	217,125	253,864	208	119
2001	188,958	290,458	210	158
2002	200,333	232,250	262	267
2003	224,958	260,917	266	345

Source: Bruce Schaller, *The New York City Taxicab Fact Book,* 3rd ed. (New York: Schaller Consulting, 2004).

TABLE 3
TAXI FARES SINCE 1952

	Initial Charge	Mileage Charge	Wait Time	Mile	Charge per Minute	Average Fare
Before 1952	$0.20 first 1/4 mi.	$0.05 per 1/4 mi.	$0.05 per 2 min.	$0.20	$0.03	$0.83
July 1952	$0.25 first 1/5 mi.	$0.05 per 1/5 mi.	$0.05 per 90 sec.	$0.25	$0.03	$1.06
Dec. 1964	$0.35 first 1/5 mi.	$0.05 per 1/5 mi.	$0.05 per 90 sec.	$0.25	$0.03	$1.16
Jan. 1968	$0.45 first 1/6 mi.	$0.10 per 1/3 mi.	$0.10 per 2 min.	$0.30	$0.05	$1.48
March 1971	$0.60 first 1/5 mi.	$0.10 per 1/5 mi.	$0.10 per 72 sec.	$0.50	$0.08	$2.30
Nov. 1974	$0.65 first 1/6 mi.	$0.10 per 1/6 mi.	$0.10 per 60 sec.	$0.60	$0.10	$2.71
March 1977	$0.75 first 1/7 mi.	$0.10 per 1/7 mi.	$0.10 per 60 sec.	$0.70	$0.10	$3.09
July 1979	$0.90 first 1/7 mi.	$0.10 per 1/7 mi.	$0.10 per 60 sec.	$0.70	$0.10	$3.24
April 1980	$1.00 first 1/9 mi.	$0.10 per 1/9 mi.	$0.10 per 45 sec.	$0.90	$0.13	$4.06
July 1984	$1.10 first 1/9 mi.	$0.10 per 1/9 mi.	$0.10 per 45 sec.	$0.90	$0.13	$4.16
May 1987	$1.15 first 1/8 mi.	$0.15 per 1/8 mi.	$0.15 per 60 sec.	$1.20	$0.15	$5.08
Jan. 1990	$1.50 per 1/5 mi.	$0.25 per 1/5 mi.	$0.25 per 75 sec.	$1.25	$0.20	$5.70
March 1996	$2.00 per 1/5 mi.	$0.30 per 1/5 mi.	$0.30 per 90 sec.	$1.50	$0.20	$6.85
May 2004	$2.50 per 1/5 mi.	$0.40 per 1/5 mi.	$0.40 per 120 sec.	$2.00	$0.20	$8.65

Source: Bruce Schaller, *The New York City Taxicab Fact Book*, 3rd ed. (New York: Schaller Consulting, 2004).

Notes: Average fare based on 2.8 mile trip with 4.77 minutes of wait time.

Surcharges and flat fares:
• A night surcharge, applying to trips beginning between 8 p.m. and 6 a.m., was added in May 1981. The surcharge was rescinded in January 1982 for all but the 2,300 fleet cabs. The $0.50 night surcharge was extended to the entire industry in May 1987.
• A $1 surcharge for trips beginning between 4 p.m. and 8 p.m. was added in May 2004.
• A $30 flat fare from JFK airport to Manhattan was adopted in January 1996 and increased to $35 in 2001 and $45 in 2004.
• The surcharge for trips to Newark Airport was increased from $10 to $15 in 2004.

Table 4
AVERAGE FLEET DRIVER EARNINGS, 1913–1978

Year	Earnings
1913	$2.50/day + tips, 12-hr. day
1916	$2.50/day + tips, 10-hr. day
1917	$2.70/day + tips, 10-hr. day
1922	35% commission
1930s	$2.00/day + tips (40%)
1933	$15.60, including tips/wk.
1937	$15.00/wk. days, $18.00/wk. nights
1938	40% commission ($3.00/day)
1940	42% commission
1945	$70.00–80.00/wk.
1949	42½% commission, booking $17.22 ($35.00–$40.00/wk., including tips)
1952	45% commission
1960	44–45% commission
1966	46% commission ($20.00/day)
1967	47% commission ($89.00/wk. commission, $47.00 tips)
1970	$150.00/wk. including tips (42–50% commission)
1973	43–50% commission
1978	43–50% commission ($213.15 commission + tips, 5-day wk.)

Sources: New York Times, 6 November 1913, 12, 17 January 1917, 23 August 1923, 14 February 1933, 28 February 1938, 29 October 1939, 7 June 1945, 27 June 1952, 2 October 1966, 8 November 1967; *New York World Telegram,* 24 December 1937, 29, 30 March 1949; *New York Journal American,* 10 December 1961; *New York Daily News,* 10 November 1970; Edward G. Rogoff, "Theories of Economic Regulation Tested on the Case of the New York City Taxicab Industry" (Ph.D. diss., Columbia University, 1980), 112.

TABLE 5
NUMBER OF LICENSED DRIVERS, 1918–1979

Year	Number	Year	Number
1918	8,780	1939	30,438
1919	9,261	1947	33,000
1920	15,000	1949	35,000
1921	15,500	1952	30,000
1922	15,223	1956	30,000
1923	24,000	1959	35,000
1926	24,896	1960	37,000
1927	53,015	1965	44,000
1928	61,432	1966	30,000
1929	65,147	1967	34,000
1930	69,397	1969	36,500
1931	73,626	1973	43,000
1932	75,000	1974	36,000
1934	53,713	1975	36,000
1935	48,916	1979	34,500
1937	47,000		

Source: Edward G. Rogoff, "Theories of Economic Regulation Tested on the Case of the New York City Taxicab Industry" (Ph.D. diss., Columbia University, 1980), 185.

Notes

Introduction

1. For the concept of spectacle in New York City, see Marshall Berman, *On the Town: One Hundred Years of Spectacle in Times Square* (New York: Random House, 2006).

2. *New Yorker*, 23 May 2005.

3. Kate Daniels, "My Father's Desk," *The White Wave* (Pittsburgh: University of Pittsburgh Press, 1984).

4. Fred Davis, "The Cabdriver and His Fare: Facets of a Fleeting Relationship," *American Journal of Sociology* 65 (1959): 158–65; Diditi Mitra, "Rotating Lives: Indian Cabbies in New York City" (Ph.D. diss., Temple University, 2002), 66–67. I have benefited from the useful observations about the genealogy of servant behavior in Greta Foff Paules, *Power and Resistance among Waitresses in a New Jersey Restaurant* (Philadelphia: Temple University Press, 1991). For a good example of training a cabdriver, see Michael Santee, *Taxi Driving Made Simple: How to Do It Profitably, Pleasurably, and Professionally* (Oakland, CA: Round Robin Press, 1989).

5. Davis, "The Cab Driver and His Fare"; Clancy Sigal, *Going Away: A Report, a Memoir* (Boston: Houghton Mifflin, 1962), 473.

6. Here I am adapting the five-class model articulated in R. S. Neale, *Class and Ideology in the Nineteenth Century* (London: Routledge & Kegan Paul, 1972), 30. For class culture, see Raymond Williams, *Keywords: A Vocabulary of Culture and Society*, revised edition (New York: Oxford University Press, 1985), 68.

7. *Taxi Times*, July 1964, as quoted in Abraham Nash, "The Making of the New York City Taxi Drivers' Union" (M.A. thesis, Columbia University, 1967), 6–7.

8. James Sanders, *Celluloid Skyline: New York and the Movies* (New York: Knopf, 2001); Steven Ross, *Working-Class Hollywood: Silent Film and the Making of Class in America* (Princeton, NJ: Princeton University Press, 1998); John Bodnar, *Blue-Collar Hollywood: Liberalism, Hollywood, and Working People in American Film* (Baltimore: Johns Hopkins University Press, 2003).

9. For insights into the world of truckers, see Lawrence Ouellet, *Pedal to the*

Metal: The Work Lives of Truckers (Philadelphia: Temple University Press, 1994). For comments on *luftmenschen,* see Nash, "Making of the New York City Taxi Drivers' Union," 5–6.

10. A sampling of children's books on taxi drivers includes Betsy Maestro and Guilio Maestro, *Taxi: A Book of City Words* (Boston: Houghton Mifflin, 1990); Lucy Sprague Mitchell, *The Taxi That Hurried* (New York: Simon & Schuster, 1946); Eugene Baker, *I Want to Be a Taxi Driver* (Chicago: Children's Press, 1969); Carl Best, *Taxi! Taxi!* (New York: Orchard Books, 1996); Betsy Franco, *Tina's Taxi* (New York: Scholastic Books, 1994); Debra Barracca and Sal Barracca, *The Adventures of Taxi Dog* (New York: Penguin, 1990); and Annie McKie, *Teddy and the Little Yellow Taxi: A Teddy Taxi Book* (London: Granddreams, 1996).

11. Dave Betts, *I'm Lucky at That, by Dave Betts the Taxi Philosopher* (Garden City, NY: Doubleday, Doran, 1930), 146.

12. Important examples include Gorman Gilbert and Robert E. Samuels, *The Taxicab: An Urban Transportation Survivor* (Chapel Hill: University of North Carolina Press, 1982); Charles Vidich, *The New York Cab Driver and His Fare* (Cambridge, MA: Schenkman Publishing, 1976); Joshua Mark Lupkin, "Constructing the 'Poor Man's Automobile': Public Space and the Response to the Taxicab in New York and Chicago" (Ph.D. diss., Columbia University, 2001); Edward G. Rogoff, "Theories of Economic Regulation Tested on the Case of the New York City Taxicab System" (Ph.D. diss., Columbia University, 1980).

13. Joshua B. Freeman, *In Transit: The Transport Workers Union in New York City, 1933–1966* (New York: Oxford University Press, 1989); and Freeman, *Working-Class New York: Life and Labor in New York City Since World War II* (New York: New Press, 2000).

14. Thomas Bender, *The Unfinished City: New York and the Metropolitan Idea* (New York: New Press, 2002).

15. See Biju Mathew, *Taxi! Cabs and Capitalism in New York City* (New York: New Press, 2005) for this contemporary development.

16. Stanley Walker, *The Night Club Era* (New York: Frederick A. Stokes, 1933), 246–48.

1. The Creation of the Taxi Man, 1907–1920

1. *Taxi Weekly,* 30 October 1947. On fortieth anniversary, see *Taxi Weekly,* 2 October 1947. On Sullivan, see Kenneth T. Jackson, ed., *The Encyclopedia of New York* (New Haven, CT: Yale University Press, 1995), 1141.

2. *New York Times,* 27 March, 26 April, 26 June, 25 August, 5 September, 2 October, 18, 25 December 1907. For debate on rudeness of hack men, see *New York Times,* 22 August 1865; 23 July 1872; 4 November, 12 December, 8 August 1874. For concerns over rate-gouging, see *New York Times,* 22 July 1865; 24 November and

12, 15, 17 December 1874; 26 December 1876; 18 July 1885; 1 December 1887. For early history, see Rogoff, "Theories of Economic Regulation," 54–56; Vidich, *New York Cab Driver and His Fare*, 59–60; Gilbert and Samuels, *Taxicab*, 33–35; Lupkin, "Constructing the 'Poor Man's Automobile,'" 48–51.

3. *New York Times*, 12 September, 4–27 October 1908. For beatings, bombings, and killings, see *New York Herald*, 8–22 October 1908.

4. *New York Times*, 7–20 November 1908; *New York Herald*, 7–15 November 1908; *New York Evening Post*, 16 November 1908. For Allen's failure, see *New York Times*, 11 June 1910; 11 March 1911.

5. *New York Times*, 19–24 December 1908.

6. Clay McShane, *Down the Asphalt Path: The Automobile and the American City* (New York: Columbia University Press, 1995), 41–55; *New York Times*, 23 August 1869; Gilbert and Samuels, *Taxicab*, 25–38; James Flink, *The Car Culture* (Cambridge: MIT Press, 1975), 34–37.

7. McShane, *Down the Asphalt Path*, 81–101; Flink, *Car Culture*, 7–9, 19.

8. Edward Spann, *The New Metropolis: New York City, 1840–1857* (New York: Columbia University Press, 1981), 189–91, 289–95; Clifton Hood, *722 Miles: the Building of the Subways and How They Transformed New York* (New York: Simon & Schuster, 1993), 37–42.

9. Robert Ernst, *Immigrant Life in New York City, 1825–1863* (New York: King's Crown Press, 1949), 216; Howard B. Rock, *Artisans of the New Republic: The Tradesmen of New York City in the Age of Jefferson* (New York: New York University Press, 1979), 216–18; Graham Russell Hodges, *New York City Cartmen, 1667–1850* (New York: New York University Press, 1986).

10. *New York Times*, 5, 11, 19, 22, 27 June 1894; 21 May, 2 July 1895; Hackney Coach Drivers License Books, 1845–1865, Municipal Archives of New York (MARC).

11. Vidich, *New York Cab Driver and His Fare*, 57–60; Gilbert and Samuels, *Taxicab*, 33–35; Irving Lewis Allen, *The City in Slang: New York Life and Popular Speech* (New York: Oxford University Press, 1993), 96; Theodore Dreiser, "The Horseless Age," in *Selected Magazine Articles of Theodore Dreiser*, vol. 2, ed. Yoshinobu Hakulani (Rutherford, NJ: Fairleigh Dickinson University Press, 1987); *Taxi Weekly*, 13 July 1949. For a full account of the early history of the electric car and preference for horse-drawn cabs, see David A. Kirsch, "The Electric Car and the Burden of History: Studies in the Automotive Systems Rivalry in America" (Ph.D. diss., Stanford University, 1996), 67–68, 2121–24.

12. Vance Thompson, "The New York Cab Driver and His Cab," *Outing Magazine*, November 1906. For Maxwell, see *New York Times*, 22 November 1936. For Pearson, see 15 December 1948.

13. Philip Warren, *The History of the London Cab Trade: From 1600 to the Present Day* (London: Taxi Trade Publications, 1993); G. N. Georgano, *A History of the London Taxicab* (Newton-Abbott, UK: David and Charles, 1972).

14. Thomas Kessner, *The Golden Door: Italian and Jewish Immigrant Mobility in*

New York City, 1880–1945 (New York: Oxford University Press, 1977): 16–20, 32–40, 57; Reports of the Immigration Commission, 20:128–29, 134–35, 246–47; 28:278–82. For later estimates, see *Taxi Weekly,* 23 July, 17 September 1928.

15. *New York Times,* 5 October 1907; 22 November 1936; William R. Taylor, *In Pursuit of Gotham: Culture and Commerce in New York* (New York: Oxford University Press, 1992), 39; Lupkin, "Constructing the 'Poor Man's Automobile,'" 31–34; Allen, *City in Slang,* 96.

16. For merger talks, see *New York Times,* 15–18 March, 15 April, 9 July 1909. For strikes, see *New York Times,* 8 November–16 December 1909, and 8 November–11 December 1910. For windfall, see 18 November 1910.

17. Vidich, *New York Cab Driver and His Fare,* 80.

18. Lupkin, "Constructing the 'Poor Man's Automobile,'" 84–88; *New York Times,* 11 December 1910, 17 January–17 February 1912; *Taxicab Inspector Examination Instruction Manual* (New York: Civil Service Chronicle, 1913), 31–35.

19. Chanoch Shreiber, "The Effect of Regulation on the Taxicab Industry" (Ph.D. diss., Columbia University, 1973), 37.

20. Jean Sprain Wilson, *All About Tipping* (New York: McFadden, 1965), 19; William Rufus Scott, *The Itching Palm: A Study of the Habit of Tipping in America* (Philadelphia: Penn, 1915), 9, 33–34, 50, 90; Kerry Segrave, *Tipping: An American Social History of Gratuities* (Jefferson: McFarland & Company, 1998), 53.

21. *New York Times,* 3 June 1913; Lupkin, "Constructing the 'Poor Man's Automobile,'" 87; Courtlandt Nicoll, "New York Cab Situation," *National Municipal Review* 11 (April 1913), 101–2; Rogoff, "Theories of Economic Regulation," 59–66; Shreiber, "Effect of Regulation," 37.

22. Vidich, *Cab Driver and His Fare,* 6–7; Hazard, *Hacking New York* (New York: Scribner's, 1929), 54. For reference to the "cabby's Magna Carta," see *New York Times,* 22 November 1936.

23. Shreiber, "Effect of Regulation," 44–46.

24. For ex-convicts, see *New York Times,* 22 February 1912. A similar number was reported ten years later; see 12 October 1921. For robbery, see James H. Collins, *The Great Taxicab Robbery: A True Detective Story* (New York: John Lane, 1912); Kevin Mumford, *Interzones: Black/White Sex Districts in Chicago and New York City in the Early Twentieth Century* (New York: Columbia University Press, 1997), 23. For schemes, see *Taxicab Inspector Examination Instruction Manual.*

25. Box 34, Committee of Fourteen Records, New York Public Library Manuscript Collection. For discussion of the committee's intentions and history, see Lewis A. Ehrenberg, *Steppin' Out: New York Nightlife and the Transformation of American Culture, 1890–1930* (Westport, CT: Greenwood Press, 1981), 62–64.

26. Box 34, Committee of Fourteen Records.

27. For borrowed cab see Captain Cornelius W. Willemse, *Behind the Green Lights* (Garden City, NJ: Garden City Publishing, 1931), 100–101.

28. Nancy Groce, *New York: Songs of the City* (New York: Watson-Guptill Publications, 1999), 123; Willemse, *Behind the Green Lights,* 83.

29. E. S. Clowse, "Street Accidents—New York City," *Publications of the American Statistical Association* 13 (1913): 449–56.

30. Steven J. Ross, *Working-Class Hollywood: Silent Film and the Shaping of Class in America* (Princeton: Princeton University Press, 1998), 43–45.

31. *The American Film Institute Catalog of Motion Pictures Produced in the United States: Feature Films, 1911–1920* (Berkeley: University of California Press, 1971), 29, 4, 5, 29, 102, 161, 183, 215, 240, 304, 362, 442, 505, 645, 730, 880.

32. *American Film Institute Catalog, 1911–1920,* 41, 132.

2. Hack Men in the Jazz Age, 1920–1930

1. *Cab News,* May 1922.

2. Dave Hazard, *Hacking New York* (New York: Scribner's, 1929), 127–28; Dave Betts, *I'm Lucky at That by Dave Betts, the Taxi Philosopher* (Garden City, NY: Doubleday, Doran, 1930); *Taxi Weekly,* 15 October 1928.

3. Hazard, *Hacking New York,* 24–25, 50–51, 211.

4. Hazard, *Hacking New York,* 54, 137–38; Betts, *I'm Lucky at That,* 112.

5. Hazard, *Hacking New York,* 108–11.

6. *Taxi Weekly,* 9 July 1928.

7. Hazard, *Hacking New York,* 24, 31–33, 112–14, 149–58.

8. Betts, *I'm Lucky at That,* 249.

9. Morris Markey, *Manhattan Reporter* (New York: Dodge, 1935), 266–74.

10. *New York Times,* 27 February–19 April 1919; 22, 24 February 1920; 20 September–4 October 1921; 1 April 1922; *New York Herald,* 27, 28 February 1919.

11. Charles Vidich, *The New York Cab Driver and His Fare* (Cambridge, MA: Schenckman Publishing, 1976), 81–82. For attitudes about tipping in the 1920s, see Dorothy C. Cobble, *Dishing it Out: Waitresses and Their Unions in the Twentieth Century* (Urbana: University of Illinois Press, 1991), 41–42.

12. *New York Times,* 4–25 February 1923; Edward G. Rogoff, "Theories of Economic Regulation Tested on the Case of the New York Taxicab Industry" (Ph.D. diss., Columbia University, 1980), 68.

13. Rogoff, "Theories of Economic Regulation," 65–69; Chanoch Shreiber, "The Effect of Regulation on the Taxicab Industry" (Ph.D. diss., Columbia University, 1973), 51–55.

14. Rogoff, "Theories of Economic Regulation," 68. *New York Times,* 12 October 1921; 2 February 1923, *New York American,* 4 February 1923.

15. *New York Times,* 22 February 1925; Stanley Walker, *The Night Club Era* (New York: Frederick A. Stokes, 1933), 246–48; Markey, *Manhattan Reporter,* 55–58; Louise Berliner, *Texas Guinan: Queen of the Night Clubs* (Austin: University of Texas

Press, 1993), 96–105; Caroline F. Ware, *Greenwich Village, 1920–1930: A Comment on American Civilization in the Postwar Years* (Boston: Houghton Mifflin, 1935), 275, 357–59; Stephen Graham, *New York Nights* (New York: George H. Doran, 1927), 90–94.

16. For law and debate over police control, see *New York Times*, 8, 9, 12, 14, 17, 18, 24 April 1925. For insurance decision, see *New York Times*, 1 May 1927.

17. *New York Herald Tribune*, 14, 15, 16 December 1926; *New York Post*, 15 December 1926; *Taxi Weekly*, 12 December 1926.

18. *Taxi Weekly*, 2, 9, 30 July 1928; *Time*, 7 July 1930.

19. *New York Times*, 20, 26 January, 23 September 1927; *Taxi Weekly*, 6 August 1930.

20. For uniform and fitness, see *New York Times*, 4, 14 June 1925. For Cody, see *New York Times*, 8, 11 May 1924. For Kuebler, see 19 August 1926. For awards, see 28 July 1926; 24 November 1926; 15 January, 27 March 1927. For attacks on women, see 19, 24 December 1926; 19 October 1927. For arrests for meter tampering, see 24 January, 16 February 1927.

21. For meter violators, see *New York Times*, 24 January, 6 February 1927. For attacks, see 22 May 1921.

22. "Stories, Poems, Jargon of the Hack Drivers," *American Memory Histories: Manuscripts from the Federal Writers' Project* (Washington, DC: Smithsonian Institution), 3. Betts, *I'm Lucky at That*, 122.

23. Box 34, Committee of Fourteen Records, New York Public Library Manuscripts Collection; *The American Film Institute Catalog of Motion Pictures Produced in the United States* (New York: R. R. Bowker, 1971), 1814; Roaring Twenties Press book, Billy Rose Theater Collection, New York Public Library for the Performing Arts; Graham, *New York Nights*, 34.

24. Boxes 34, 35, Committee of Fourteen Records; Frederick Lewis Allen, *Only Yesterday* (New York: Harper and Bros., 1931), 221–53; Jimmy Durante with Jack Kofoed, *Night Clubs* (New York: Knopf, 1931); Captain Cornelius W. Willemse, *Behind the Green Lights* (Garden City, NY: Garden City Publishing, 1931), 78, 91; Graham, *New York Nights*, 242–55.

25. Box 35, Committee of Fourteen Records.

26. "Stories, Poems, Jargon of the Hack Drivers," 9; Graham, *New York Nights*, 66.

27. "Hey Taxi," in *Short Stories of Conrad Aiken* (New York: Duell, Sloan, and Pearce, 1934), 107–16.

28. Paul G. Cressey, *The Taxi-dance Hall* (Chicago: University of Chicago Press, 1932), 5, 14, 142, 178, 182–85; Irving Lewis Allen, *The City in Slang: New York Life and Popular Speech* (New York: Oxford University Press, 1993), 172; Markey, *Manhattan Reporter*, 17–24.

29. Blair Niles, *Strange Brother* (New York: Liveright, 1931), 37, 63, 65; *The American Film Institute Catalog of Motion Pictures Produced in the United States: Feature Films, 1921–1930* (Berkeley: University of California Press, 1997), 786.

30. Cressey, *Taxi-Dance Halls*, 31, 146–77.

31. Kevin J. Mumford, *Interzones: Black/White Sex Districts in Chicago and New York City in the Early Twentieth Century* (New York: Columbia University Press, 1997), 23 for go-betweens and passim for other comments.

32. Hazard, *Hacking New York*, 18–21, 102; F. Scott Fitzgerald, *The Great Gatsby* (New York: Scribner's, 1925), 31; Graham, *New York Nights*, 53.

33. Niles, *Strange Brother*, 182–83; Graham, *New York Nights*, 53.

34. Nancy Groce, *New York: Songs of the City* (New York: Watson-Guptill Publications, 1999), 123.

35. Fitzgerald, *Great Gatsby*, 62.

36. Ruth Prigozy, "The Unpublished Stories: Fitzgerald in his Final Stage," *Twentieth Century Literature* 30 (1974): 69–90.

37. George Agnew Chamberlain, *Taxi: An Adventure Romance* (Indianapolis: Bobbs-Merrill, 1920). For the movie version, see *The American Film Institute Catalog of Motion Pictures Produced in the United States: Feature Films, 1911–1920* (Berkeley: University of California Press, 1989), 911.

38. James Sanders, *Celluloid Skyline: New York and the Movies* (New York: Knopf, 2001), 40–41; *American Film Institute Catalog, 1911–1920, 787.

39. *Taxi Weekly*, 9, 16, 23 July, 6, 13, 20 August 1928.

40. *Taxi Weekly*, 30 July, 6 August, 3 September, 22 October 1928.

41. Shreiber, "Effect of Regulation," 62–67, 71, 73.

42. Betts, *I'm Lucky at That*, 249–51.

3. The Search for Order during the Depression, 1930–1940

1. See appendix, table 5, for numbers. See also Frederick M. Binder and David M. Reimers, *All the Nations under Heaven: An Ethnic and Racial History of New York City* (New York: Columbia University Press, 1995), 177–80.

2. Morris Markey, *Manhattan Reporter* (New York: Dodge, 1935), 222–24; Meyer Berger, *The Eight Million* (New York: Simon & Schuster, 1942), 167.

3. Edward G. Rogoff, "Theories of Economic Regulation Tested on the Case of the New York City Taxicab Industry" (Ph.D. diss., Columbia University, 1980), 81–83; Chanoch Shreiber, "The Effect of Regulation on the Taxicab Industry" (Ph.D. diss., Columbia University, 1973), 75–79. For Whalen plan, see *New York Times*, 5 May, 13 June 1920.

4. Hawley S. Simpson, "The Taxicab Industry Faces a Crisis," *American Electrical Railway Association*, May 1932.

5. *Minutes of the Meeting of the Mayor's Commission on Taxicabs*, 5–7, 30 September 1930 (New York: City of New York, 1930).

6. "A Nationwide Survey of Taxicab Regulation," *American Electric Railway Association Bulletin* 389, 34–35.

7. *Report of the Mayor's Commission on Taxicabs,* September 23, 1930 (New York: City of New York, 1930), 26–27; Shreiber, "Effect of Regulation," 72–79.

8. For quotes and testimony, see *Report of the Mayor's Commission on Taxicabs,* 41.

9. William B. Northrup and John B. Northrup, *The Insolence of Office: The Story of the Seabury Investigation* (New York: Putnam, 1932), 264–68; Herbert Mitgang, *Once Upon A Time in New York: Jimmy Walker, Franklin Roosevelt, and the Last Great Battle of the Jazz Age* (New York: Free Press, 2000), 169; Rogoff, "Theories of Economic Regulation," 84; Arthur Mann, *LaGuardia Comes to Power 1933* (Philadelphia: J. P. Lippincott, 1965), 38–40; Raymond S. Tompkins, "The Taxi Runs Amok," *American Mercury* (1932): 392–94.

10. "Police Department Interviews with Cab Drivers, 1932," Papers of Mayor Fiorello LaGuardia, 1933–1945, Municipal Archives of the City of New York.

11. "Police Department Interviews with Cab Drivers, 1932"; Shreiber, "Effects of Regulation," 92–95; Ronald H. Bayor, *Neighbors in Conflict: The Irish, Germans, Jews and Italians of New York City,* 2nd ed. (Urbana: University of Illinois Press, 1988), 10–13. For horse hiring, see "Stories, Poems, Jargon of the Hack Drivers," *American Memory Histories: Manuscripts from the Federal Writers' Project* (Washington, DC: Smithsonian Institution), 9; *Directory for Taximen and Flat Rates for Out of Town, 1930–1931* (New York, 1930).

12. *New York Times,* 18 February 1934. On Parmelee, see *Taxicab Industry Monthly,* September 1953; Gorman Gilbert and Robert F. Samuels, *The Taxicab: An Urban Transportation Survivor* (Chapel Hill: University of North Carolina Press, 1982), 49–60.

13. Mann, *LaGuardia Comes to Power,* 110–15; Bayor, *Neighbors in Conflict,* 130–33; Thomas Kessner, *Fiorello H. LaGuardia, and the Making of Modern New York* (New York: McGraw Hill, 1989), 250.

14. For nickel tax and subsequent developments, see Rogoff, "Theories of Economic Regulation," 85–86.

15. "Transport Workers Union Scrapbook, 1933–1949," Transport Workers Unions Manuscripts, Tamiment Library, New York University; *Taxi,* 9 January 1933; Rank and File Coalition Tapes NS 13, Tamiment Library, New York University.

16. *Taxi Age,* 29 December 1933. For appeals and instructions about the survey, see LaGuardia Papers, Reel 117, and Reel 230: images 1939–40. The Fusion Party reminded cabdrivers of Tammany support for the nickel tax the following year in an election for city comptroller. See New-York Historical Society Broadside Collection, #50.

17. "Police Department Interviews with Cab Drivers, 1933," and Lester Stone to LaGuardia, 17 January 1934, both in LaGuardia Papers; Shreiber, "Effect of Regulation," 97.

18. *New York Post,* 3 February 1934.

19. *New York Post,* 2 February 1934.

20. Jeff Kisseloff, *You Must Remember This: An Oral History of Manhattan from the 1890s to World War II* (San Diego: Harcourt Brace Jovanovitch, 1989), 466; *Daily Worker* (New York), 3 February 1934.

21. Taxi Strike Folder, 1934, LaGuardia Papers.

22. United Auto League, Inc. of Drivers and Owners to Mayor Fiorello LaGuardia, 4 February 1934; and Columbus Circle Taxi Group to Mayor Fiorello LaGuardia, 6 February 1934, both in LaGuardia Papers, Reel 230. See also Matthew J. Jones, Driver 22921, to Mayor LaGuardia, 6 February 1934, in LaGuardia Papers, Reel 230; *Taxi Age* (New York), 5, 12 February, 5, 13 March 1934; *New York Post*, 2, 3 February 1934.

23. *New York Times*, 3, 4 February 1934; *New York Post*, 2 February 1934; Kessner, *Fiorello H. LaGuardia*, 353–54.

24. *New York Times*, 5, 6, 7, 8 February 1934; *New York Post*, 7 February 1934; LaGuardia Papers, microfilm roll 240; and *Taxi Age*, 12 February 1934 for full list of actions against strikebreakers. For Harlem garage, see Juliet E. K. Walker, *The History of Black Business in America: Capitalism, Race, Entrepreneurship* (New York: MacMillan Library Reference), 196.

25. Joshua B. Freeman, *In Transit: The Transport Workers' Union in New York City, 1933–1966* (New York: Oxford University Press), 43–73.

26. *Daily Worker*, 5, 6, 7, 8 February 1934.

27. *The Militant* (New York), 2 February, 7 April 1934, as quoted in Abraham Nash, "The Making of the New York City Taxi Drivers' Union" (M.A. thesis: Columbia University, 1967), 132–34.

28. *New York Times*, 12, 13, 14 February 1934.

29. *New York Times*, 13, 15, 17, 18 February, 5, 7, 8 March 1934; *Taxi Age*, 5, 12 February 1934; *Daily Worker*, 8 February 1934.

30. *New York Times*, 10, 16 March 1934; *New York Daily News*, 23 March 1934; *Taxi Age*, 13, 22 March 1934; *Daily Worker*, 12, 13 March 1934.

31. *New York Times*, March 19–26, 1934; Shreiber, "Effect of Regulation," 96–101.

32. Joseph North, "Taxi Strike," *New Masses*, 3 April 1934, as quoted in Vijay Prasad, *The Karma of Brown Folk* (Minneapolis: University of Minnesota Press, 200), 196–97; *Daily Worker*, 15–17 March 1934; *New York Daily News*, 27 March 1934.

33. *New York Daily News*, 27 March 1934; *Daily Worker*, 19–24 March 1934; LaGuardia Papers, Reel 0117: images 0203–0216; Transport Workers Union Files, Box 47, Tamiment Institute, Ben Josephson Library, New York University. Accusations of union racketeers extorting protection money from the independent drivers persisted into the late 1930s. See *New York Post*, 5 April 1938.

34. For lists of revocations and suspensions, see LaGuardia Papers, Reel 230.

35. *New York Times*, 28, 30, 31 March, 1, 11, 12 April, 10, 11 July, 4 August 1934; *New York Herald Tribune*, 18, 21, 22, 23 March 1934; *Taxi Age*, 16 April 1934; *New*

York Daily News, 24 March 1934; *New York Post,* 24 March 1934; *Daily Worker,* 30 March, 2 April 1934; Freeman, *In Transit,* 51.

36. *New York Times,* 8 March, 13 April, 14, 16 May, 18, 27 July, 7 November 1935.

37. Charles Vidich, *The New York Cab Driver and IIis Fare* (Cambridge, MA: Schenkman Publishing, 1976), 83–87.

38. Record of Joseph Smith, 2 April 1934, and Samuel Spiro, 16 April 1934, to Mayor LaGuardia, both in LaGuardia Papers and *Taxi Age,* 23 April 1934.

39. Albert Halper, "Scab," *American Mercury* (June 1934).

40. *American Film Institute Catalog of Motion Pictures Produced in the United States: Feature Films, 1931–1940* (Berkeley: University of California Press, 1993), 2132.

41. *Six Plays of Clifford Odets* (New York: Modern Library, 1962), 5–13. For reviews of Odets's play, see *New York Herald,* 27 March 1935; *New York Daily News,* 27 March 1935; *New York Post,* 27 March 1935. See also William B. Scott and Peter M. Rutkoff, *New York Modern: The Arts and the City* (Baltimore: Johns Hopkins University Press, 1999), 210–15; Michael Denning, *The Cultural Front: the Laboring of American Culture in the Twentieth Century* (New York: Verso, 1966), 365–66; Jane Livingston, *The New York School: Photographs, 1936–1963* (New York: Tabor & Chang, 1993).

42. On the re-release of *Taxi,* see *New York Evening Standard,* 21 May 1936; *New York Daily Mirror,* 22 May 1936. On Cagney, see Robert Sklar, *City Boys: Cagney, Bogart, Garfield* (Princeton: Princeton University Press, 1992), 13, 37; *Taxi* Scrapbook, Billy Rose Theater Collection, New York Public Library for the Performing Arts.

43. Sklar, *City Boys,* 37, 49–50; *Taxi* Scrapbook; John Bodnar, *Blue-Collar Hollywood: Liberalism, Democracy, and Working People in American Film* (Baltimore: Johns Hopkins University Press, 2003).

44. *American Film Institute Catalog, 1931–1940,* 1:154–55.

45. Ibid., 2:239.

46. Ibid., 2:916, 2173.

47. Ibid., 2:2042–43. See also 1:361.

48. *American Film Institute Catalog of Motion Pictures Produced in the United States: Within Our Gates: Ethnicity in American Films, 1911–1960* (Berkeley: University of California Press, 1997), 971.

49. *American Film Institute Catalog, 1931–1940,* 146, 1379.

50. Ibid., 444–45, 1374, 1660; Bodnar, *Blue-Collar Hollywood,* 15.

51. "Stories, Poems, Jargon of the Hack Drivers," 9–10; *New York Times,* 1 November 1936.

52. *New York Times,* 22 November 1936.

53. "Stories, Poems, Jargon of the Hack Drivers," 2.

54. Rogoff, "Theories of Economic Regulation," 89–99; Rogoff, "Regulation of the New York City Taxicab Industry," *City Almanac* 15 (1980): 4; Shreiber, "Effect of Regulation," 110–11; LaGuardia Papers, Reel 230; *Brotherhood Register* (New York),

7 March 1937; *Taxi Age*, 15, 22 February, 5 March, 17 May 1937; *New York Times*, 17 February, 10, 31 March, 15 April, 11 May 1937. For licenses, see Graham Russell Hodges, *New York City Cartman, 1667–1850* (New York: New York University Press, 1986); Howard B. Rock, *Artisans of the New Republic: The Tradesmen of New York City in the Age of Jefferson* (New York: New York University Press, 1979).

55. Rogoff, "Regulation of the New York City Taxicab Industry," 5.

56. For developments in the late 1930s, see Freeman, *In Transit*; TWU File, Box 47, Tamiment Library; LaGuardia Papers, Reel 230:2239; *New York Times*, 12, 13, 24 June, 2, 16, 30 July, 11, 31 August, 1, 24 September, 10, 14, 15, 16, 18, 26 October, 16, 17, 18, 20, 22, 24, 25, 29 December 1937, 5 , 6, 7, 12, 13 March, 19 April, 6 May 1938; *New York Herald Tribune*, 14, 17 October 1937; *New York Post*, 15–24 December 1937; *New York Mirror*, 20–25 December 1937; *New York Sun*, 24–26 December 1937; Vidich, *New York Cab Driver and His Fare*, 86–90; *Taxi Age*, 14, 28 June, 30 August, 20 September 1937; *Brotherhood Register*, 7 September 1937; "To the New York Public," ca. 1938, New-York Historical Society Broadside Collection #36.

57. TWU File, Box 47.

58. *New York Post*, 5 April 1938; TWU File, Box 47.

59. Freeman, *In Transit*, 44–54, 132. For negotiating team, see *New York Times*, 9 December 1937; TWU File, Box 47; LaGuardia Papers, Reel 230: images 2301, 2216, 2227. Connolly's name appears frequently in accounts of negotiations in 1937. For comments on LaGuardia, see Kessner, *Fiorello LaGuardia*, 386- 88. Freeman argues that LaGuardia's later hostility towards the TWU was usually caused by his animosity toward Mike Quill. See *In Transit*, 217–18.

60. Freeman, *In Transit*, 113–25.

61. TWU Archives, Box 47; "Stories, Poems, Jargon of the Hack Drivers," 4; Vidich, *New York Cab Driver and His Fare*, 90.

62. Bradford F. Kimball, "Trends of Immigration to New York State, 1920–1935," *Bulletin of the University of the State of New York* 1134 (Albany: State University of New York, 1938), 32.

63. Faber's life is chronicled in "Manhattan Hackie," *Fortune*, July 1939. For Mrs. Roosevelt, see *New York Times*, 5 October 1996.

64. TWU Files, Box 47; *New York Times*, 4, 5, 6, 29 January, 6 April 1939. For arrests and convictions, see 7, 8 February, 1 July 1939. See also *PM Magazine*, 14 April 1939; *New York Herald Tribune*, 2 June 1939.

65. Shirley Quill, ed., *Mike Quill—Himself, A Memoir* (Greenwich, CT: Devin-Adair, 1985), 111–13.

4. Prosperity during Wartime, 1940–1950

1. Edward G. Rogoff, "Theories of Economic Regulation Tested on the Case of the New York City Taxicab Industry" (Ph.D. diss., Columbia University, 1980), 124–

25; Chanoch Shrieber, "The Effect of Regulation on the Taxicab Industry" (Ph.D. diss., Columbia University, 1973), 105–7; *Taxi Age* (New York), 11, 23 January, 7 June, 30 August 1943, 4 December 1944; Medallion Issues, 1937–1941, Municipal Archives of the City of New York.

2. *Business Week,* 10 February 1940.

3. *New York Times,* 25–29 April 1940; TWU File, Box 47.

4. For strike, see *New York Times,* 6, 12, 26, 28, 29 May 1940; *New York Herald Tribune,* 28 May 1940; *New York Daily News,* 28 May 1940. For problems at the World's Fair, see Kenneth T. Jackson, ed., *Encyclopedia of New York City* (New Haven: Yale University Press, 1995), 1275–76.

5. *Taxi Bulletin,* April-May 1944; 28 June 1944. *Taxi Age,* 11 November 1944; Shirley Quill, ed., *Mike Quill—Himself, A Memoir* (Greenwich, CT: Devin-Adair Publications, 1985), 112.

6. *New York Times,* 11 April, 3 July 1943.

7. Shreiber, "Effect of Regulation," 115–16; *New York Times,* 20 February 1949.

8. Gorman Gilbert and Robert E. Samuels, *The Taxicab: An Urban Transporation Survivor* (Chapel Hill: University of North Carolina Press, 1982), 76–78; *New York Times,* 21 March, 30 August, 10 September 1942; *New York Herald Tribune,* 5 September 1941. For difficulties surrounding ride sharing in snowstorm, see *New York Times,* 17 January 1945.

9. Ruth Sulzberger, "Adventures of a Hackie (Female)," *New York Times,* 8 July, 28 September, 28 November 1941; 21 February 1942.

10. Edith Martz Clark, M.D., *Confessions of a Girl Cab Driver* (New York: Vantage Press, 1954), 18–19, 80–81, 128–29, 137–41, 171, 194–95. For unwanted requests for dates, see 20, 28–29, 40, 42, 98, 104, 111.

11. *Taxi Weekly,* 21 August 1944. For traffic lights, see 29 April 1946.

12. *Taxi Age,* 23, 28 February 1944.

13. *American Film Institute, Catalog of Motion Pictures Produced in the United States, Feature Films, 1941–1950* (Berkeley: University of California Press, 1999), 428–29, 1034, 1137. See also 1208 and 2164.

14. Ibid., 325, 1513, 2445; *Broadway Orchids; McGuerins of Brooklyn;* and *Taxi, Mister!* Scrapbook Collections, Billy Rose Theatre Collection, New York Public Library for the Performing Arts.

15. John Bodnar, *Blue-Collar Hollywood: Liberalism, Democracy, and Working People in American Film* (Baltimore: Johns Hopkins University Press, 2003), 79–80.

16. *Taxi Weekly,* 3 September, 8 October 1945; *Taxi, Mister!* Scrapbook, Billy Rose Theatre Collection.

17. George Lipsitz, *Rainbow at Midnight: Labor and Culture in the 1940s* (Urbana: University of Illinois Press, 1994), 282–83.

18. *American Film Institute Catalog, 1941–1950,* 1278.

19. *New York Times,* 8 January 1946.

20. *New York Times,* 14 May, 10 June 1945.

21. *New York Times,* 24 February 1947.

22. Rogoff, "Theories of Economic Regulation," 128–29. For end of wartime profits, see *New York Times,* 30 July, 19 August 1946. For requests, see 25 February 1947; 14 August 1948. For scholarship, see 13 May 1948.

23. Rogoff, "Theories of Economic Regulation," 132–34; Shreiber, "Effect of Regulation," 115–19.

24. *New York Times,* 26 February 1947; 6 March 1948.

25. E. B. White, *Here is New York* (New York: Harper, 1949), 48–50; Jan Morris, *Manhattan '45* (New York: Oxford University Press, 1987), 24–25.

26. *New York Times,* 20 March 1949.

27. Joshua B. Freeman, *Working-Class New York: Life and Labor Since World War II* (New York: New Press, 2000), 40–43.

28. *Ibid.,* 43.

29. *New York Post,* 1 April 1949.

30. *New York Times,* 1, 3 April 1949; *New York Post,* 1 April 1949.

31. See the perceptive article by Joseph Glazer and John Gould, "Why the New York Taxi Strike Failed," *Labor and Nation,* July 1949, 33–34. See also *New York Times,* 6, 7, 8 April 1949.

32. *New York Post,* 3–10 April 1949; *New York Times,* 10 April 1949.

33. Rogoff, "Theories of Economic Regulation," 193–95; Shreiber, "Effect of Regulation," 117–20; *New York Times,* 8 July 1948; 22, 26, 29, 30 April, 1–9 March 1949; *New York Post,* 13 April 1949; Freeman, *Working-Class New York,* 47–48.

34. *New York Times,* 20 March 1949. For the success of other transit workers in this period, see Joshua B. Freeman, *In Transit: The Transport Workers Union in New York City, 1933–1966* (New York: Oxford University Press, 1989).

35. Bud Johns and Judith S. Clancy, eds., *Bastard in the Ragged Suit: Writings of, with Drawings by, Herman Spector* (San Francisco: Synergistic Press, 1977). For prestige, see Abraham Nash, "The Making of the New York City Taxi Driver's Union" (M.A. thesis, Columbia University, 1967), 94–95.

36. *Taxi Weekly,* 28 September 1949.

37. *Taxi Weekly,* 29 March 1950.

38. *New York Times,* 3 February 1948; Eliot G. Fay, "Saint Exupery in New York," *Modern Language Notes* 61 (1946), 458–62.

39. On Thenstead, see *Taxi Weekly,* 11 December 1947; *Taxicab Industry Monthly,* December 1953, September 1964. For other successful African American cab operators around the nation, see Juliet E. K. Walker, *The History of Black Business in America: Capitalism, Race, Entrepreneurship* (New York: Macmillan Library Reference, 1998), 252–54.

40. Julian Mayfield, *The Hit* (New York: Vanguard Press, 1947), 87–88.

41. On "Singing Cabbie," see *Taxi Weekly,* 16 November 1949. For Faust, see 8 April 1945; on LOMTO dance, see 13 April 1943. For scholarship, see 21 September 1949; on vacation, see 30 November 1949. On film, see *American Film Institute*

Catalog: Within Our Gates: Ethnicity in American Feature Films, 1911–1960 (Berkeley: University of California Press, 1997), 387.

42. Morris, *Manhattan '45*, 189–91.

43. Freeman, *Working-Class New York*, 36; Morris, *Manhattan '45*, 28–29; *This Place on Third Avenue: The New York Stories of John McNulty* (Washington, D.C.: Counterpoint, 2001), 147.

44. McNulty, *This Place on Third Avenue*, 148–50.

45. Damon Runyon, *In Our Time* (New York: Creative Age Press, 1946), 13–15; Daniel R. Schwarz, *Broadway Boogie Woogie: Damon Runyon and the Making of New York City Culture* (New York: Palgrave, 2003), 96.

46. *Taxi Weekly*, 13 December 1950 (Carroll); 21 March 1951 (D'Angiolitto); 6 September 1950; 17 October 1951 (Kreloff) (Festa); 21 May 1951 (Kronowitz); 30 May 1951 (Caruso).

47. *New York Times*, 1 April 1948.

48. *New York Daily Mirror*, 25 August 1950, quoted in *Taxi Weekly*, 8 September 1950.

5. The Creation of the Classic Cabby, 1950–1960

1. Jan Morris, *Manhattan '45* (New York: Oxford University Press, 1987), 166, 189–91.

2. On working-class accomplishments in this period, see Joshua B. Freeman, *Working-Class New York: Life and Labor Since World War II* (New York: Free Press, 2000), 99–167; Frederick M. Binder and David M. Reimers, *All the Nations Under Heaven: An Ethnic and Racial History of New York City* (New York: Columbia University Press, 1995), 202–3.

3. Charles Vidich, *The Cab Driver and His Fare* (Cambridge, MA: Shenkman Publishing, 1976), 173–75; Edward G. Rogoff, "Theories of Economic Regulation Tested on the Case of the New York City Taxicab Industry" (Ph.D. diss., Columbia University, 1980), 195–97; Chanoch Shreiber, "Effect of Regulation on the Taxicab Industry" (Ph.D. diss., Columbia University, 1973), 127; *Taxi Weekly*, 11, 18 February, 27 May, 16 June 1953; 11, 18, 25 January 1956; *New York Times*, 3, 11, 14, 18, 19, 20, 26 March 1956; *New York Herald Tribune*, 18, 19 June 1956; *New York Daily News*, 18, 19 January 1956.

4. Shirley Quill, ed., *Mike Quill—Himself, A Memoir* (Greenwich, CT: Devin-Adair Publications, 1985), 113–14.

5. "From the Driver's Seat: It's No Easy Life," *Business Week*, August 23, 1951.

6. *Taxicab Industry Monthly*, May 1958.

7. Discussion of movie is in John Bodnar, *Blue-Collar Hollywood: Liberalism, Democracy, and Working People in American Film* (Baltimore: Johns Hopkins University Press, 2003), 151–53.

8. James Maresca, *My Flag Is Down* (New York: E. P. Dutton, 1946), 56–59, 141–50; Maresca, *Mr. Taxicab* (New York: Bantam Books, 1958), 22–31.

9. Maresca, *My Flag Is Down*, 102.

10. Maresca, *Mr. Taxicab*, 61, 102–9.

11. Ibid., 19–20, 48–50, 58–59, 86–87.

12. *New York Times*, 4 December 1960. Adler later sold a play to the CBS serial *East Side/West Side*. See *New York Times*, 22 August 1963.

13. *Taxi Weekly*, 3 March, 26 May 1954. For Uswelk, see 6 August 1958, 11 March 1959. See also *Taxicab Industry Monthly*, May 1958, April 1959; *New York Times*, 30 July 1958.

14. Richard Yates, *Eleven Kinds of Loneliness* (New York: Vintage Books, 1989), 189–230; David Castronovo and Steven Goldleaf, *Richard Yates* (New York: Twayne, 1996), 28, 73–75; Blake Bailey, *A Tragic Honesty: the Life and Work of Richard Yates* (New York: Picador, 2004), 103–4.

15. J. D. Salinger, *The Catcher in the Rye* (Boston: Little, Brown, 1951), 81–82.

16. *Taxi Weekly*, 10 July 1961; *Taxicab Industry Monthly*, August 1961.

17. For development of tipping, see Dorothy C. Cobble, *Dishing It Out: Waitresses and Their Unions in the Twentieth Century* (Urbana: University of Illinois Press, 1991), 42; Kerry Segrave, *Tipping: An American Social History of Gratuities* (Jefferson: McFarland & Company, 1998), 88–89.

18. Maresca, *My Flag Is Down*, 104; Jean Sprain Wilson, *All about Tipping* (New York: MacFadden, 1965), 19, 73.

19. Seagrave, *Tipping*, 88.

20. Fred Davis, "The Cabdriver and His Fare: Facets of a Fleeting Relationship," *American Journal of Sociology* 65 (1959): 158–65; Leo P. Crespi, "The Implications of Tipping in America," *Public Opinion Quarterly* 11 (1947): 4, 24–35; Segrave, *Tipping*, 85–88.

21. Hy Gardner, *Champagne before Breakfast* (New York: Henry Holt, 1954), 194–95.

22. *Taxi Weekly*, 3 October 1961; *Taxicab Industry Monthly*, October, December 1961; February, March 1962; *Los Angeles Times*, 10, 15 April 1962; *Chicago Tribune*, 13 December 1964. For obituary see *New York Times*, 28 February 1968.

23. *Taxi Weekly*, 14, 28 January 1953 (reviews); *Taxicab Industry Monthly*, January 1953; Twentieth Century Fox Final Script for *Taxi*, in author's possession; *Taxi* Clipping File, Billy Rose Theater Collection, New York Public Library for the Performing Arts. For later commentary, see *Taxi Weekly*, 31 July 1957. For Golden, see *Taxi Weekly*, 25 November 1959. For Downs, see 14 August 1961. For Como, see *Taxicab Industry Monthly*, January 1958. For McGuire, see November, December 1958.

24. *Hy Gardner's Offbeat Guide to New York* (New York: Grosset and Dunlap, 1964), 41–43.

25. Gardner, *Offbeat Guide to New York,* 42; Hy Gardner, *So What Else is New* (Englewood Cliffs, NJ: Prentice-Hall, 1959), 18–20.

26. Gardner, *Champagne before Breakfast,* 126.

27. Wallace Markfield, *To an Early Grave* (New York: Simon & Schuster, 1964), 124–33.

28. Julian Mayfield, *The Hit* (New York: Vanguard, 1947), 91–93. For Amos, see Melvin Patrick Ely, *The Adventures of Amos 'N' Andy: A Social History of an American Phenomenon* (New York: Free Press, 1991).

29. *Taxi Weekly,* 24 November 1954. For Fishbein, see 5 February 1956. For filling in for sick husband, see *Taxicab Industry Monthly,* April 1958.

30. George Lipsitz, "The Meaning of Memory: Family, Class, and Ethnicity in Early Network Programs," *Cultural Anthropology* 1 (1985): 355–87.

31. Mayfield, *The Hit,* 161; *Taxi Weekly,* 22 July, 5, 12 August 1953.

32. *New York Times,* 23 June 1958, 18 February, 11 March, 25 June, 14 August, 31 October, and 31 December 1959; *Taxicab Industry Monthly,* February, March 1958, March-May 1959.

33. *New York Times,* 4 December 1960.

6. Unionization and Its Discontents, 1960–1980

1. Edward G. Rogoff, "Theories of Economic Regulation Tested on the Case of the New York City Taxicab Industry" (Ph.D. diss., Columbia University, 1980), 135–37; Chanoch Shreiber, "Effect of Regulation on the Taxicab Industry" (Ph.D. diss., Columbia University, 1973), 142–49; *Taxi Weekly,* 6 November 1961; 26 February, 23 April, 7 May 1962; *New York Times,* 17 September 1960; 3 September 1961; *Taxicab Industry Monthly,* July, November, December 1960.

2. *Taxi Industry Monthly,* August 1962; February, April, September, October 1963; *Reader's Digest,* February 1965.

3. *Taxi Industry Monthly,* December 1963.

4. Ibid., July 1960, July 1963.

5. Abraham Nash, "The Making of the New York City's Taxi Driver's Union" (M.A. thesis, Columbia University, 1967), 94–95, 108–12.

6. For discussion of Van Arsdale's career up to this point, see Gene Ruffini, *Harry Van Arsdale, Jr.: Labor's Champion* (Armonk, NY: M. E. Sharpe, 2003), chapters 1–11.

7. *Taxi Industry Monthly,* March 1965. On Van Arsdale and Wagner, see Joshua B. Freeman, *Working-Class New York: Life and Labor Since World War II* (New York: New Press, 2000), 103; Ruffini, *Harry Van Arsdale, Jr.,* 179. For interviews, see Nash, "The Making of the New York City Taxi Drivers' Union," 190–93.

8. John Ellis, "Victory after 33 Years," *Free Labour World* (1967).

9. Rogoff, "Theories of Economic Regulation," 198–200.

10. *New York Times,* 15 March, 14 August 1962; 24 February, 3 September 1963;

29 July, 15, 26 September, 1, 2, 20, 3 November 1964; *Taxicab Industry Monthly,* April 1965. For Central Labor Council see Freeman, *Working-Class New York,* 100.

11. Ruffini, *Harry Van Arsdale, Jr.,* 179–81.

12. Rogoff, "Theories of Economic Regulation," 152, 200–202. For strike, see *New York Times,* 24 March, 17, 28 May, 28–30 June, 1–5 July 1965; *New York Post,* 24, 25, 28 March, 19, 20 May, 25, 28, 29, 30 June 1965; *New York Daily News,* 25 March, 16 May 1965; *Taxicab Industry Monthly,* May, June, August, September, October, November 1965.

13. Mann quoted in Ruffini, *Harry Van Arsdale, Jr.,* 184–85.

14. *New York Times,* 5 January, 15, 24 May, 12 June, 22 November 1967.

15. *Taxi Drivers' Voice,* June 1968–March 1969.

16. Stern quoted in Ruffini, *Harry Van Arsdale, Jr.,* 187.

17. *New York Times,* 4 August 1969.

18. On other tensions between "hard hats" and students, see Freeman, *Working-Class New York,* 228–56.

19. *New York Times,* 12 February 1973.

20. Harry Chapin, *Taxi,* musical score (New York: Warner Bros. Publications, 1975).

21. *New York Times,* 17 December 1970.

22. *New York Times,* 3 November 1965.

23. For Cambridge, see *New York Post,* 26 December 1969; *New York Times,* 26 December 1969; 21 March 1973.

24. Willie Morris, *New York Days* (Boston: Little, Brown, 1993), 138–39.

25. Rogoff, "Theories of Economic Development," 164–68; Shreiber, "Effect of Regulation," 129–36. For an earlier case, see *New York Times,* 27 March 1961. On Booth, see *New York Times,* 5 March, 8 April 1966; *Taxicab Industry Monthly,* January 1965.

26. *New York Times,* 28 February, 9, 10 July 1968; Rogoff, "Theories of Economic Development," 170–71; Shreiber, "Effect of Regulation," 166–67.

27. *New York Times,* 27 August, 28, 30 September 1970. For reference to Williams, see *New York Times,* 20 January 1971; Charles Vidich, *The New York City Cab Driver and His Fare.* (Cambridge, MA: Shenkman Publishing, 1976), 161. For other murders, see *Taxi Drivers Voice,* 20 March, 6 June 1968; *Time,* 3 February 1967; 21 September 1970. Three unemployed men were arrested for the killing of a cabdriver; see *New York Post,* 15 June 1968. For further commentary by Gore, see *Taxi News,* 15 March 1977.

28. *New York Times,* 4, 6, 8, 21, 22 December 1970.

29. Shreiber, "Effect of Regulation," 185–89; *New York Times,* 21, 22 January, 20 February, 2–3 March 1971.

30. *New York Times,* 20 January 1971, 1 October, 13 November 1973.

31. Shreiber, "Effect of Regulation," 133.

32. *New York Times,* 18, 22 May, 16 July, 4 August, 9 September, 4 December 1972; 23 July 1976; Vidich, *New York City Cab Driver,* 101.

33. Shreiber, "Effect of Regulation," 131, 140, 145.

34. *Taxi Industry Monthly,* April 1963, March 1965.

35. Shreiber, "Effect of Regulation, 193, 204–5; Gorman Gilbert and Robert E. Samuels, *The Taxicab: An Urban Transportation Survivor* (Chapel Hill: University of North Carolina Press, 1982), 92.

36. *Time,* 8 April 1974.

37. *Time,* 21 June 1976.

38. Emilio Ambasz, *The Taxi Project: Realistic Solutions for Today* (New York: Museum of Modern Art, 1976). For Arthur Gore comment, see *New York Times,* 9 July 1975; for disinterest of the fleets, see 16 June 1976.

39. Ruffini, *Harry Van Arsdale, Jr.,* 189; *Hot Seat,* June 1972. For a recent review of the rank and file, see *Village Voice,* 15 February 2006.

40. Vidich, *New York City Cab Driver,* 110–16; *Taxi at the Crossroads* (New York: Rank and File Coalition, 1974), 3; Rank and File Coalition Audio Tapes, 1, 3, and 14, March 21, 1978, Tamiment Library.

41. John Gordon, "In the Hot Seat: The Story of the New York Taxi Rank and File Coalition," *Radical America* 17 (1983): 27–43.

42. *Taxi at the Crossroads,* 7–9, 23–28.

43. Rogoff, "Theories of Economic Regulation," 204–5; Shreiber, "Effect of Regulation," 156–57; *New York Times,* 18 April 1971; on opposition to Van Arsdale, see 14 October, 15 November 1971; on contract, see 28 December 1972.

44. *New York Times,* 7 July, 13 September 1974; see also 23 May, 24 November 1976. For Scher, see 9 August, 19 September 1976. For transit policeman, see 21 December 1976. For McCall, see 22 December 1976.

45. *New York Times,* 2 December 1979. For other stories, see 17 October 1977, 11 April 1979.

46. Bruce Schaller, *The New York City Taxicab Fact Book,* 3rd ed. (New York: Schaller Consulting, 2004), 25.

47. Rogoff, "Theories of Economic Regulation," 157–59; *Committee on Taxi Regulatory Issues, Preliminary Paper,* October 22, 1981 (New York: City of New York, 1981), 17–19, 25–26, 30; Schaller, *Taxicab Fact Book,* 25.

48. Gerri Hirshey, "Uneasy Riders: the Taxi Perplex," *New York Magazine* (May 1980).

49. Hirshey, "Uneasy Riders." On gold line, see *New York Times,* 3 February 1977; Tom Wolfe, *Bonfire of the Vanities* (New York: Farrar, Straus & Giroux, 1987). On irritation, see *New York Times,* 30 June 2002.

50. Morris, *New York Days,* 156.

51. *Al Held Taxi Cabs* (New York: Robert Miller Gallery, 1959).

52. Arthur G. Danto, Timothy Hyman, and Marco Livingstone, *Red Grooms,* (New York: Rizzoli, 2004), 8–9, 233–34.

53. Frank Lovece and Jules Franco, *Hailing* Taxi: *The Official Book of the Show* (New York: Prentice-Hall Press, 1988), 3, 194–98.

54. In Richard Elman's novelization, Betsy suggests that Travis call her sometime, leaving a reconciliation open. Richard Elman, *Taxi Driver* (New York: Bantam, 1976), 146.

55. John Bodnar, *Blue-Collar Hollywood: Liberalization, Democracy, and Working People in American Film* (Baltimore: Johns Hopkins University Press, 2003), 185–88; James Sanders, *Celluloid Skyline: New York and the Movies* (New York: Knopf, 2001), 136; Colin McArthur, "Chinese Boxes and Russian Dolls: Tracking the Elusive Cinematic City," in *The Cinematic City*, ed. David B. Clarke (London: Routledge Publishers, 1997), 31.

56. Elman, *Taxi Driver*, 20, 31.

57. Schrader, as quoted in Sanders, *Celluloid Skyline*, 395. For Canby review, see *New York Times*, 15 February 1976.

58. Schaller, *Taxicab Fact Book*, 18, 37.

7. The Lease Driver and Proletarian, 1980–2006

1. Edward G. Rogoff, "Theories of Economic Regulation Tested on the Case of the New York City Taxicab Industry" (Ph.D. diss., Columbia University, 1980), 206–7; *New York Times*, 15 February 1979.

2. Allen Russell Stevens, "A Study of Leasing" (Ph.D. diss., City University of New York, 1991), 20, 95–105; *New York Times*, 21, 22, 28 February, 6 August, 24 October, 14 December 1980; for tour bus, see 27 July 1989. On the union, see Bruce Schaller, *The New York City Taxicab Fact Book*, 3rd ed. (New York: Schaller Consulting, 2004), 27.

3. Stevens, "Study of Leasing," 50; *New York Times*, 6 March 1980.

4. Stevens, "Study of Leasing," 56–70; Christina Oxenberg, *Taxi* (London: Quartet Books, 1986), 7; Iva Pekarkova to author, 6 February 1993, in author's possession. On suit, see *New York Law Journal*, 21 April 1993.

5. Biju Mathew, *Taxi! Cabs and Capitalism in New York City* (New York: New Press, 2005), 64–68; *Committee on Taxi Regulatory Issue, Preliminary Paper*, October 22, 1981 (New York: City of New York, 1981), 35–38.

6. Schaller, *Taxicab Fact Book*, 25; "Taxi and Limousine Commission Files," Papers of Mayor Edward Koch, 1980–1992, Reel 220, New York Municipal Archives and Records Administration; *National Law Journal*, 24 January 2005.

7. *New York Times*, 7 April, 21 May, 6 August 1980. For attacks, see *New York Times*, 19, 22 October, 30 December 1981. On African Americans and loans, see *New York Times*, 8 January 1983; on schools for cabbies, see 28 September 1983; 8 April 1984. For clothing rules, see 18 June, 22 August 1987 and "Taxi and Limousine Commission Files," Koch Papers, Reel 220.

8. *New York Times*, 16 February 2006. For Checkers, see *New York Times*, 27 March 1997.

9. Schaller, *Taxicab Fact Book,* 28.

10. *New York Times,* 11, 17, 26 June, 14 November 2005.

11. For Koch plan, see *New York Times,* 16 January 1985. For medallion cost, see 16 December 1985. For Baker, see 12 October 1985. For blockades, see 18 November, 3 December 1986. For letter from Stoppelmann to Gilbert, see "Taxi and Limousine Commission Files," Koch Papers, Reel 220.

12. Schaller, *Taxicab Fact Book,* 28. On wheelchair accessible cabs, see *New York Times,* 26 August, 24 September, 10 October 2004.

13. *New York Times,* 28, 29 February, 2 March 1980.

14. *Committee on Taxi Regulatory Issues,* 47–51; *New York Times,* 13, 23 March, 23 October 1980; on strike see 17 March, 8 April 1983.

15. Jack Lusk, *Taxicab Fare Review: Fare Analysis and Recommendations, New York City Taxi and Limousine Commission,* 12 October 1989 (New York: City of New York, 1989).

16. *New York Times,* 19 February 1982; 4 April 1987; Schaller, *Taxicab Fact Book,* 26.

17. Iva Pekarkova, *Gimme the Money: The Big Apple as Seen by a Czech Taxi Driver* (London: Serpent's Tale, 2000), 89–93. See also Vladamir Lobas, *Taxi from Hell: Confessions of a Russian Hack* (New York: Soho Books, 1993), 96–100.

18. For blind woman, see *New York Times,* 7 March 1983. For actress, see 15 March 1983. For anger over cab unavailability, see 10 July, 7 August, 12 September 1984. For Xiao Qian, see R. David Arkush and Leo Ou-fan Lee, *Land without Ghosts: Chinese Impressions of America from the Mid-Nineteenth Century to the Present* (Berkeley: University of California Press, 1989), 283.

19. Colson Whitehead, *Colossus of New York* (New York: Doubleday, 2003), 63–64. Pekarkova, *Gimme the Money,* 47–48.

20. For typical passenger, see *New York Times,* 3, 8 March 1981.

21. Pat Hackett, ed., *The Andy Warhol Diaries* (New York: Warner Books, 1989).

22. Bernice Kanner, "Hack Work: Bernice Kanner Drives a Cab," *New York Magazine* (May 1988).

23. Oxenberg, *Taxi,* 16–17. For Eisenstein, see *New York Times,* 4 January 1983; 7 March 1984. For Levenson, see *Village Voice,* 7 April 1998.

24. *New York Times,* 3 August 1980.

25. Kanner, "Hack Work," 50; Gerri Hirshey, "Uneasy Riders: The Taxi Perplex," *New York Magazine* (May 1980).

26. For working in community, see Hanoch Teller, *"Hey, Taxi!" Tales Told in Taxis and Recounted by Cabbies* (New York: New York City Publishing Company, 1990), 277. For university, see Nik Cohn, *The Heart of the World* (New York: Knopf, 1992), 5. For Max and others, see Annelise Orleck, "The Soviet Jews," in *New Immigrants in New York,* ed. Nancy Foner (New York: Columbia University Press, 1987), 288–89.

27. Oxenberg, *Taxi,* 19.

28. Ashish Rajadhyaksha and Paul Willemen, *Encyclopedia of Indian Cinema* (New Delhi: Oxford University Press, 1994), 42, 316; Mathew, *Taxi!* 151–53.

29. *New York Times,* 22 January 1995; Fidel Del Valle, "Who's Driving New York?: A Profile of Taxi Driver Applicants," *Migration World* 23 (1995): 12–15; Diditi Mitra, "Rotating Lives: Indian Cabbies in New York City" (Ph.D. diss., Temple University, 2002), 79–91.

30. Mitra, "Rotating Lives," 75–77; Roger Waldinger, *Still the Promised City: African Americans and the New Immigrants in Postindustrial New York* (Cambridge: Harvard University Press, 1996), 141–53, 219–53.

31. Mitra, "Rotating Lives," 63–70, 92–99, 115–24; Mathew, *Taxi!* 26.

32. Mathew, *Taxi!* 21–26, 177.

33. Schaller, *The Changing Face of Taxi and Limousine Drivers* (New York: Schaller Consulting, 2004), 31–35.

34. Ibid., 25–30.

35. Pekarkova, "The Book of Iva" (unpublished); idem, *Truck Stop Rainbows* (New York: Farrar, Straus, and Giroux, 1992); idem, "Wheels of Fortune," *New York Times Sunday Magazine,* 16 January 1994; idem, *Gimme the Money;* Schaller, *Changing Face of Taxi and Limousine Drivers,* 29.

36. Kanner, "Hack Work," 47.

37. Ibid., 47.

38. Ibid., 49–51.

39. Lobas, *Taxi from Hell,* 98.

40. Oxenberg, *Taxi,* 26–27, 40–41, 45–46, 49.

41. Denise Levertov, "Poet Power," *Breathing the Water* (New York: New Directions, 1987), 6.

42. Oxenberg, *Taxi,* 72, 78, 81.

43. David Bradford, *Drive-By Shootings: Photographs by a New York Taxi Driver* (Kohn, Germany: Konneman, 2000). For "the Photographer," see Oxenberg, *Taxi,* 16–17.

44. Ryan Weideman, *In My Taxi: New York after Hours* (New York: Thunder's Mouth Press, 1991); *New York Times,* 13 December 2002. For Higgins, see *New York Magazine,* 11 January 1999.

45. Ambrose Clancy and Peter M. Donahoe, *The Night Line: A Memoir of Work* (New York: New Amsterdam Books, 1990).

46. For discussion of Allan and his self-published book, see *New York Times,* 20 April 2000.

47. David Owen, "Old Hack," *New Yorker Magazine,* 26 January 2004; *New York Times,* 15 November 1990; 6 January 1998. For feats with numbers, see *New York Times,* 29 May 2005.

48. Jim Pietsch, *The Cab Driver's Joke Book* (New York: Warner Books, 1986–1988) 2:56, 68, 122; *New York Times,* 9 December 1987; 8 July 2005.

49. Risa Mickenberg, *Taxi Driver Wisdom* (San Francisco: Chronicle Books, 1996).

50. *New York Times,* 2 April 1996; Pekarkova, *Gimme the Money,* 18–49.

51. *New York Times,* 11 August 1996. For *My Life's in Turnaround,* see 12 June 1994.

52. Tom Zaniello, *Working Stiffs, Union Maids, Reds and Rifraff: An Expanded Guide to Films about Labor* (Ithaca: ILR Press, 2000), 364–65, 386–87; *New York Daily News,* 19 August 2001.

53. Vijay Prasad, *The Karma of Brown Folk* (Minneapolis: University of Minnesota Press, 2000), 195–203; Mathew, *Taxi!* 11–35, 129–41; *American Lawyer,* June 2003; *Wall Street Journal,* 14, 15 May 1998; Milyoung Cho, "New York Cabbies Start an Organizing Drive," *Third Force* 1 (1993): 5. On female leadership, see Mitra, "Rotating Lives," 14–17. On Lazarus, see *Village Voice,* 15 February 2006.

54. Freeman, *Working-Class New York,* 327. For a good discussion of the mayor's contradictory rhetoric, see *New York Daily News,* 19 May 1998. For court decision, see *New York Times,* 26 June 1998. For fleet owners' complaints, see Mitra, "Rotating Lives," 55–58.

55. *New York Times,* 10 December 1987; 12 January 1988; 20 December 1993; 4, 5 December 1994; Cornel West, *Race Matters* (Boston: Beacon Press, 1993), xv; Holder quoted in Oxenberg, *Taxi,* 91; Jill Nelson, "I've Got Your Number," *Village Voice,* April 1983. For Marable, see *Journal of Blacks in Higher Education,* 21 (1998): 68.

56. *New York Times,* 7, 11 November, 6 December 1999.

57. Schaller, *Taxicab Fact Book,* 15, 19.

58. For Glover, see *New York Daily News,* 21 November 1999. For other quotes, see Mitra, "Rotating Lives," 57–59.

59. *New York Times,* 12, 13, 19 November 1999. For profile of Desai, see *New York Times,* 8 December 1999; *World Press Review,* May 2000.

60. *Newsday,* 19 November 1999.

61. *New York Times,* 13, 19 November 1999; Lobas, *Taxi from Hell,* 97–99.

62. *New York Times,* 25 January 2004.

63. Mathew, *Taxi!* 131–36.

64. Nancy Foner, *From Ellis Island to JFK* (New York: Columbia University Press, 2000), 157–60.

65. Diego Gambetta and Heather Hamill, *Streetwise: How Taxi Drivers Establish Their Customer's Trustworthiness* (New York: Russell Sage Foundation, 2005), 160–70; Ian Ayers, Frederick E. Vars, and Nasser Zakiriya, "To Insure Prejudice: Racial Disparities in Taxicab Tipping," *Yale Law Journal* 114 (May 2005): 1613–73; Glenn C. Lourie, *The Anatomy of Racial Inequality* (Cambridge: Harvard University Press, 2002), 30–31, 59.

66. Mathew, *Taxi!* 3–5, 153–55.

67. *New York Times,* 29 January 2004; Mathew, *Taxi!* 5–7.

Epilogue

1. See for example, the furor raised when a hack man dropped off a female passenger, then drove off with the back door open and the passenger's child on the backseat. *New York Times,* 17, 22 February 2006.

2. Biju Mathew, *Taxi! Cabs and Capitalism in New York City* (New York: New Press, 2005), 166–75.

3. Saskia Sassen, *The Global City: New York, London, Tokyo* (Princeton: Princeton University Press, 1991). For proposal, see *New York Times,* 9 August 2005. For lack of conversation see *New York Times,* 17 July 2003.

4. Bruce Schaller, *The New York City Taxicab Fact Book,* 3rd ed. (New York: Schaller Consulting, 2004), 1–2.

5. *New York Times,* 14 November 2005; 34 July 2006.

6. *Village Voice,* 31 May 2006.

Essay on Sources

Taxis and cabdrivers are as ubiquitous in print and visual materials as they are in the streets. Most important to the understanding of cabbies are their own words. While cabdriver memoirs are a genre unto themselves, I found their words in a variety of manuscript and magazine sources. In creating this book, I leaned most heavily first on two classics about the 1920s: Robert Hazard, *Hacking New York* (New York: Scribner's, 1929), and *I'm Lucky At That, by David Betts the Taxi Philosopher* (Garden City, NY: Doubleday, Doran, 1930). There are no cabbie memoirs from the 1930s, but for a fine magazine article by one, see Harry Farber, "Manhattan Hackie," *Fortune Magazine*, May 1939. Cabdriver voices recalling strikes and the Depression can be found in "Stories, Poems, and Jargon of the Hack Drivers," *American Memory Histories: Manuscripts from the Federal Writers' Project* (Washington, DC: Smithsonian Institution). A strong sense of the bitterness of hackwork in the 1930s may be found in Bud Johns and Judith S. Clancy, eds., *Bastard in the Ragged Suit: Writings of, with Drawings by, Herman Spector* (San Francisco: Synergistic Press, 1977). Compiled at a later date, this book includes Spector's excoriating essays on cabdriver characters and his evocative drawings. In the early 1940s, female cabdrivers told their stories. See Ruth Sulzberger, "Adventures of a Hackie (Female)," *New York Times Magazine*, November 1943, and Edith Martz Clark, M.D., *Confessions of a Girl Cab Driver* (New York: Vantage Press, 1954). Most important for understanding the wise-guy cabby of the 1950s are the two memoirs by James Maresca: *My Flag is Down* (New York: E.P. Dutton, 1946) and *Mr. Taxicab* (New York: Bantam Books, 1958). The Transport Workers of America archive at the Tamiment Library, New York University, is an important collection of materials about cabdriver organization from the 1930s to the 1970s and includes the Rank and File Coalition audiotapes of interviews with cabdrivers in the 1970s. Important for understanding hack men later in the century are Vladimir Lobas, *Taxi From Hell: Confessions of a Russian Hack* (New York: Soho Books, 1993); Hanoch Teller, *"Hey Taxi!" Tales Told in Taxis and Recounted by Cabbies* (New York: New York City Publishing Company, 1990); Andrei Frolov, *The Stories of a Taxi Driver* (New York: Vantage Press, 1994);

and Iva Pekarkova's novel about driving a cab in New York City, *Gimme the Money: The Big Apple as Seen by a Czech Taxi Driver* (London: Serpent's Tale Books, 2000).

Cabdrivers have become inveterate photographers as well as talkers. Among the best books of photography by hack men are Ryan Weideman, *In My Taxi: New York After Hours* (New York: Thunder's Mouth Press, 1991); Ambrose Clancy and Peter M. Donahoe, *The Night Line: A Memoir of Work* (New York: New Amsterdam Books, 1990); and David Bradford, *Drive-by Shootings: Photographs by a New York Taxi Driver* (Kohn, Germany: Konneman, 2000). Cabbies have recorded their humor as well. See Jim Pietsch, *The New York City Cab Driver's Joke Book,* 2 vols. (New York: Warner Books, 1986, 1988), and Pietsch, *The New York City Cab Driver's Book of Dirty Jokes* (New York: Warner Books, 2005). See also Risa Mickenberg, *Taxi Driver Wisdom* (San Francisco: Chronicle Books).

Along with sizable troves of articles about cabdrivers in such New York City daily newspapers as the *New York Times, New York Daily News, New York Post, New York Herald Tribune,* and *Wall Street Journal,* there are specialized imprints aimed at the hack men themselves. Microfilms of the indispensable *Taxi Weekly* (also formerly known as *Taxi News* and *Taxi Age*) and the *Taxicab Industry Monthly* are located at the New York Public Library Science and Technology Branch. Both were printed beginning in the 1920s. Found at the same place are union newspapers including the *Taxi Bulletin, Taxi Driver's Voice,* and the *Brotherhood Register.* The Transport Workers Union Collection at New York University has files of the radical *Hot Seat* from the 1970s.

The TWU files at NYU are not the only archives of cabdriver material. The mayoral papers of James J. Walker, Fiorello LaGuardia, and Edward Koch at the New York Records and Archives Commission in lower Manhattan have sizable holdings about cabdriver regulations and activities.

Academic study of cabs starts with Gorman Gilbert and Robert F. Samuels, *The Taxicab: An Urban Transportation Survivor* (Chapel Hill; University of North Carolina Press, 1982). There are excellent doctoral dissertations on taxi regulation in New York City, including Edward G. Rogoff, "Theories of Economic Regulation Tested on the Case of the New York City Taxicab Industry" (Ph.D. diss., Columbia University, 1980), which is partially summarized in his "Regulation of the New York City Taxicab Industry," *City Almanac* 15:3 (August 1980). Other valuable dissertations about regulation include Chanoch Shreiber, "The Effect of Regulations on the Taxicab Industry" (Ph.D. diss., Columbia University, 1973) and Allen Russell Stevens, "Taxi Driving: A Study of Leasing in New York City" (Ph.D. diss., City University of New York, 1991). A fine portrait of mid-twentieth-century cabbies and union organization can be found in Abraham Nash, "The Making of the New York City Taxi Driver's Union" (M.A. thesis, Columbia University, 1967). A good historical review of the early evolution of the taxi industry is Joshua Mark Lupkin, "Constructing the 'Poor Man's Automobile': Public Space and the Response to the Taxicab in New York and Chicago" (Ph.D. diss., Columbia University, 2001). On more recent cabbies, see Diditi Mitra, "Rotating Lives: Indian Cabbies in New York City" (Ph.D. diss., Temple University, 2002). The invaluable studies of Bruce Schaller are compiled in his essential *New York City Taxicab Fact Book,* 3rd ed. (New York: Schaller Consulting, 2004). Finally, anyone interested in contemporary cabdrivers and the brave efforts of the New York Taxi Workers Alliance to improve their lot must read Biju Mathew, *Taxi! Cabs and Capitalism in New York City* (New York: New Press, 2005).

Index